SEVEN KINGS

How it Feels to be a Teenager

Fran Abrams

ATLANTIC BOOKS
LONDON

First published in Great Britain in 2006 by
Atlantic Books, an imprint of Grove Atlantic Ltd.

1 3 5 7 9 8 6 4 2

A CIP catalogue record for this book is available
from the British Library.

ISBN 10: 1 84354 445 8
ISBN 13: 978 1 84354 445 6

Printed and bound in Great Britain by William Clowes Ltd, Beccles, Suffolk

Atlantic Books
An imprint of Grove Atlantic Ltd
Ormond House
26–27 Boswell Street
London WC1N 3JZ

SEVEN KINGS

Contents

The name Seven Kings contains both legend and dream. The legend is that in Saxon times seven kings met at a cool, clear stream in the forest which covered the area. Out for a day's hunting, the 'kings', or regional overlords, let their horses drink and then moved on.

www.7kings.co.uk

FOREWORD

It feels a long time, now, since this book was conceived. When I first thought of writing a book based around a school, I thought its central aim would be to describe today's education system. At the time, in early 2004, I had been rereading a groundbreaking piece of educational research, completed a quarter of a century ago by academics at the University of London. It was summed up in a book called *Fifteen Thousand Hours. Secondary Schools and their Effects on Children*.

What it said was extraordinary and controversial: that schools actually made a difference to children's lives. Nowadays, this would seem so obvious as to be banal, but during the 1960s education theorists had argued that a school was a mere vessel: put in bright-eyed, motivated children from 'good' homes and it would produce a predictable number of O levels; put in tardy, scabby-kneed underachievers and jail fodder would come out. Schools, then, could do little to mitigate the overwhelming effects of poverty, family dysfunction and inbred underachievement.

Fifteen Thousand Hours turned that view on its head. Schools *could* make a difference, it said. To a measurable extent, pupils' behaviour, attitudes and academic success could be determined by the qualities of the school they attended. The researchers spent long periods in a number of London schools, and reported that each had a distinct ethos, a sort of essence that coloured the life of everyone who passed through its corridors. Even a school with pupils who, on paper, appeared virtually untameable could have an orderly atmosphere if its essential nature was orderly.

It is hard to overestimate the effect of this work on the education system. It was published in 1979, just as Margaret Thatcher came to power. Yet despite Thatcherism's free-market, *laissez-faire* approach, its ideas worked their way into the nation's political consciousness. Britain's schools became increasingly centralized and controlled: the national curriculum, Ofsted, league tables, all nodded towards the researchers' revelation. So central now is this belief in a school's individual character that it has become one of the great truisms of our time. The embracing, pulsating, tenacious personalities of our schools have been regulated to bring them as close as possible to an accepted ideal. They have been forced to focus increasingly on measurable results such as exam grades and exclusions.

I found myself wondering how it would feel now inside a school. This might seem odd, given that I had spent the previous fifteen years, on and off, visiting schools and writing about them. Yet I had never spent more than a couple of hours at a time in one, or not since my own schooldays. I wondered who, in the computer age, now stood in the space once occupied by the tweed-jacketed, elbow-patched teacher of old. I thought about the children, and how their lives might differ from those who went before.

I could never have attempted to replicate the scale or rigour of *Fifteen Thousand Hours*. But I did wonder what an outsider would find now, sitting at the backs of classrooms as those researchers had, simply recording what occurred. I called John Dunford, general secretary of the Association of School and College Leaders, who gave me a list of five or six likely schools. Two responded positively to my initial approach: Seven Kings High School in Ilford, and Royal Docks High School in London's Docklands. At Seven Kings I discussed the project with the school's headmaster, Alan Steer, and met some of the staff and children. At Royal Docks I spent a day following the head teacher, Pat Bagshaw, and watched a literacy lesson in which a twelve-year-old boy struggled to sit still for long enough to grapple with a list of one- and two-syllable words. Pale, drawn and heavy-lidded, he looked as if he had been up half the night.

By now I was beginning to think my book might encompass something more than just the life of a school: it might paint a broader picture of growing up in an urban area in the twenty-first century. It might reflect on who the children were, and where they went when their lessons ended. It might ask who their parents were, and what had been their personal journeys. It might delve a little into their dreams and futures.

In the end, Royal Docks decided not to participate. It had a challenging year ahead – though it seems to me that in Docklands every year is a challenge – and the staff had enough on their plates. Meanwhile, at Seven Kings the head and governors were enthusiastic – which seemed a strong recommendation. I had quickly learned how stretched schools can be, and I needed a deep level of commitment from them in terms of time and trust.

Seven Kings was a fascinating prospect in other ways, too. Its location in an area that was neither leafy nor grim, the very niceness and ordinariness of its pupils, made it feel fresh and intriguing. An excellent Ofsted report, too, was a spur: what about its daily life had contributed to its success?

In the UK we hear so much about failure. We feel familiar, from media reports, with areas where social problems seem insurmountable. And we think we know, from television dramas, about the lives of the wealthy and successful. We hear far less about the lives of hard-working families who have demanding if unglamorous jobs. We know little about the roots of aspiration and achievement. By spending a year at Seven Kings, I felt I could begin to redress that balance. I hoped I could say something new about how teenagers grow up in today's urban world, and how they make sense of the future laid out before them.

With Alan Steer I drew up a list of staff and pupils whose daily comings and goings I could record. We decided the book should focus on four key adults, including himself, and a number of pupils. Doug Harrison, an assistant head and the school's head of pastoral support, would introduce me to the school's pupils and, with more than thirty years' service behind him, would provide a long view. Debbie Adams, recently arrived from teacher-training college, would help me to see it from the point of view of a newcomer. Alan Steer would take me through the strategic issues and policy decisions that all head teachers face, and would help me to grasp the vision he had had for Seven Kings in the twenty years since he had arrived as its new headmaster.

We decided that the fourth staff member would be the school's head of welfare, Angela Cassidy. A former nurse, she now ran the medical centre and looked after pupils with special needs.

Decisions on which pupils to follow proved rather more random. There were one or two obvious choices. On my first visit I had met Perin Patel, a bright sixth-form boy who was keen to take part, and Anthony, a fifteen-year-old, who came into Alan's office for a dressing down. His earlier school career had been somewhat chequered, and he had arrived at Seven Kings, aged fourteen, from another local comprehensive. The third boy, Tyrone, was thirteen, a likeable boy who tended to drift a bit academically.

Of the three girls we chose, Kessie seemed shy but I was told she was an exceptional student, hard-working and determined. Shivanie, then twelve, was going on a trip to an activity centre in the Lake District, which the school was keen for me to accompany. Ruhy had just come up from primary school, and was one of a few children at Seven Kings who came from refugee families.

We selected one more pupil when it was suggested that I should follow seven rather than six: so the 'seven kings' of local legend from whom the school took its name would be mirrored by these future movers and shakers. And so Jemma, feisty and full of opinions, came into my life.

None of us – least of all me – knew what was in store. I worried that the pupils would find my presence irritating or, worse, intimidating. None of us knew what might occur during the year to make our adventure fraught or exciting. This book tells the story of our journey and – I hope – points also to the road that lies ahead.

Fran Abrams,
Suffolk, April 2006.

INTRODUCTION

Ilford is a place through which people pass on their way out of London. The Romans came through here on their way to Colchester, and the Great Eastern Railway has been trundling past since 1839. Nowadays the town is framed to its north by the A12 trunk road, along which the traffic crunches slowly towards the M25 and beyond.

London's East-Enders, Jews, Poles and Irish have all been here and left their mark, but they are being replaced now by the children and grandchildren of Indians, Pakistanis and Africans. So, in a sense, this book is about a group of modern-day travellers on a well-worn route. 'It seems Ilford exports people,' someone has written in the Knowhere Internet guide to the area.

It is the story of a year in the life of seven young people from an area of Ilford called Seven Kings. Like the Saxon rulers who are reputed to have gathered here, drawn succour from the clear waters of a stream and left again, they all have one thing in common: they are all pupils at Seven Kings High School, and will be together here for a limited time – just this year, in fact, for one has just arrived and two are leaving.

Five were born in Britain; two were not. Between them they have their origins in England, India, Africa and the Middle East, but their future is likely to have one common feature: for the most part, if history is anything to go by, they will keep moving on.

Our seven young people have much in common with each other. They are growing up in the grid of streets around their school; they share certain tastes, dreams and aspirations. And yet there is also much to divide them. Of the three boys, only one can count his education so far an unqualified success. The girls are all doing well – even though one sometimes clashes with her teachers – and they have clear ideas about what they would like to do when they leave.

Their story, ethnically and geographically, might be that of any Greater London district in the early twenty-first century. But it also points to a much more fundamental story in the life of Great Britain. It is the story of people on the move, and also of those who will – or might – be left behind. In the course of their daily lives these young people demonstrate, often without knowing it, the attributes, traditions, abilities and passions they will take with them as they find their places in the urban world of tomorrow. They hint, too, at the possible future shape of the nation as their generation moves on, moves up and moves out.

This is the story, too, of Seven Kings High School, which in many ways is an ordinary school. The educational ability of its pupils, so far as we can tell, is close to the national average. Its intake is based on its catchment area, and there is no selection. Its buildings, with some additions and modernizations, are standard-issue 1920s grammar school. But the school is on the move: fifteen years ago its GCSE results were average; now Seven Kings is close to the top of the comprehensive-school league table.

Our seven pupils will help us to discover the core of Seven Kings High School and show us how it feels to travel its corridors each day. They will show us the face school shows to them, the multiplicity of minor everyday interactions that weave pattern and texture into their daily lives.

Around 1300 pupils attend the school, all of whom have their own stories to tell, and we will meet many of them too. We will be introduced to some by the four members of staff who will take us with them through their daily lives, meeting as they go the successes and failures, dramas and traumas of the children in their care.

This book reflects just a year in the life of a group of young people within one particular school. But it aims to travel with its characters into the country that Britain – or, at least, parts of it – could be in twenty years' time.

SEPTEMBER

SHIVANIE

The sun is slapping the hot Tarmac, kicking back off the white clapboard house fronts at the end of the terrace. In a little square car park, framed by garages and a brick wall, two girls are bashing a football about. Their shouts rise above the rumpus of the traffic on Seven Kings High Road, which is above them, beyond another brick wall. Whenever the ball hits a car in the nearby parking area, they squeal.

'OK. Your turn. No! Aaaaah! Missed!'

The ball rolls under a car and Shivanie peers underneath. She is wearing prescription sunglasses, flared jeans, a T-shirt with 'Cheeky' on the front and 'Monkey' on the back, and white trainers, with pink and green straps. Small for her age and slight, she is on the brink of her teens. On Monday she will put on her uniform again: blazer, navy blue with school badge; trousers, navy blue, straight cut; blouse, light blue, traditional design with collar and school tie; shoes, black, low-heeled; jewellery, sleeper earrings, one per lobe. Then she will be another Shivanie. She will not be cheeky, funny, scatty, dreamy, sparky, loopy Shivanie, or little sister, youngest daughter, always-ready-to-play Shivanie. She will be one pupil in the crowd at Seven Kings High School, beacon school, leading edge school, specialist technology school.

Her mum has emerged from the house and is standing by the gate. 'Do you know where your pencil case is, Shivanie?'

'Mum! You put it somewhere!' The last time she saw her schoolbag it was on the floor in the hall by the radiator, full of detritus from the end of last term.

She opens the front door, with the little plate that says, 'Jai Shri Ganesh', and goes into the hall, then to the big cupboard under the stairs, she fishes out a bag, empty now, then another, which is heavier. Her pencil case is pink and covered with writing. 'Sheena. No. 1 Sister. Louise, aka Pooh Bear.' She pulls out her pens: a silver one with a fluffy white feather at the top and a sparkly, bouncing 'S'; a more studious red Parker – her favourite. Biros are not allowed at Seven Kings High School.

She has been bored during the holidays but she does not want to go back – to sit in class, facing the front – yet somehow she is looking forward to it. Either way, she will go without protest, because in this family education matters. Her family is well qualified. One of her uncles is a professor.

Her dad pushes her, she says, but not in a bad way. He assumes she will do well. He works in the offices, now, at the postal sorting office, but perhaps if he had more qualifications he would not be there.

Her mum and dad had to leave school before they were ready. Her mum missed a lot because her own mother was ill after they came to Britain, and she had to stay at home to look after her. Her dad did his A levels in Kenya. Her mum's grandfather was friends with her dad's grandfather, and both men watched over their grandchildren's education. They went to the Christian school, and after they came home at three o'clock they went for extra tuition. School, then more school. 'You had to go', her mum told her, 'because if you didn't you think, What am I going to say to Grandad? Studying always came first.'

Her dad had had to leave school to work in the family business because *his* father was ill. He wants more for his daughters. He came here in 1984 to marry her mum. Her mum arrived when she was ten.

This afternoon when Dipti and Sheena left for the shops, Shivanie had told her mum she didn't need anything for school. Now, fiddling with the items in her pencil case, she remembers: ink cartridges.

'Dipti will have to get you some in the morning.' Her mum grumbles, cheerfully. 'It's always the same with you, Shivanie. You never remember anything till the last minute.'

'I do my homework! You don't have to tell me to!'

'I do. Otherwise you don't remember.'

'I do, because I look at my planner... On my report it said I meet all my deadlines. I think I work hard, but you don't.'

'You think if you come home with bad marks Mum will be angry. But as long as you do the best you can, that's fine. That's what Daddy always says.'

'I probably work harder than most of my class, because they're boys and they make jokes all the time,' she says. 'Rajiv is going to be the next Mr Bean.' She admires him for that. 'I saw these boys outside the staffroom. And they were going,

6

"Your sister Sheena's so *clev*er, man. How did she get to be so *clev*er, man? Have you got any tips?"'

'Man?' her mum says. 'What is all this "man"? Why don't you talk properly?'

'I'm not talking, Mum! I'm imitating!'

Her mum is sitting next to her on one of the big leather sofas in the living room. Above Shivanie's head her four-year-old self stares solemnly down from a formal family portrait. In it her mum is wearing the brightly coloured sari she keeps for special occasions, while Dipti and Sheena, her sisters, are in dresses with white collars. There is also a picture of the guru Sathya Sai Baba in an orange robe.

Her mum is teasing her now about the review she had at the end of last term: 'And when Mrs Cassidy asked what you'd like to be, you sat there and said you wanted to be an actor. And then you said, "But maybe my mum would rather I was a doctor!"' Her mum thought that was funny, if a bit embarrassing – as if Shivanie's parents might push her to do something she didn't want to do.

'I don't think I really want to be a doctor,' Shivanie says. 'You have to check people's heart rates and stuff. And I don't want to be stuck in an office. Maybe I could be a secret agent.' She smiles at the thought. 'I *would* quite like to be an actor. But I'd have to be an English actor – I couldn't go to Bollywood because then I'd have to learn Hindi.'

'So long as you do your best, Shivanie, it really doesn't matter,' her mum says.

Sometimes Shivanie flicks through her mum's Argos catalogue, looks at the ladies in suits and thinks, I'd like to be someone like that. I'd like to go to work in a suit.

Her mum laughs when she mentions this. 'Sometimes I

don't know where it all comes from. When they see me going out to work looking smart in my trousers and blazer, they say, "Oh, Mum, *you* look smart." Sheena says she's going to have a suit and a briefcase and she's going to be a lawyer. And Dipti is going to be an accountant.'

'I have to get married too, though, when I'm twenty-five or twenty-six,' Shivanie says. What sort of man would want to marry her? She isn't sure. 'I don't think my husband will be normal, though.'

Her mum looks at her sharply. 'That's not right! Just because you have a visual disability…'

Dipti, seated now on the other big sofa, looks up from her Sudoku book. 'Mum,' she says, mock weary, 'she means because of her personality.'

TRAINING DAY

At Seven Kings High School, next to the wheelchair ramp beside the bright, modern reception area, a granite-and-slate water feature murmurs as a slim man comes up the drive past the tennis courts. As he enters Reception, Alan Steer spots him, and mentally raises an eyebrow: it is past 8.30 a.m. One of the new arrivals is late.

Alan will not concern himself with this now. He's at the far end of the school hall, checking his pre-term powerpoint presentation to the staff. Behind him the proscenium arch is filled with a screen shaded sky blue with mountains at the bottom. 'Where Are We Now?' the caption asks.

At eight thirty-nine the staff file in and sit down on the neat rows of chairs. He greets them with the usual pleasantries, then holds up an A5-size laminated booklet entitled *Seven Kings High School. Teaching and Learning Policy*. Several staff members are holding a copy.

'This is the most important of all our school policies,' he says. 'It is not advisory. It is mandatory. It is to be followed by all colleagues throughout the school. Not just occasionally, but constantly.' Then he thaws. He confesses that he fears he may sometimes be considered rather authoritarian. He doesn't think of himself like that because inside he still feels like a liberal.

The staff laugh politely and he moves on. 'What does Seven Kings do well?' There is plenty to report: the latest GCSE results, in which more than 150 of the 180 pupils got five A–C grades; an excellent list of university places for the sixth form; Seven Kings among the top ten schools in the country for 'added value' – that is, higher than average results from pupils whose academic ability and achievement were close to the national average when they entered the school; good behaviour; a caring ethos.

Weaknesses? A few pupils who do not get five basic GCSEs; disparities between – perhaps even within – departments; homework sometimes not set according to the timetable. Consistency is the key, he says. Someone once said – and this is crucial, he thinks: 'The problem is not that we do not know what to do but that we must begin to do what we know.'

He looks down at his notes, mentally ticking off the points:

Celebrate success.
Be tough with ourselves.
What are our weaknesses?
Conservatism.
Individualism.

Focus on students.

Examples – sixth-form lessons ending early, punctuality.

Our responsibility to create change – no processing.

Can train children out of bad habits.

Homework: a force for good, or bad?

Then he hands out some inspirational new posters that have just arrived: 'Never Settle For Less Than Your Best!' 'Never Stop Asking: Why?'

He finishes with a couple of his regular motifs: 'Children don't come here as a privilege, they come here as a right. This school does not exist for adults.' And another favourite: 'Did you know that herrings have to keep swimming or they can't breathe?'

There is a little skirmish as everyone disperses.

Alan collects his laptop and walks along the corridor, looking out of the window at the fading grasses in the wildlife garden. In his office he helps himself to some of the food that has been prepared for the staff: samosas, sausage rolls. He shouldn't be eating it: he's supposed to be on the Atkins diet.

His first walkabout of the autumn term will be different from all those that follow. Later he will be checking on the pupils but today only the staff are about. Everywhere little clusters of teachers are gathering, flicking the switches of electronic whiteboards, inspecting newly painted classrooms. In the English department, the high, arched, cast-iron beams are a calming shade of green. 'It's "Warm Meadow",' a woman flings over her shoulder. Her head is buried in a cupboard of books where Maya Angelou jostles with Shakespeare and Harper Lee.

The English department, like others in the school, has seen

change over the years. Two decades ago if you had looked in that cupboard you would have found little else but short stories, nothing pre-twentieth century. English teachers used to think they could do exactly as they liked.

Alan casts his mind back to the early days of his headship, when he would pad through the school in the early morning with his master key, opening doors, investigating. Now it seems strange that he felt the need to do so. But that was an age when it was unthinkable for the headmaster to discuss results with a departmental head. He remembers difficult 1980s staff meetings in which acrimony was common: 'It isn't your role to question how we teach in the classroom.' It is now.

Not that Seven Kings was ever a bad school, but the kids arrived, hung around for five years and left with no greater sense of achievement or aspiration than they had arrived with. The staff had not talked much about raising levels of attainment. Twenty years ago, when they were first introduced, fewer than a third of the pupils left with five good GCSEs. When Alan asked if he could see the neighbouring schools' results, there were shocked faces. Later someone slipped him a copy in a brown envelope. Now they are published in the local paper.

Change has been constant. In the early days of the national curriculum the debates were all about what should be taught and when. Should children learn about Admiral Horatio Nelson in year nine? Now people discuss *how* children learn. At Seven Kings the staff want pupils to know why they do what they do, and how they can improve.

Alan feels that guilt is a big part of being a head teacher: you read something in the paper, or you hear someone talking at a conference, and think: Oh, no, that's me. When the *Guardian* claimed that 60–70 per cent of pupils had said that no one talked to them about their learning, he arranged regular interviews for all his pupils.

He leaves the main, pre-war building by the back door. Ahead, his view is blocked by a huge tarpaulin and some scaffolding. There is the tinny sound of a radio, accompanied by hammering. The science block is being extended, though it will be months yet before the job is finished. 'Are you up there, Terry?'

'Yeah.'

'Good. I'll come and see you later.'

He likes to keep a close eye. Some of the staff joke that it is his hobby, building things.

Seven Kings High School. Teaching and Learning Policy.

Teachers must ensure a purposeful learning environment:

- Punctuality is essential for staff and students.
- Students must enter and leave the classroom in an orderly way at the instruction of the teacher.
- Teachers must have a seating plan for every class.
- Lessons must last the full duration and students must not be dismissed early.
- Teachers must ensure that classrooms are left clean and tidy.
- Teachers are responsible for managing stimulating displays, which should be changed regularly.

SHIVANIE

Monday morning has dawned hot and wet. Shivanie sits at the kitchen table sipping milky coffee and examining her tie. The little crowns on it are interspersed with large pale spots. Geeta is here, talking to Dipti about her brother's GCSE results.

'...Yeah, I know. All As and A stars. He is *sooo* clever...'

Shivanie sniffs. 'Urgh. There's something all over it – I'll have to clean it.' She goes to the sink and tries to sponge her tie without taking it off. Her dad left for work hours ago and her mum has gone, too.

'...And then when Justin showed his dad his results, his dad started crying...' Now they are talking about *Hollyoaks*.

'It feels weird going to school,' Shivanie says, as they set off.

They don't live in the Seven Kings catchment area but Shivanie and Dipti were admitted to the school because they have sight problems and it has facilities for the physically disabled. Sheena got in because she was their sister. They turn the corner and cross the road by P.G. Creed and Son, iron-mongers – plastic chairs and dustbins are stacked outside the shop. Next door the Apna Punjab Meat Market is open for business too.

'I just have this feeling of weirdness,' Shivanie repeats. 'Geeta, what have you got in your bag?'

'My science books.'

Shivanie's bag contains only her pink pencil case.

The girls head down Benton Road, with its traffic and big houses. Outside a peeling, pebbledashed semi, a television set has been abandoned in the weeds beside a pile of old car parts. The adjoining house has new Tarmac, an extension with sliding doors and a double garage. Geeta and Dipti are talking about Geeta's cousin, who goes to the fifth best grammar school in the country, in Kent. 'They have a 99.8 per cent pass rate, or something...'

They pass the allotments. Near the big, painted sign that says, 'Grow Your Own Fresh Fruit and Vegetables. Rents from

£12 per year', runner beans are scrambling into the branches of a dead tree. A dark red bra hangs on the chain-link fence.

Near the school gate someone has planted rosemary and bright orange canna lilies along the edge of a concreted garden. Like most of the houses that surround the school, this bay-fronted 1920s terrace was built from brick, but is now pebbledashed, with a hint of grime from exhaust fumes.

As they near the gate Dipti fishes in her bag for her student card. This is a frontier point and sometimes she must prove her identity to be admitted. Today, though, they pass unchallenged into the playground where little swirls of pupils greet each other. At the front of the main building stands a large, silent crowd of younger children with wide eyes: new year-sevens. Last September Shivanie stood among them.

She needs to find a safe point in this sea of blazers. Her best friend, Jas, will not be here yet. Sarah, she thinks. She slips inside and down the corridor to her new classroom, but it is too early and no one is there. She wanders out again, into the yard at the back, and eventually spots her friend coming through the gate in a knot of girls. Sarah's voice rises in a thin crescendo of excitement and she runs towards Shivanie. They give each other a little stylized hug, then walk off arm in arm towards the school building.

DEBBIE ADAMS

In the dark corridor the fresh gold braid on the children's blazers shines like cats' eyes on a road. Several times Debbie makes them practise lining up and filing into the classroom. They are not unwilling – quite the reverse – but in the struggle to co-ordinate they perform a jerky little dance. A boy rocks from foot to foot, unable to stand still.

At the fourth attempt she lets them in and directs them to their seats. She is apprehensive. She has read the list of names over and over again, but can she pronounce them?

'Satrajit,' she begins. 'Over here. Masheer? Down here. Pakriti? Here. Jonathan... Jonathan? Over here. Femi? Here. Natasha?... Natasha? Does anyone know if Natasha is here?... Oh. OK. Amrit?'

She finishes the list with a mixture of relief and concern. Three children are still standing just inside the door. They look at her anxiously. She allocates seats to them and takes a breath.

'OK! Welcome! I'm Miss Adams, and I'm new too, so we can all be new together.' Despite that, she is in charge now. Classroom management is one of her fortes, she believes. Her straight brown hair is pulled back from her face, and her pinstripe trousers are of a severe cut.

She has always wanted to teach. Even at home, with her two sisters and brother, she was the bossy one. When they played school she was always the teacher. Last year she commuted from her flat in Holborn to the University of East London to do teacher training. Now she will make the same journey to work.

She rolls the board round. 'These are my rules on how to behave in the classroom.'

1. Arrive on time for lessons.
2. Bring your pencils and dictionaries.
3. Copy all work off the board.
4. Complete assignments on time.

5. Use your listening skills – focus on the person speaking.

6. Ask questions.

7. Use your teacher.

8. Make sure you know what you are being asked to do.

The children copy them into their books. 'Mark, you're already disobeying rule number five,' she says. 'Deal with it.' Then: 'We're goin' to be a good, hard-workin' class, aren't we?'

The rest of the lesson is a get-to-know-you session. They talk about their hobbies. Hers is going to the theatre. Theirs are swimming, singing, cricket, karate, dancing, photography, football, cooking and Playstation Two.

She supports Chelsea. They support Arsenal, Tottenham, Chelsea and Manchester United, but mostly Manchester United.

Her favourite food is Chinese roast duck. They like jelly babies, beefburgers, fish and chips, chicken burgers, chocolate, cake and cauliflower cheese – but their top favourite is pizza.

Between lessons, the classroom breathes out. There is a different kind of quiet; the energy flows out into the corridor. Today Debbie will be teaching year seven, a couple of year-eight groups, year nine – she has heard there are one or two difficult pupils in the latter. She goes through the seating routine with year nine G. 'Who's being shy after the holidays?' she asks.

'Me!'

She directs her eye to the voice: Mayur, at the back, seated alone – maybe she should have put him nearer the front. She might review that. Before she can speak, one of the girls fixes him with a cold stare. 'For a little boy you ain't 'alf got a big mouth.'

He's bored with copying out the classroom rules: 'Miss, this is too much.'

'You should see how much they have to copy in year ten.'

A couple of minutes later he asks, 'Miss, what do we do when we've finished?'

'Read them over again, Mayur.'

'I ain't finished, Miss. I'm just saying.'

They talk. She discovers that year nine G enjoys maths, playing football, laughing, watching telly, Playstation Two, basketball, talking to friends, cricket, entertaining people and staying at home. It dislikes maths, chatterboxes, computers, football and swimming.

They talk about what they read yesterday. She marks it up on the board, adding to the numbers as they go round the class:

Magazine: 11

Book: 9

Teletext: 1

Newspaper: 6

Text message: 1

Coco Pops Packet: 1

Mayur says, 'Miss, I read this man was a playboy and Victoria is *preg*nant.' She ignores him.

They're working quietly now, writing lists of reasons why they read. The sound of the wind rustling the late-summer leaves in the tree outside fills the air. One of her display posters falls off the wall. She smiles apologetically and puts it back up. Later she hands out copies of a book the group will study this term: *Gulf*, by Robert Westall. 'What do you think it's about?'

'Afghanistan.'

'An aeroplane?'

'The Gulf War.'

'One of the key places on this map on the cover. Baghdad.'

'War!' the class choruses.

'Mayur,' she says. 'You are breaking rule number five.'

'Sorry, Miss.'

'It isn't good enough, because you have already broken rule number two on your first day. We're going to have problems. You've got to be careful.'

'Sorry, Miss.'

Tonight she will work until ten or eleven, preparing for tomorrow. At the moment, she feels like a fraud. Her predecessor won an award. Those kids are so going to miss her.

But everyone is nice. At one of the schools where she did teaching practice, she would sat down in the staffroom and someone told her that that chair belonged to someone else. It wouldn't happen here. People are enthusiastic, and everyone seems young at heart. At other schools you meet teachers who hate teaching.

TYRONE

Tyrone bounces down the stairs with a series of thumps, and flops on to one of the worn leather sofas in front of *Coronation Street*. He is pleased with the way he looks tonight. Black Nike jacket. Black Nike tracksuit pants. Grey T-shirt. Nike Air Force One trainers. A big square diamond ear stud. He had his hair plaited last week, tight against his head with little bits left at the ends. His pants are pulled up round his waist. His mum hates it when the crotch droops round his knees. They call them low battys.

He is back at school. He missed the first few days of term – he always does, he reflects, with a frisson of satisfaction. This year they were in Florida and there was a hurricane. They went to the airport but there was a foot of water on the runway so they couldn't come home.

He gets up, ambles into the kitchen, rummages in the fridge for a soft drink, then ambles back and flops again. It is a busy house, one of the big, bay-windowed, early-twentieth-century terraces that surround the school. His mum is bustling about. His dad has just arrived to drop his sister Tamia home. His mum's partner drifts in and out.

He thinks that his best friend Jerome would say he is friendly, bouncy, a laugh. He's big for his age, which is thirteen going on fourteen, not tall, but chunky. He's a follower of fashion, sets the trend for his friends.

When he was in year seven, he had a jacket with loads of different symbols on it. Everyone said he looked like Dizzee Rascal. When they had non-uniform day he wore his leather jacket and a balaclava. At the moment he's trying to get every Nike tracksuit so he doesn't have to wear anything else. Altogether he has... He counts on his fingers. Four... five... seven. He only wears them outside school, of course.

In the morning his alarm will go off at seven forty. He will run around getting ready, then chill in front of the telly until it's time to wander up to Jerome's house. His mum laughs at him sometimes, as she gets into the car to go to work. 'Look at you! You'd think you had nowhere to go!'

He usually gets to Jerome's just after ten past eight, but his friend is never ready. So he waits. Jerome usually takes at least six minutes. By the time they make it into registration it's often past eight thirty, and they're late.

School will be better this year, he thinks. He isn't going to mess around so much. It's hard, not talking in class. Sometimes he puts his hand up to answer a question, but sometimes he doesn't, even though he knows the answer. Maybe he'll talk a bit in class, but not so much.

He thinks more about his school work than some of his friends do. Some of them mess around too. Once Wesley tried to tackle the PE teacher, and Tyrone laughed because the teacher said Wesley had a hole in his sock. Usually he keeps his friends under control.

'And I've already had some merit marks, haven't I, Mum?' he says.

'Yes, darling. Maybe you'll get an achievement award for me this year.' She sits down next to him and gives him a hug. 'Make me proud,' she says. 'I already *am* proud, but I'd be even more proud if you won an award. Like Tamia. Tamia's won an award for effort every year.'

Tamia sits down at the computer and starts her food-technology homework – she has to design a beefburger. She's aiming for really good grades in her GCSEs. Her friends all push each other to do well.

He thinks for a minute, with a ripple of concern. Maybe he can get that award. But maybe it would be easier next year. He has SATs in the spring. He doesn't think he can do them. His mum says he can: he just has to work hard and he'll be fine. But he's not sure. There are six or seven pages to the paper, and you have to read all of it in fifteen minutes. He doesn't like reading. His mum buys loads of books but he never looks at them. He likes *Auto* magazine.

He has to choose his GCSE options this year. There might be a course on construction. That would be good: licensed to build! But he doesn't want to do ICT. He is *not* doing ICT. Other people in the class would be smarter than him, and he won't give them that opportunity.

'You'll just have to work at it, Tyrone,' his mum says.

He stretches his legs, surveys his trainers and looks glum. 'Yeah. I'll do my schoolwork at home and that will be my life over.'

'Tyrone, if they tell you to write two hundred words, you write two hundred words. You never write two hundred and one.'

'In my geography test, you were supposed to write a hundred words, right? No more, no less.'

His mum supports the school, tells them they should be strict with him. If he comes home and says he's been naughty, he's got a detention, and can she write a letter to get him out of it, she says no. 'Take your punishment,' she says. 'Teachers need to be able to set the kids on the straight and narrow.' Some of his friends write their own letters and pretend they come from their mum, but his mum always puts her work phone number at the bottom of hers, so they know.

His mum didn't go to school in Britain. She was born here but her parents sent her to school in their native Ghana because they thought she would get a better education there. Then, she says, the education system in Ghana was second to none. There was no such thing as failure. If you didn't pass you stayed down until you did.

If he hasn't done his homework, she will say, 'If you were in Ghana, you would have done it. If you were in Ghana, you would never not listen because if you didn't, you'd be hit.

21

I never got hit. I was good. But I'd love them to whip you,' she says, with a big smile. She doesn't mean it.

She doesn't push him, like her parents pushed her. They wanted her to be a doctor or a lawyer but in the end she decided she had to do her own thing and trained as a legal secretary. Whatever he chooses to do with his life, she will support him. But she won't make it easy for him if he drops out at sixteen. 'You won't be living the high life, Tyrone, if you do that. You'll soon realize it isn't easy to have seven track-suits if you haven't got a job or a college place.'

Tamia gets up from the computer, comes to the sofa, sits on her mother's knee and wraps her arms round her. 'Tyrone and Tamia are like chalk and cheese,' his mum says. She tells people at work about them. She thinks in the end that people grow up as they want to, not as you bring them up. 'Jump up now, darling,' she says to Tamia, after a minute or two, and pushes her off gently.

Tyrone is a good cook. Not long ago he made a fruit cock-tail for his mum, with strawberries. He got some of that stuff you use for strawberry milkshakes, mixed it with strawberries and water. Then he gave it to her with a strawberry on the side as a garnish. His mum says he's good with money, too: he saves up to buy the stuff he wants.

Tamia says: 'I can see your head expanding, Tyrone.'

'Just because you're always phoning your friends... And I *do* have friends to ring,' he says, with a glance that recalls an ongoing cheerful quarrel.

They are not meant to take their mobiles to school but they do, of course. There's been a craze for 'happy slapping': someone hits someone else, then sends pictures on their phone. Tyrone gets some. His mum thinks it's awful.

The doorbell rings. Tyrone rushes out, slamming the door behind him. A minute later he's back, carrying a dark purple baseball cap with devoré on the back.

'It's gay!' His mum laughs.

But he likes it. 'It's not! It's cool!' He flops back on the sofa, the hat in his hand. 'I'm not bad, am I, Mum?'

'You're not bad, Tyrone. You like to act like a gangsta, but you're a perfect gentleman, really. You like to pretend you're streetwise, but you're really loving.' She smiles again. 'A fake gangsta. A plastic gangsta!'

He rubs his head on her shoulder, puppyish. 'No! I'm fully fledged!' he says. 'But I'm a good boy, really.'

ANTHONY

All morning Anthony has been stacking wafer-thin turkey in the chiller cabinets. They like him at the Sainsbury's super-market in Barkingside. It's only been a few days – it's late September and he's on work experience – but they've said they'd have him back.

Now, lunchtime nearly over, he's sitting in the canteen, his six-foot-three-inch frame hunched in a plastic chair. A packet of ten Benson & Hedges Low Tar Silvers sits beside him on the table. He is trying to cut down. He fiddles with his mobile, looking at a rap he's written.

> *Dis Song is a Weed an' Bredrin*
> *Dedication*
> *We ain't a cru just a blazin'*
> *Segregation.*

The door opens and the guy from the cold store comes in, the one he was chatting to earlier. He waves. 'Awright, mate?'

'Yeah, I'm good thanks.' Anthony looks up and smiles diffidently. Yeah, it *is* boring, but he's making friends. He's good at that.

Yesterday lunchtime he was sitting like this, listening to Fat Joe and smoking a cigarette, and the door opened. It was Mr Harrison, doing the rounds, checking everyone was OK. Anthony freaked, of course, dropped his cig and started fanning the air. And Mr Harrison laughed. 'You're not at school now, Anthony. It's OK.'

He had thought it would be all right here. His mum had fixed it up for him. And it is. It's fine. Everyone's friendly. Maybe he'll come back at the end of the year after his GCSEs. He doesn't know.

At the moment he can see two futures: maybe as a rap artist, or maybe working in a shop like this one. Or maybe he'll stay at school. Go to university, even. His mum would like that.

His mate, Romy, has a relative who works in a recording studio. They might go down there, record something. Maybe they could put it out for him, but probably he'd have to go to America because that's where the money is. His English teacher, Miss Ranson, is cool. She often asks how it's going.

> *The rap game*
> *I don't think*
> *I'll ever quit it*
> *Fuck English sport*
> *Like cricket*
> *Like green*
> *Play the game clean.*

I blaze, rap and live in IG3
And I'm not a menace
To society
When it comes to exotic erotic chronic hot comet girls
I got a wide variety
Like a KFC
Bucket.

English is one of his best subjects, that and art. He hasn't thought what he might do at A level.

He strokes his stubble. At school he has to shave, and he has to grow his ash-blond hair. This morning he was outside the barber's at ten past eight: He likes his scalp about a millimetre all over – at the moment it has geometric patterns on the sides.

He waves across the room to the old guy who pushes the trolleys. 'Awright? Yeah, later. You take care, now.'

He had trouble about his hair when he moved to Seven Kings at the start of year ten. Miss Handley, the year head, kept telling him, but he didn't do anything about it. They even announced it in Assembly, and everyone looked at him. Then one day he came home and there was a message on the answerphone for his mum and dad. 'Can Anthony please shave his beard and moustache? Miss Handley says she's happy to let him keep the sideburns. And, since he asks, no, she doesn't require him to shave his legs.'

And he had a bit of bother when someone started a rumour that he was prejudiced against Muslims. About twenty Asian kids started calling him racist. He just laughed. He had an Asian girlfriend then. Now everyone's cool with him. He gets on with everyone – some of his mates are white, like him, others aren't. The teachers were on his back a lot last year, though. It was like they were marking his card, letting him know he wasn't getting away with anything, because of his history. Because of what happened before.

He had got in with the wrong crowd. In years seven and eight, he was small, but in year nine he'd got to be a big person because of this boy he hung around with, who gave him skunk to smoke. Six of them were permanently excluded from his old school for smoking weed on the school field. They were not caught, more set up. The teachers never saw him smoking but later they made him sign a statement admitting it.

His mum and dad were really worried and upset. They had to come to Seven Kings to see Mr Steer, and he was so stern they didn't think he would give Anthony a place. He and Miss Handley had said things like he wouldn't be able to behave that way or talk the way he talked, at Seven Kings.

That had annoyed him. It gets to him when people go on about the way he talks and say he sounds like a rapper. But the way he sees it, it's a generational thing: he talks the way teenagers talk. His mum told him he shouldn't talk like that at Seven Kings because people wouldn't like it. So he thought about it. But then he realized he just had to be himself. He's been into rap for years, since he was eleven or twelve. Mobb Deep, Notorious BIG, Tupac. He's been reading on the Internet about how Tupac died, how it could have been a fake death, outside that casino in Las Vegas.

This is his bit on MSN. He wrote it a year or two back, when he was younger.

I'm 14 an' my name is Blaze King
I obviously love Blazing

I'm all about rappin' freestyle
Fuck Eminem this is 3-mile
I can't be bothered to walk the extra 5.

Blaze King is his tag, like Biggy's really called Christopher Wallis. At home he has his own doorbell, so his friends can ring and he'll hear them up in his attic room. On the little label, it says, 'Anthony: Blaze King'. His mates are always round the house, relaxing on the sofa and the double bed in his room. Listening to music. Chatting on MSN. After a while they'll go out. He always sends a text to let his mum know where he is.

He likes a drink and a smoke but he keeps out of trouble nowadays. That one time, a year or two back, wasn't serious but it shook him. Like so many things that happen in his life, he wrote a rap about it:

Yo back in the day I was convicted with a reprimand
Got tackled to the floor forcefully and with demand
By three big policemen
I was only a little boy shouting out please man
Get the fuck off
Stop treating my neck like a phone line cos its gonna get
*   cut off*
Well I weren't convicted
Just pulled out an illegal knife and got shifted
Got chased and thrown in a meat-wagon.

In the police cell there's bare graffiti and bear grimy
I don't eat the police food cos it's slimy, probably been
*   spitted in*

I go for a piss in the toilet and notice it's been shitted in
I jus lay with no possessions, going to sleep
With my hood up so my head don't get dirty cos the
  blanket and pillows cheap
Look to the ceiling there is a number and message
  saying crime-stoppers...

He is not proud of this. He used to smoke far too much skunk but he's cut down. His mum would prefer him not to do it at all. And he doesn't, at home. His mum is hoping it's a phase and it was, at first. But now he sometimes feels like he isn't here. He tried to stop once, but he only managed about ten days. It wasn't a physical thing, just lack of willpower. Now everyone else smokes, too. It makes him a bit annoyed. He thinks some people do it because they want to be gangsters. He does it because he can't stop.

He has his own style, he doesn't just wear the things everyone else wears. Today, when he's not in uniform, he'll be in a long-sleeved silky white top, white trousers, his big crucifix. It's a rapper style, but his own. You get these people who wear baggy trousers and chains and stuff. That's just gay. He buys his clothes from Foot Locker and JD, and he has a little diamond stud for his ear.

His mobile rings. The ringtone plays 'Witness The Fitness' by Roots Manuva. He answers. 'Awright? Yeah, man. Cool. Cool. No. Later.'

He has matured over the summer. His mum says he's a lot more grown up than she was at his age. But his parents worry: they know what it's like out there, with house prices and so on. His dad says if he doesn't get the qualifications now he'll regret it in ten years. His dad knows because he doesn't have them. He can do his job, which is carpentry, but he doesn't have the pieces of paper to prove it. He wants Anthony to have those pieces of paper.

They both trust him to get on and do his homework. They don't really push him. They understand because they didn't enjoy school all that much themselves. His mum says she was picked on a bit because of her red hair. His dad went out to work at fifteen. When there was a strike at the Ford plant, he had to take round the telegrams telling the workers when they had to go back.

Now his mum works at a special school. The head is funding her in a psychology degree she's doing part time at the University of East London. So, Anthony and she will both be doing exams this year.

Sometimes he winds her up, but not as much as he used to. Like the other night. She was in the kitchen making dinner. Anthony eats most things, but his little brother John's a bit picky. And his dad eats meat, but his mum doesn't. So she gets fed up of having to make four different meals. And he did something, he can't even remember what it was now, and it just pushed her over the edge. The next thing he knew, she'd thrown frozen peas all over the kitchen.

That was when he realized he was growing up: he knew what to do. He went straight to the freezer for some ice. 'Mum,' he said, 'you need a drink so I'm going to make you one.' Then he picked up the frozen peas.

OCTOBER

RUHY

They are wedged into the dark space between the mobile class-rooms at the back of the school, clutching their bags as if they might bolt. Their energy is tempered by the uncertainty they still feel after a few weeks in their new surroundings.

Ruhy gives her friend Gita a surreptitious shove, and Gita murmurs: 'You'd better watch out if you want to come to my party.' Eyes narrowed, mock-sinister.

The drama teacher, Mr Lord, arrives. When he opens the door they rush inside and sit on the floor in a circle. Their routines are set: there will be warm-up exercises, improvised plays, a performance. 'OK,' he says. 'Today is all about friendship.'

They are all familiar with this kind of role-playing. Ruhy, serious with her long black hair pulled into a ponytail, makes a group with her new friends Gita, Waseme and Ayesha. They all speak at once. 'OK! OK! Waseme! Waa-se-me... So, Gita, you're the teacher, right? And me and Waseme are the cool girls. And Ayesha is the new girl.'

Ruhy sits down again with Waseme and Ayesha. Gita says in an imperious tone, 'Who knows what is ten divided by five?'

Ayesha calls out, 'Me, Miss! It's two!'

And Ruhy and Waseme sing: 'Ooo-ooh!' in a crescendo of condescension.

They are immersed, enjoying themselves.

Around the room other groups are acting out the same scene.

'Eieee – teacher's pet!'

'Do you wanna fight?'

When they act for the class they are solemn. Ruhy doesn't want to giggle, except when Gita asks if anyone knows what ten divided by five is, and a boy's hand shoots up. Then they all laugh.

Mr Lord sits on the edge of a table, seemingly relaxed, but when they finish he is quizzical. Twenty pairs of eyes gaze up at him from the floor.

'Why's it cool to be dumb?' he asks.

Silence.

'Who here wants to be dumb?'

Six hands go up.

'Who wants to be average?'

Eight more hands. Three belong to Ruhy's friends.

'Who here wants to be clever?'

Ruhy has not put up her hand yet. Now she raises it. Two of her friends follow suit, having changed their minds.

Mr Lord waits for a long minute. 'Why?' he says.

'Well, if you're clever, people might pick on you or beat you up,' says a boy who wants to be dumb.

Waseme's arm is waving. 'I want to be clever *and* average, because I believe there should be a balance. A lot of people make assumptions that when you're clever you have to wear glasses and you don't have any fun.'

A boy with sticking-up hair says, 'I want to be dumb because you can join in the groups and everything.'

They are all warming up.

'I'd rather be average because if you have a clever person and they have lots of friends, people who are not clever get jealous.'

'I want to be dumb and average and clever. Dumb so I won't get picked on, average so I'll be all right, and clever so I'll be in the top set.'

Ruhy puts up her hand. 'I think it's good to be clever because you can get better marks and get what you want. But if people bully you it's because they are jealous of you.'

The boy with the sticking-up hair puts up his hand again. 'Sir, can I change to average?'

'You can change to clever if you want.'

The boy looks uncertain.

In the corridor, on the way to English, Ruhy and Gita push each other affectionately. Ruhy pulls the clip out of Gita's hair, which falls round her shoulders.

'Right. So you're definitely not coming to my party.' Gita smiles. There will be pizza and bowling. Maybe they will do their nails and hair. Ruhy's mum put some highlights in hers last week. And Gita still has the big box of makeup her dad bought her in the Summer holidays.

In English Ruhy sits next to Ayesha. She has brought a CD for Mr Ford to play, a song called 'My Favourite Things'. Last week they were writing about their favourite things, but today the CD-player won't work. In her book she has written a long list of her favourite things:

Food: Pizza
Animal: Dolphin
Film: *Freaky Friday*
Author: Michael Morpurgo
Teacher: Miss Ioannou
Sport: Swimming
TV programme: *My Wife and Kids*
Subject: Art
Country: Sweden
Clothing: Pedal-pushers
Celebrity: Beyoncé
Actor: Leonardo di Caprio
Jewellery: Gold hoop earrings
Smell: Strawberry
Song: 'My Favourite Things'

And she has written:

My happiest memory was when I was three and a half and I went on my first holiday. I remember holding my mum's hand and going up the stairs on to the aeroplane.

Ambitions. To be a fashion designer, to be a beautician. To be a teacher. To go scuba diving. To own a holiday villa in Hawaii. To take a gap year and explore the Amazon. To have my handprint in the Hollywood Walk of fame. To have a nose job.

Fantasies. To be a dolphin, to become a princess, to live for ever. To touch the bottom of the Pacific Ocean. Another fantasy is I have got ten children. I would like to do that because I'm an only child and that makes me want to have lots of children. When I was little I had all the names and descriptions of my children.

Pink is one of my favourite colours because it makes me feel warm and happy inside. Another of my favourite colours is blue because it reminds me of the sky. Lilac is also one of my favourite colours because it just is.

When she thinks what her friends would say about her, she thinks mostly they would say she is a bit weird, because sometimes, when they're walking down the street, not talking about anything in particular, she will say, 'I've got a dog in Iran.' That makes Gita laugh. But then she hugs her and says she's lovely, too.

Her friends would also say she studies quite hard: she gets good marks and comments from the teachers. But she chats a lot in class – she finds it hard not to. Her life story? 'It's been happy,' she says.

The first thing she remembers is going up the stairs of the aeroplane with her mum, the day they left Iran. She was happy because she was going on holiday. She was going to visit her auntie in Sweden. It was like... a big adventure. She only found out later that her Mum had known they were not going back.

Mostly she remembers nice things – like when they were in Sweden and her auntie's neighbour was so lovely she was like a grandma. While they were there, she had her fourth birthday and this lady gave her a red purse. She kept it until last year, when she lost it. Her auntie in Sweden used to be a journalist. Sometimes she thinks she might be a journalist, too, instead of a fashion designer. Her auntie worked on a newspaper in Tehran.

There is one thing she can remember about Iran: the nursery she went to. They had bunk beds for when they went to sleep. A little boy had a plastic ball. He put it in his mouth, then took it out again and said, 'Do you want to play with it?' And she was, like, 'No, thanks.'

She doesn't remember anything about why they came here, but her mum has told her. When the revolution happened, Ruhy's mum was in England, taking a secretarial course. Then she went back to Iran to study Persian literature at university. She wore the same clothes as everyone else but they told her she did not look right. She did not walk or talk like a religious person. One day she was in an exam and the examiner came up to her and hissed at her to cover herself. She felt her hair but it was all under her scarf. 'You are showing your body,' the woman said. Then she saw where her eye had fallen: her ankle was showing. She wanted to tell the woman to shut her mouth, but she could not. She never went back to university.

Instead she worked as a secretary, and it was OK. In the office they were all women together and could relax. If a religious visitor came they were warned and would cover themselves.

But Ruhy's mum says she doesn't want her daughter to grow up like that. At school Ruhy would have studied Islam and played behind a high wall where no one could see her. She would never have worn nail varnish, or a short skirt, or highlights in her hair. She would not have plucked her eyebrows like some of her friends do. In class when the bell went she would have stood up straight and not moved.

Ruhy doesn't remember arriving at Heathrow. But her mum does. She says that when they came into the arrivals area the man who had brought them disappeared, and she didn't know what to do. So she sat down for about an hour to think. Then she went to the immigration officers and said, 'I have no passport. I am a refugee.'

They came to England in August and Ruhy started nursery school in September. On the first day she met her friend Elizabeth. Her mum had stayed outside in case she cried, but after an hour they told her to go home. When she came back Ruhy and Elizabeth were playing together so well that you wouldn't have known they didn't speak the same language. Ruhy doesn't remember not being able to speak English.

When she left primary school her head teacher wrote in her book: 'When you came here you could not speak English. Now you speak more than anyone.'

At home she thinks in Farsi, but at school she thinks in English. When they first came here her mum spoke English to her, to help her learn, but now they can speak Farsi together. And she speaks to her dad on the phone in Farsi. He still lives in Iran, but he phones every day. And he visits. Sometimes he takes her to the park and tries to teach her to play football. And she's like, yeah, yeah. OK. Sometimes he takes her out to a restaurant in Kensington. But best of all is when he takes her shopping.

Mr Ford still cannot make the CD-player work, so they will have to listen to her song next time. When the bell goes she swings her bag over her shoulder and trips down the corridor with Fazia and Gita. They are teasing Fazia: 'Fazia fancies Yusuf.' Ruhy skips around her. They have reached their classroom.

'You and Yusuf, sitting in a tree—' Ruhy breaks off, dashes to Gita and grabs her hairclip again. Gita, giggling, rushes to her and trickles some Fanta over Ruhy's head from a bottle she's holding. Ruhy shrieks, flapping her hands in the air.

Before she can look up, everything goes silent. She stands up straight, looks at the teacher who has entered the room and doesn't move.

DOUG HARRISON

Doug Harrison's face is set in a stern expression – a professional tool, not his natural demeanour. Given the choice, he would assume a much more relaxed air, but right now there is discipline to be dispensed.

It is just a few weeks into the autumn term but already this small boy is in trouble. Doug finishes reading the paper that has been placed reluctantly in his outstretched palm, and lowers it with an air of disappointment. 'Tell me what sort of person you are,' he says.

The boy stares at the floor.

'If I was to ask your teacher, what would she say?'

'She'd say I talk too much, sir.'

'Are you rude?'

'No.'

'Are you well behaved in lessons?'

'Sometimes.'

His expression hardens. 'Only sometimes?'

The boy squirms. 'Because sometimes I get distracted.'

'Tell me why I have a note to say that your behaviour at the beginning of the last lesson was appalling.'

'I was talking—'

Doug interrupts, an edge in his voice: 'The word here is "appalling". Do you understand what that means? It means something far worse than simply talking.'

'Well...' he stumbles, '...when he came in I pushed Arif. Then he pushed me. Then we were talking, loud.'

'That's not very good, is it? What would your parents say if I rang them up?'

'Disappointed, sir,' he mumbles.

'Yes. I'd be disappointed if I was your dad. So, what are you going to do?'

'Apologize, sir.'

'Yes. That's exactly what you're going to do. You're going to go back to your teacher and apologize.'

He dismisses the boy.

In room two, his year seven class is waiting. They are about to embark on an assignment about the area where they live. He casts his eye around them. 'Samir, could you go to my office and find my briefcase? It's disguised as a Tesco bag. Thanks.'

In the classroom he takes the register. 'Gita... Wah-se-may? I'm sorry, I'll get it right before the end of term... Luke?... "Sir", please, not "yup"... Thank you. So, what's the first thing to do in geography if we want to find out about a place?'

'Go there?'

'Well, that would be nice. I'd quite like to go to Antarctica.' A little ripple of amusement. 'What else?'

'Books?'

'Maps?'

'The Internet?'

They talk a bit about where they are: urban or rural? Residential, retail, industrial?

'Where is London?'

'In the south.'

'And where is Redbridge?'

'Zone four...'

He talks about how the Romans named Ilford: Hill Ford, because it is situated on a hill and in a place where they would have crossed the river Roding.

Samir reappears, carrying the 'briefcase'. 'I couldn't find it, sir. I thought you said Sainsbury's.'

Doug holds it up so that everyone can see it. It is a Tesco Bag for Life, with spring lambs frolicking on it. Not bad, but he still misses the heavy-duty Woolworths bags they had in the 1970s: thick and red, with white writing on them. Someone gave him a Harrods bag once, but it was useless.

He pulls out the worksheets and hands them round. Each is an A4 piece of paper with boxes for the children to fill in details of the area where they live. The marking scheme is attached, so they can see how many marks are allotted to each question and what they have to do to get them: one mark for saying there is a supermarket, another for naming it.

The usual hands are up. Someone wanting to know for the fourth time what the title is. Someone else wanting to know if it is all right to put that he lives on 'kind of an island'. Doug gives one of his shrugs: shoulders raised, upper arms straight, lower arms splayed. This is his small shrug. The big one is like the Angel of the North. 'I'm losing the will to live.' His eyebrows arch and he glances at the ceiling.

The class laughs appreciatively. At the front, Ruhy giggles.

He has slung his suit jacket on the back of a chair, and his shirt sleeves are rolled up. Suits are a part of the job, these days, especially for senior staff, but his does not sit comfortably on him. The trousers tend to wrinkle at the ankles.

The lesson over, he puts the jacket on and pulls up a boy for carrying his blazer over his shoulder. 'I've put mine back on. You can do the same.'

He slings his bag into his office and makes for the canteen. It is Ramadan, so the straggly queue is shorter than usual.

'Packed lunches? Away you go… Yes, Everton, man and boy… Since Rooney's gone… Lindsay, how many badges is that?'

'Five, sir.' Lindsay's face is open and cheerful, as always. A slick of blue eyeshadow. Lip gloss. Dangly earrings. He could comment on half a dozen things, but Lindsay has other issues in her life. Indeed, he might choose to congratulate her on having made it to school today because sometimes she doesn't. But sarcasm is not in his nature. 'But two of them are relevant!' she adds, and puts her finger on the one that says 'School Council'.

He grins. 'I'm not quite sure what the rest are for,' he says, and lets her go.

Behind her, a new girl looks pained. 'Sir, my shoes are hurting. I ain't never had to wear shoes till I came here. I only wear trainers usually.'

Tyrone is jostling and larking with his friend Calvin. 'Sir, I've been to Amsterdam,' Calvin says. 'Do you know why?'

'I can't think. Must have been the canals.'

'It was educational, sir. Urban science.'

Doug waves him on without comment.

Wesley, walking behind, offers a clenched-fist greeting. Doug clenches his own and responds in kind, with a light fist-to-fist touch.

After all these years, Doug Harrison jokes sometimes that

he's still thinking about what he wants to do with his life, but that's not true. He's still teaching because when he gets up in the morning he feels happy to go to work. At grammar school in North Wales someone suggested teacher training, so that was what he did. Then a group of them at college decided to stick together and teach in Redbridge. That was 1969, four of them. One's dead now. One moved to Lincolnshire. The other teaches part time at Redbridge College. Doug started his teaching career at Downshall Secondary Modern School for Boys. Things came along at the right times – becoming a year head, then pastoral head of this school. Now he teaches geography half the time, does pastoral work the other half. Discipline. Attendance. Welfare. Unhappy parents. Pastoral is not a sexy word any more, but it's what he does.

Being pastoral is about dealing with things before they come up. With his year group, year ten, he always has something individual to say to each child when he meets them around the school. A word about a brother or sister, or something that's going on in their life. It's a hard thing to measure, and if you tried you'd probably stop doing it. If you counted up the hours he spends, having a little chat here, a word about the football there, lending an ear somewhere else, you'd say it cost too much money. Yet it's the bedrock on which so much else is built. It's the difference between walking about the school barking orders, and quietly letting the kids understand the structure. If they know you, and they know you like them, they tend to buy into the system. You don't often hear teachers shouting at Seven Kings.

Teaching used to be a vocation, now it's a profession. The quality of teaching is far better. Teachers are better prepared. The lessons are more innovative. His first CSE syllabus had been on agriculture: he had a list of ten different types and went through them, one by one. Downshall Secondary Modern wasn't a bad school, but there was only one football in the place. You'd set up a lesson that needed a projector, and the room you were in wouldn't have the right plug. You spent hours making posters, getting things together. Now there is more money, and there is the Internet.

When Downshall's boys moved here, they formed an at-first uneasy alliance with Beal Grammar School's girls. It was a strange time – boys who wouldn't have been looked at twice by those girls now walking down the corridors like peacocks with one on each arm; grammar-school teachers struggling to adjust to mixed-ability teaching. Some were arrogant, and most didn't really teach, just dictated. Quite a few left. But it was always a good school. Kids knew they were valued. There was a structure, and they responded to it. Even those who might have become a problem knew where they stood.

Are children worse than they used to be? People often ask him that. He doesn't think so. The big difference is that peer pressure is more of a problem. You can speak to some pupils on their own and they're nice as pie, but put them in a group and it's a different matter. They're with their mates. They can't lose face. You need to be aware of that.

You also need to be aware that every evening the gossip and intrigue of the day will spread and grow on MSN. It will leap from house to house like a virus. There's something about the semi-anonymity of the computer screen that dampens inhibition. Things are said, feelings are hurt. Someone gets upset, and trouble spills into school the next morning.

There are other networks, too, that spread beyond the school boundaries. There are websites that the black kids in different schools subscribe to. When a message goes out, and five or six kids from each school in the district respond, the next thing you know twenty or thirty kids are hanging around the Exchange shopping centre, waiting for the scrap. It happens right across London.

And there are local problems. Last night two pupils excluded from another school tried to force their way into Seven Kings. Doug had met them before and so had the school caretaker, Dave Starkey. Doug and Dave caught them in the school not long ago, stealing laptops. So, when Dave spotted them outside the gate, he wouldn't let them in. They threatened him. He stood his ground. Eventually they left, saying they would return today 'to cut him up'. The police have been informed, but their concern hasn't stretched to any visible presence at the school. So, Doug's day will end as it began, at the gate, having a word or two here and there, scanning the traffic. Marking the all-important boundary between street and school.

SHIVANIE

She leans her forehead against the cool glass and drinks in the view. Below, Bassenthwaite lake is spread out, its blue-black water dappled at the end with clumps of boggy grass. October has crept in and the Lakeland mountains are wearing autumn coats, dark orange and rust woven into the deep green of the pines. When she scrunches up her eyes she can make out wisps of cloud, drifting below the line of the ridge. 'This is fantastic,' she says. 'It's *sooo* good waking up in the morning and seeing this.' Her best friend Jas nods, mutely compliant.

They have been here for two days, at a special outdoor pursuit centre for the disabled, and they are tired. The hour between five and six is the only time they have to chill out in the whole day. They are busy all the time. They spent the afternoon in the woods, carrying cups of water round the assault course, trying not to spill them, helping each other under and over logs. David eyed the cups hopefully: 'Is that petrol? Are we going to blow something up?' They screamed with laughter as they swung down the aerial runway and over the stream, the teachers splashing them with water as they flew across. Sparring with Jack on the way round. Me first. No, me. Jack leaning over and licking her face. Eurgh. She rubs her cheek again. Jack has Down's syndrome and doesn't understand he musn't do it.

She searched under the trees in the rain for conkers, smooth chestnut spots on a rough chestnut background of fallen leaves, telling everyone, cheerfully, 'I have a sight problem. I can't really do this.' But she came back with pockets full. She put them straight into the sink to wash them in case of slugs. Jas's side of the room is neat and tidy. Shivanie's is a big jumble of clothes.

There are several things wrong with her eyes: photophobia, which means she's blinded by bright light, and partial colour-blindness. Its overall name is rod monochromatism. The consultant at Moorfields Eye Hospital explained it to her like this: basically there are rods and cones in your eyes, like two triangles. One lot of triangles are from rods, and the other lot are from cones. They send out information to your eye. If they aren't working properly not all the proper information can be sent. Her cones aren't working properly. They call that cone dystrophy. Her sister, Dipti, has it too. So, she wears these

44

purple-framed glasses and sometimes she looks at the world through half-closed eyes. But she has learned to recognize all the different colours. And it's getting better: she can do just about anything she wants to.

When she was little she went to a special nursery called Joseph Clarke. It had a little swimming-pool, and she had two friends called Lucy and Sana. Sana loved red but Lucy loved yellow, and so did Shivanie. And there were two school buses, one red, one yellow. When the yellow bus came Shivanie and Lucy would shout, 'Yellow!' And when the red bus came Sana would shout, 'Red!' Shivanie liked it there. But it was kind of weird. If she went there now she'd feel like an invalid.

At school sometimes one of the boys calls her evil because of her squint. One day she bumped into two boys from her year and they laughed. So she said, 'It's not my fault. I have an eyesight problem.' They said they hadn't forgotten and started laughing again. That made her really annoyed. But here, on this trip, she has reigned supreme. Yesterday she won the chocolate bar for being the bravest on the climbing wall. She went right to the top and waved. Later, when she is launched in a swing from the ceiling of the gym, she will scream with the sheer joy of flying through the air.

She is still staring dreamily at the view. 'It makes me think of being in an aeroplane. You know when you're in a plane and you can see the sun shining on the clouds and it's so cool? I want to ask for the plane to stop so I can get out and just sit on the clouds.'

She has been on a plane about five times; three or four times to India, once to Kenya. Kenya was beautiful. Her dad says in Kenya he used to live in a really big house... What was it? The size of two football pitches? She's not sure. Her auntie, her dad's sister, lives in Kenya. But her dad's mum lives here, round the corner.

'Jas,' she says, 'what do you call your grandfather?'

'Babaji. And Dad is Dadaji.'

'In Gujerati my grandmother is Ba.'

She has known Jas since her first day at primary school. It's eight years now since she saw her sitting there, needing someone to talk to. So she talked to her, but Jas couldn't talk back because she didn't speak English then. Jas's mum comes from South Africa, and at home she speaks Punjabi. At school they go everywhere together.

'Swimming now, Jas.' They trot to their room to root out their costumes.

At lunch they are all handed little brown envelopes with their money in, to spend in Keswick. She has twenty pounds. Maybe she will buy some jewellery for the disco tonight. She will wear her pink cords, a pink top and a white poncho that belongs to Jas. In the minibus she and Jas wonder idly which member of Busted is the nicest.

'You like Charlie.'

'No, I don't.'

'Yes, you do... Which member of Busted do you think Mr Whiteson looks like?'

They both collapse in giggles.

The good thing to do would be to save some of her twenty pounds to give away. She goes to a Saturday school where they learn about different religions, do drama and stuff like that. They are collecting for people to have eye operations in India. It costs five hundred pounds to cure one person's cataracts.

The minibus parks and they all jump out, then run up the pedestrianized street to Woolworth's. 'Three ninety-nine for a single? Give me a break.' They drift past the jewellery – 'This stuff's all rubbish' – and spend a few minutes examining a Halloween mask that looks like an elongated skull, captured mid-scream.

Shivanie wanders outside with Jas. At a stall in the street she buys a little pot full of scented rocks and a scented candle, and the lady gives her a lavender bag for free. When she gets back to the minibus she has twelve pounds fifty left. Far too much to give to her Saturday-school project.

David is dwarfed by a huge scythe, like the one the Grim Reaper carries, but it's made of foam rubber. Jack is clutching a brown-paper bag. He puts in a hand and reveals the head of a chocolate Santa Claus, covered with silver paper. 'For my mum.' Its hips and legs are already missing. Someone puts on a tape of really old songs, and they all sing at the top of their voices.

ANGELA CASSIDY

As usual she was here before eight, sitting at her desk in the medical centre, writing furiously. She looks up from the learning-support assistants' daily timetables and glares with undisguised animosity at the fish tank. At this time in the morning its inane babbling fills the air. A pasty pink creature stares rudely at her with bulging eyes. Beneath it, another sucks the green algae from the glass with an oddly prehensile mouth. Mutants, she thinks, then checks herself – and laughs. She doesn't believe in being politically correct.

When she started here eleven years ago there were two PD children at the school – the borough centre for children with physical disabilities – and one learning-support assistant. One of the two children was barely disabled at all. Angela was so bored that twice within the first week she picked up the phone to tell Alan she was leaving. He wasn't there. Otherwise she would have gone.

After the hurly-burly of nursing at the Royal London Hospital, she thought she was calcifying. One day, anything from road accidents to machete attacks, the next, almost nothing. But the senior welfare officer's job grew. Now there are thirty-eight PD kids, six full-time wheelchair-users, a few with quite severe learning difficulties and twenty-six learning-support assistants. Last week several went on an autumn trip to Keswick; this week they're back to normal.

Nowadays she manages all that as well as dealing with child protection and attendance – plus the constant stream of pupils who drift in with grazed knees, toothache, or need to phone home because they've forgotten their games kit. Or because they're feeling a bit vulnerable and want some time out.

A jumble of lost property and other jetsam – a multi-coloured fluffy duster on a stick, a cricket bat, five metres of electric cable – sits in a corner. Most of the small, lost things in the school wind up here eventually. She makes a virtue of it. Sometimes she'll spot a child out there, beyond the pale wood double doors of the medical centre, and send a PD kid to fetch them in. What if it was one of her own? She'd want to know they had somewhere to feel safe.

At eight forty she has her first customer. A girl with a headache.

'Can I have a paracetamol, Miss?'

'I'm sorry, I'm not allowed to dispense drugs. Is there anyone at home who can bring you some in?'

'No, Miss.'

She looks at her watch. 'Have you got any money?'

'Yes, Miss.'

'You'd better walk up to the shop to get some. Report back to me before nine.'

The girl leaves. As Angela glances at her retreating back, someone else catches her eye. A small boy is hovering uncertainly outside her door. 'My teacher sent me, Miss.'

'And what can I do for you, er...?' She looks at him expectantly.

'Arron, Miss. I was upset... in registration.' He shifts awkwardly from one foot to the other, gazing at the floor. His face twists.

'I see. And why was that?'

'It was my dad, Miss. And my stepmum.'

'You'd better come in and sit down.' She closes the door behind him. 'What's happened?'

'Well, I had an argument with my stepmum because I tore my school trousers. And then she hit me. And my dad locked me in my room and made me stay on my knees all night, praying.' She can see he has been crying. He is calmer now but his voice is barely audible and he is playing with a piece of tissue. 'I'm not going back,' he says.

She promises to help, and sends him to sit in the medical room next door. Social Services will have to be involved, but first she must phone Dad. She taps her keyboard, looking for the number on the screen. Lifts the phone and dials.

'Hello – Mr Samuel? It's Mrs Cassidy here at Seven Kings High School. I deal with child protection... Yes, well, I've had Arron here. He's quite upset... about being hit and locked in his... Yes. I'm sure there is. But I have to take that seriously.

He says he won't return home so I'll have to call Social Services... No, I'm not at the minute... He's not here.' She glances through the glass between her office and the medical room. She can see the back of Arron's head.

She puts down the phone quietly. What will Social Services do? It's complicated. Arron has also told her that last night's crisis was not the first. The family has moved around but she wants to ensure that he is placed in care in Redbridge. He needs to come to school. It is one of the few places he feels safe and secure.

It seems so incongruous. Here is this boy, with his London street accent, his sculpted hair, the same uniform as everyone else, yet he goes home to a father and stepmother who believe he has demons inside him. A regularly administered punishment has reduced him to this clenched state. It makes her angry. Sometimes it's hard to make these calls calmly.

She lifts the phone again to ring Social Services and ask them to send someone to fetch Arron. She goes next door to tell him what's happening, and asks if he wants to go to his lesson. He shakes his head miserably.

As she returns to her office she meets Doug Harrison coming the other way. He needs to talk about Amina Simpson. Last week they had her in with her mum and explained to them that Mrs Simpson will be in court before the end of term if Amina does not attend school regularly.

She's a puzzle, that girl. She's very bright, popular with the other pupils in year nine, doesn't seem unhappy, yet when they ask why she's hardly ever here she just shrugs. Her mum makes all the right noises, but claims she has not received any of the letters that have been sent.

Amina is supposed to check in with Angela every morning.

A piece of paper is taped to the side of her computer screen, which Amina is meant to sign. But so far she has not been in. Angela picks up the phone again. 'Mrs Simpson? It's Mrs Cassidy. Is Amina coming to school?' She can hear a murmured conversation down the line: 'Are you going to school, Amina?'... 'Of course I am.' There is surprise that anyone should have felt the need to ask. Her attendance since September stands at 30 per cent, one of the lowest in the school.

She also needs to make one of her frequent calls to Mrs Ambrose. She sighs. What's the point? Six kids, and the oldest girl already has one foot in Holloway: drugs, prostitution. And Angela is phoning to ask why her fourteen-year-old brother is not at school. He's slightly deaf and gets learning support, but as often as not when she schedules an assistant for him he doesn't turn up. It's been going on for years, with one child or another from that family. You get cynical. How many meetings can you have to say the same things time and time again? It makes absolutely no difference. You go through the motions, then you move on to the next child and do the same thing.

On the first day of term, the youngest Ambrose boy arrived at eleven o'clock. When Angela asked why, he said it was because his mum hadn't bought him any shoes. On the morning term started she'd given him some money, but he had to go out and get them himself so he was late. And he is missing again today. She dials. Ansaphone. They're always on ansaphone. 'It's Mrs Cassidy. I'm wondering about Robbie – he's not at school. Can you ring me, please?' She replaces the receiver and sighs.

At eleven thirty, Amina arrives in a rush.

'Here at last!' Angela exclaims.

'Miss! I had to go to the dentist! I got up late!'

Still no sign of anyone from Social Services. She phones them again. Again, they assure her someone will be there soon. On the other side of the glass, she can still see Arron's bowed head.

At lunchtime, the usual group of physically disabled kids arrive and skitter into her office to pull belongings from the cupboard. David produces a carrier-bag and hands his Tesco microwaveable burger to a learning-support assistant to heat up for him. He could use the canteen, but he chooses not to. Some of them prefer it here: it's calmer, safer. Out there, they can feel threatened by the crowds. In here there is space, light and an assistant to help.

Sometimes they get out of hand. Sometimes there are food fights. Then she gets very stern and throws them out. But usually they're back after about ten minutes: they can feel isolated out there, in the crowd.

With the best will in the world, some of these kids find it hard to mix. When they are eleven or twelve the ones in wheel-chairs tend to be well looked after by their friends. Perhaps they're a bit of a novelty. But then they hit the disco years and it's all nightclubs, street cred and what-do-I-look-like-in-this. That's when they don't necessarily get invited to the right clubs and parties. It's just the way it is. It's life, and it's horrible.

As lunchtime ends, she clears out the medical room and sends a couple of pupils back to class. That leaves a girl with stomach-ache, and Arron. Someone has brought him some work to do and he's looking at it blankly.

Still no sign of Social Services. She phones them again. Now they tell her no one's available to come over. She'll have to take him herself. Poor kid. She knows that Social Services will do everything in their power to persuade him to go home. And the shocking thing is that it's probably the best place for him. Why? Because most of the care places available will probably be just as bad, one way or another.

They're just about to leave when her phone rings. Arron's dad is in Reception. He seems agitated. She swears inwardly. She'd had the impression when she spoke to him that he might be on a short fuse.

She tells Arron they'll leave by the back door. They get outside and into the car park, but at this time of day the back gate is locked for security reasons. As they drive past the front of the school, Arron tenses. 'Miss, that's my dad's car... That's my stepmum.'

She sees a thin woman sitting in the front passenger seat and hits the accelerator, ignoring the speed bumps on the drive. Behind her, a man is emerging from Reception. She's keeping calm, chatting to Arron, trying to let him know that she's in control, everything's OK. But she's constantly looking in her rear-view mirror. Is she being followed? Arron sits hunched in the passenger seat.

It seems like hours later when they finally pull up outside the Social Services office and park on double yellow lines. She takes Arron inside, restraining herself from rushing him through the doors. The social worker who greets them is reassuring, takes them upstairs, tells Arron he'll be safe there.

They sit down and talk for a few minutes. Arron is starting to breathe again. He tells the social worker, as he told Angela, that he won't go home. 'But what about my sisters? The little one was locked in her room all last weekend and they didn't even give her any food most of the time. And my dad has a stick with a leather thong on the end. He threatens to use that on us, too.'

The social worker makes reassuring noises. Then she takes Angela aside and tells her that Arron's father is downstairs. She shows her how to get out of the building without meeting him, and warns that the car will probably have been clamped. Before she leaves Angela gives Arron a hug. Suddenly they feel like comrades.

Her heart is pounding as she closes the door behind her, but she heaves a sigh of relief when she finds her car free and unclamped. She gets in and drives away, knowing Arron will almost certainly go back to face his father and stepmother tonight.

What has she done for him? Nothing. He came to her because he thought and hoped something would change. When it happens again, will he come to her? Why should he? In the end, she could not help him. That is how they lose children.

KESSIE

At lunchtime the ground-floor of the sixth-form block is not where she chooses to be. The music pounds – she can hear it now or maybe she's feeling it in the soles of her feet, a muffled, rapid thump, vibrating up through the floor. Her place is here, in the first booth in this row, next to where the supervisor sits. In study periods, at morning break, at lunchtime, she needs to work. She has an exam next week. At Seven Kings they keep you busy.

Grace is with her, of course. They're always together. There is a companionable feeling about sitting together like this, in their adjoining booths, heads down. As usual they are both wearing long, parka-type anoraks with fur round the hood. Underneath Kessie is in a plain white shirt and beige trousers. Her hair is straightened and highlighted, pulled back tight round her head with a tortoiseshell clip.

Sometimes she has to go down and edge through the crowd, maybe for food, maybe to see Miss Jones, who is head of the sixth form and also Kessie's maths teacher, to ask her to explain again some problem she has been wrestling with. And again, if need be. The way she sees it, she comes to school to work. Sometimes it's hard, and she has to push and push, but she knows there's nothing she can't do.

It's mid-October and she's applying for university places for next year. She has chosen pharmacy, maybe at Manchester or Nottingham. In the past few weeks she and her dad have been to both cities to have a look. She quite liked Nottingham, but she's not sure. The campus is big, green and open. She prefers the hubbub of the city. Manchester was far away from home, and it cost a great deal to get there. Maybe she'll go to Aston, in Birmingham.

She talks to her dad a lot. If she falters, it's her dad she turns to. He talks about President Kennedy, how he never gave up. When he lost, he asked, 'How did I lose? Was it the way I campaigned? Some mistake somewhere?' And he came back and he was one of the best presidents. In life, you have to struggle. You must never give up. And, he says, she has no cause for doubt. In Genesis 18:14, God told Sarah, the wife of Abraham, that in a year she would give birth to a son. And she doubted, and laughed, because Abraham was ninety-nine years old. And God told Sarah, 'Why are you laughing? There is nothing too hard for God to do.'

So, he says, there is nothing Kessie cannot do with the help of God.

Her dad says that if you think where you are is comfortable, that's no good. While you are young and have strength, there is more ahead of you that you have to do. And he says he does not want his children to be postmen like him. He wants them to go above him. He tells her that God is her foundation, her backbone. Since they have known God, their lives have got better. God says that without vision you will perish. If you just think, I'm running! you have no aim. Why are you running? You are running to get to the prize. To seal your future bright.

When she was a little girl in Ghana she'd thought she would be a doctor. She remembers going to the surgery with her mother and looking up to that man. He seemed to be respected by everyone, so she felt that was where she wanted to be. To have that respect, and that independence.

But when she was about fourteen she began to do some research. She thought about the crazy hours, the blood and gore. And she is kind of picky about what she touches. She wants to work with people, but she doesn't want physical contact with them. So, she realized it was not a doctor she wanted to be.

Her mum suggested she look into pharmacy. All she had really seen was someone standing in a chemist's shop. But there are quite a few different things she could do. She could imagine herself in a community pharmacy, maybe, running her own business.

When she came to Britain she was ten. That was in 1996. She remembers the cold, and feeling new and strange, that first day at her primary school in Stratford. She remembers, too, how rude the other children seemed. It was kind of shocking to see that at first. Not that there are no rude children in Ghana, but when they talk to a teacher they are not rude. In Ghana you stand up when you answer a question. You do not shout out, you wait to be called.

She remembers the teacher, trying to make her feel welcome, saying, 'Here is another little girl who has come from your country.' And that was Grace. There were other children in the class from Ghana, but she and Grace had a bond.

They do everything together. They went to Sarah Bonnell secondary school in Newham together, then applied for Seven Kings sixth form. They travel back and forth on the bus together, they go to church together. They share things. Even the things she can't talk to her dad about because, after all, he is her dad! She looks at Grace now and smiles.

She will always feel Ghanaian, even though she will live in Britain. It matters. If England ever played Ghana at some sport, she would be torn. At home, she speaks Twi to her dad and her auntie. Her mum is away at the moment travelling. Her younger brothers and sister understand Twi, but they don't feel confident speaking it because they were too small when they came here to have spoken it in Ghana. They are not sure their accents sound right.

She and Grace understand where the pieces of their lives fit together, where God comes in and where He stops. On one level, though, what drives her is something much more of this world: ambition. She knows where she wants to be and she knows what she has to do to get there. She wants to be able to take care of herself and her family, and she wants to earn respect.

At Sarah Bonnell they used to talk about Seven Kings in the same way that at Seven Kings they talk about Cambridge. You just thought, Wow! Even to get an interview for a sixth-form place was a big deal. It felt weird, trying to picture herself here. But it was Seven Kings, and her teachers at Sarah Bonnell had told her that if she came here she would get her work done. Guaranteed.

She was offered a place with Grace and a few others, but lots more didn't get in. Now she puts away her maths, and Grace does the same. Time for Registration, then a maths lesson. In their form room, which is in the sixth-form block, they sit quietly in their seats at the side of the room. There are fifteen minutes till the bell. Some of the others are larking about, laughing and joking, but Kessie and Grace get out their maths practice papers again. One of the other girls is doing a survey for some piece of coursework, about whether black girls feel well represented in women's magazines. What do they think? she wants to know.

Kessie and Grace look up blankly from their maths. 'We read *New Scientist*,' Grace explains, apologetic now. 'It helps with our UCAS forms.' That's partly why they did community service last year at the Springfield old people's home. Everywhere around them, people are clocking up experiences to write on the UCAS form. School council, being a prefect, playing a sport – it all helps.

In Miss Jones's maths lesson today they'll work in groups, solving problems on 'type one' and 'type two' errors. The other day Kessie went to Miss Jones's office – picking her way through the noise and chaos, ignoring the posters for the sixth-form committee elections: 'Hey! You! Vote for Rashida for President!' 'Put the P back into Party – vote for Prakash for Social Secretary!' and said to her: 'About these error types. I don't quite understand. I feel like I don't know what I'm doing.

I'm getting the answers right, but I'm not sure I understand why. Can you sit down with me and talk it through?' So Miss Jones tried to explain the concept underlying what Kessie was doing, and eventually the penny dropped.

After that Miss Jones had said Kessie was was one of the most determined people she had ever met. 'You see things behind what you're trying to do that perhaps escape other people. And you worry about it.'

Kessie smiled her quiet smile, and told Miss Jones that if she bugged her it was for the good of both of them: if Miss Jones helped her she would get good grades, which could only be good for her teacher. Miss Jones had laughed.

Today, in the classroom, she waits while the rest of the set argue about how to divide thirteen of them into four groups. Miss Jones looks at them, mock stern. 'My goodness! A-level maths and they don't know how to divide thirteen into four!'

The matter settled, they look at the problem. It's about estimating the probability, if you have a jar of black marbles and gold marbles, of correctly assessing a hypothesis on whether there are equal numbers of each. A girl and a boy start a long discussion about how they should go about solving it.

Kessie looks at the sheet. 'It's binomial, isn't it?' She starts to write down formulas, then pulls out her Tables of Cumulative Binomial Probabilities, and goes through them. 'I'm just trying to see if I can do this...' she says, almost to herself.

'So,' the girl says, 'we take everything that is more than ten or less than fifteen. Does that make sense?'

Kessie does not respond for a second. She is hesitating. She knows it doesn't, but she does not want to be rude. She smiles hesitantly. 'It makes sense...'

But the girl sees her expression. 'It doesn't, does it?'

Miss Jones materializes at her elbow, and explains why Kessie is right and the other girl is wrong.

'Sorry, Kessie,' the girl says, embarassed by her mistake. But there is no need. She needs no reassurance. There is a calm space inside her.

ANTHONY

> *Yo blud this is Blaze King*
> *Letting y'all punks know about life and drugs, ite*
> *Yo drop that shit.*

A kind of thinly controlled anarchy has taken hold in the school hall. It is dark, and the noise is deafening. There are kids, parents. Talking, shouting, yelling. The seats are banked up and coloured lights are playing across the stage. Mr Lord is trying to raise his voice above the din. He looks stressed and a bit excited. Tickets have been hard to get and already the doorkeepers have rooted out some forgeries. 'Welcome to the Seven Kings twenty-sixth annual talent show. I have been here twenty-six years, and this is my last.' There is a rising howl of booing. 'Can I ask for phones to be switched off? And please don't stand up in your seats.' He doesn't look as if he expects anyone to take much notice – or even, perhaps, as if he cares. This annual late-October event is the one night in the year when the Seven Kings culture loosens its grip.

In the crowd Anthony slouches in his seat, flanked by his friends Romy and Delroy, wearing a grey and white hooded top. His head is close-shaved; the words of the rap he wrote for this evening are inside it.

> *Yo never do weed, never do crack,*
> *Never do X, never do that,*
> *Never do drugs, never do needles,*
> *Never do LSD, cos it's illegal...*

The first act is three boys with guitars, calling themselves Levaticus. As they take the stage he is half listening, half chatting to Romy. Not really his kind of thing. But the crowd is hyped up, whistling and cheering. Delroy leans over his seat to talk to someone behind. Anthony turns, too.

'Ant! Are you doing your rap, man?' A stage whisper.

He looks sheepish. 'Nah, man. I didn't do it in time. Missed the audition.'

'Shit, man. You were good last year.'

He finished it anyway, though. Working away at one in the morning, typing it out on his computer.

> *Used 2 be hooked...*
> *then I started wantin' 2 learn and read books*
> *Still aint working, still addicted...*
> *I'm just young, high, white and gifted...*
> *quit for a few weeks, then damn I missed it...*
> *Yo I love green, ma boys and ma fam...*
> *I blaze more skunk than living in Amsterdam.*

Three girls come on and perform a dance with more enthusiasm than co-ordination. A boy gives a haunting guitar solo. A girl sings, struggling to make herself heard over the noise.

Some of the boys are laughing and chatting, but Anthony is quiet, impassive.

A girl in a boned red top, black cropped trousers and red stilettos gets up to sing. There is more whistling and stamping. Romy passes his phone to Anthony, who holds it up to take a picture. Somewhere in the middle of the crowd, the dry ice is making someone cough.

ALAN STEER

At the back of the hall Alan Steer allows himself imperceptibly to relax. The talent evening is a tense time. He cannot pretend it's his kind of thing. There have been words, with Tony Lord, in the light of past experience, along the lines, if he recalls correctly, that he does not want young girls prancing about shaking their backsides in a provocative manner. In his view it is inappropriate.

He thinks girls should not be encouraged to behave like that. It is not good for their self-image. It is exploitative. If you pushed him, he would say it was in bad taste. Just as he would say that lap-dancing was in bad taste. And he doesn't think it's good for parents to see it because it might make them uncomfortable.

He smiles resignedly. It's not to his taste, but that goes without saying. It wouldn't be much of a talent evening if it was – he can see that. But there's been nothing to concern him, really. People talk about youth culture, he reflects. And maybe they say, 'Oh, this is youth culture. That makes it OK.' Well, in his view it doesn't. Not if it's rubbish culture. If it's rubbish culture, it should be stamped on. If it's sexually explicit, or homophobic, or Anthony is writing obscenities into his raps, he feels he should not sanction it just because it is 'youth culture'.

Actually, he thinks youth culture is quite different from the sort of culture most people envisage when they use the phrase. If anything, the pupils here are quite a conservative bunch. He thinks it has to do with confidence: perhaps you get more liberal as you grow up and become more comfortable with yourself. Most of these kids want to be like their parents and grandparents. They want to do well; they want to conform.

And most of them do. But there are still those bothersome groups who seem to flounder. His eye falls on Tyrone and his friends, on their feet now despite Tony Lord's exhortations. Nice kids, but they rouse concern in him, if only because of the way they hang together, all black boys, all into the same street culture. They make friends with other black boys, older and younger.

Years ago, before they had all this technology, he used to take home entire sets of grades or reports. If it was raining or he was bored, he would count them up. He discovered that boys were ten times less likely than girls to get an A for effort in RE. The result for history was similar. Not so bad in geography, not so good in English. When you went back to the teachers you found out that they were making assumptions.

Back in the 1970s the assumptions were different: that girls were probably going to be hairdressers, for example. Now far more girls grow up believing they can do well and the boys underachieve, in particular the black and working-class white boys. It is easy to see how it happens. Nowadays girls are more self-confident and have much better social skills. It's easy to assume that a girl who is willing, articulate and – let's face it

– compliant is heading for good results. Conversely, it's too easy to assume that a boy who is noisy, lazy and sometimes difficult will fail.

So, and this is a hard question, are they failing now with the boys? Are they reading their hard-edged exteriors, their laconic attitudes, their peer-group mores that insist school is not cool and, to some extent, accepting them? It is true, he has to confess, that the girls at Seven Kings do better in exams than the boys. That, of course, is true nationally nowadays. But he resists the idea that his staff are failing to close the gap. After all, it's narrower at Seven Kings than it is in most schools, so they might feel justified in congratulating themselves on doing a good job. Yet there's still a gap, and it has to be addressed.

He would find it hard to dispute that the education system still stereotypes pupils. So many decisions sit too firmly in the comfort zone: it's too easy to assume that boys who don't value education, who don't have a strong drive to achieve, are incapable of getting top grades. He doesn't think they have low expectations at Seven Kings. Maybe the problem is that expectations can be based on faulty information. If you are still slightly programmed to see black boys as trouble... The idea bothers him. Maybe you simply have to say out loud that some of these boys need extra support.

They are thinking of ways to provide it. They have plans for staff to mentor some boys, though as yet they haven't got off the ground. They have a separate information-technology class for underachieving boys, taught by two of the school's male deputy heads. But what those pupils need more than most, he thinks, is a clear structure to their school lives. That is why he and his staff pick up constantly on little things. Some of it might not seem strictly relevant, but it is. The constant reminding of boys to tuck their shirts in is, to him, a way of preventing a lads' culture developing. The seating plans in lessons are meant to stop pupils chatting and giggling together.

But with some kids it's a struggle: they don't want to fit in with the school culture. They have to behave in a certain way for their mates. There is no simple solution to this. You just have to keep reminding them that they can do better. You have to surround them with clear rules and a strong ethos. You have to react every day to the elements of youth culture that are rubbish.

NOVEMBER

TYRONE

His walk fills the corridor – a bouncy, Tiggerish, look-at-me walk. A swagger, even, but a happy swagger. He uses his weight. Sometimes small people have to jump aside as he motors through with Jerome sloping alongside him. He wears his uniform as if he has thrown it on: top button open, tie wide and short, shirt hanging loose below his blazer. Between Registration and Mr Read's history lesson there are half a dozen of the encounters that punctuate his day.

'Hey! Shania! Where did you go for autumn half term?... What? Are you *sick*? Don't you know about anywhere further than Southend?... Kuldeep! You pushed me, man! That's the fourth time this week! I'm going to have to start bashing you up, man!' He wraps his arm around the neck of an older girl and walks her along, pretending she's his girlfriend. She is unconcerned. After a few paces, she disentangles herself good-naturedly.

In history he sits in the second row from the back, on the side of the room nearest the door. Mr Read is talking about the industrial revolution. Tyrone looks over to where Spencer sits, at the front by the window. 'Spencer,' he says. 'Hey, Spencer... *Spen*cer!'

'Tyrone,' Mr Read says, 'there is a reason why you are sitting as far away as possible from Spencer.'

He's quiet for a minute. Then he turns to look at the long-haired girl sitting behind him. When he gets no response he turns back.

Mr Read is asking: 'In eighteen hundred who was the King of France?'

'William the Conqueror?' someone offers.

'No, you're centuries out. Does anyone know when William the Conqueror was alive?'

Tyrone, engaged now, puts up his hand. 'A long time ago?'

Someone else says: 'Ten sixty-six?'

'Good.'

They start working in pairs, writing down some of the factors involved in setting up a factory. Mr Read comes down the aisle with Tyrone's green report form in his hand. 'It says here that you're meant to be on task in lessons. And I do know you just switched your conversation to one about factories, Tyrone.'

'Sorry, Sir.'

At the end of the lesson Tyrone queues to get his green form signed. 'Sir, if I'm late for French the teacher will literally kill me.'

Mr Read fills in the form: three for effort, three for attainment, the worst marks. 'Because although I told you not to, you were shouting across the room to Spencer.'

Tyrone is crestfallen. When he bursts into the corridor, a surge of anger breaks through. 'Ah, man, that teacher gave me threes. Now I've got to go to detention tomorrow.'

At break he hooks up with Calvin and heads for the canteen.

'We're just looking for someone, Mr Harrison. Can we go in?' Doug waves them on. Inside, they scoot into the crowd, greeting friends with big hand gestures. When Tyrone sees someone he knows, he holds out his hand as if to shake, then brings it down on the other's in a sharp, chopping motion. They all laugh.

Soon there is a small group around them amid the break-time throng. 'They call me Sexy T,' Tyrone announces.

Three girls standing nearby swivel their faces towards him. 'No, we don't,' they chorus. 'We call you Tyrone.'

'Well,' he continues, unabashed, 'my street name is RT9. That's what everyone calls me.' The girls continue to look at him, wordless.

After break it's his favourite lesson: PE. In the gym twenty-five boys are dressed for basketball in white T-shirts, trainers, black tracksuit bottoms or white shorts. Tyrone is in baggy white shorts, the velcro fasteners on his trainers flapping open. There is a little roll of fat under his T-shirt but he is agile. He loves handling the ball, throwing, passing. Within a minute Calvin has the ball. Then it is back and forth, quick-fire, between Tyrone, Jerome and Calvin: holding it behind their backs, running it up the wall to the basket.

Mr Bracken turns his back, watching one of the other groups. Tyrone flicks Calvin's backside and he runs off, grinning, shouting: 'Ow-ow-*ow*.' A small, skinny boy grabs the ball. Tyrone tackles him and at that moment Calvin jumps on

Tyrone from behind, locking the three of them in a tight, inextricable knot. They sway around until Mr Bracken intervenes. Then the skinny boy is complaining.

A flash of anger tightens Tyrone's face. 'Just shut up, man!' he yells. But it's a split-second thing. It subsides as quickly as it rose. A minute later he is flopped on the floor, sweating. But even in repose he is self-aware. His smile is like a searchbeam. Wherever it rests for a minute or two, there will be a comment, a cheery insult, nothing meant to cause offence. Just letting everyone know he's still here.

At the end of the game he's on his feet, arms aloft, cheering. 'Yo! Three-one! Look at me. Look at my eight-pack!'

'More like a flat pack,' the skinny boy says, fully reconciled now.

'Well, maybe a three-pack,' Tyrone ripostes. He thinks how much he's changed since he came to this school two years ago. He was a little boy then – not necessarily a geek but one of those kids who might get beaten up when they walk down the road. Now he's top boy.

He yawns. Last night he went to his dad's house, watched some music awards on television, had burger and chips for his tea. The awards were cool. Dizzee Rascal won UK act of the year, with Jamelia. He likes that kind of music. He hates pop, especially S-Club and Blink 182. And grunge.

Usually he goes home at ten o'clock, but last night it was midnight. His dad said, 'Don't blame me if you can't get up for school. Have you done your homework? And do you need any help revising for that maths test?'

'I did it at school, Dad...'

His dad likes to help him with his maths – he works in a bank. And he trusts Tyrone to tell the truth about whether or

69

not he has homework. But sometimes it's hard: the TV is on; he might prefer to play a computer game or get a drink.

'I think perhaps you ought to be doing your work at home, when you've got more time, Tyrone, rather than rushing it at lunchtime. I'm not looking for you to be up in the middle of the night doing it but if you take more time you'll get better marks.'

He'd thought about it. 'I got 16 per cent in my last maths test. I'm not going to get that again. I could go to Mr Aresti and ask him for help... Actually I'm going to do that tomorrow.'

'I struggled with maths, too, Tyrone.'

'You worked hard at school.'

'I think there were fewer distractions when I was young. There was less on TV. My dad was stricter. I had to make sure my reports were reasonable. Now there isn't as much pressure...'

'Yeah. Sometimes when the work's hard, I turn round and talk. I try to think about it, and I can't. And then I finally find a way to work it out and I get the answer wrong... But there are other times when I talk because it's easy and I can rush through my answers.'

His dad says he has lots of good qualities, but at the moment the ability to work hard is not among them. 'He's my son – I love him,' he said. 'He makes friends. He helps people. He's caring. Probably for his friends, he's a good laugh. But I think he has to be more for himself.' To Tyrone, he said, 'Tyrone, you could do a lot better. I don't think you enjoy studying, and that makes me a bit sad.'

Last year they went to a special thing the school did so the parents could look at the work they were doing. They did it over six weeks, with maths, English and science. His dad says he knows Seven Kings is a good school, but he thinks maybe Tyrone and his friends are just moseying along, going for a laugh, being the lad pack with the cool attitude. Maybe they're not achieving what they can.

'You aren't so bad you might be facing exclusion. You aren't so bad in class that the class can't go along. You're at a level where they can ignore you. And the shock at the end of it will be if you do your GCSEs and come out with nothing. And the school will say, "Well, we sent home the reports." But by then it will be too late.'

'I might go to sixth form, or to college.'

'Do you want to go to uni?'

Tyrone looked at his dad, impressed by the thought. 'Am I smart enough?'

'Who knows? It's got to come from you. You've got to see that you have to work for you, not for your dad.' He laughed. 'You never know, you could be a famous rap star or a footballer.'

After Tyrone got home last night he watched telly for a bit, something about people living on the street, he thinks. He dozed, then woke up and went to bed. At seven forty his alarm went off but his mum was in the bath so he went back to sleep. Then it was eight o'clock and he had to rush to get to school on time.

As they file out of the gym to the changing room, he remembers the maths test. An uncomfortable feeling settles in his stomach. 'Shall we go to see Mr Aresti after?' Jerome asks.

'Yeah, man.'

Back in the corridor, there are competing forces all around: their classroom, the canteen, the football field. But they have done the deal – they have made a plan to talk to Mr Aresti about the maths test. They go to his room, not hurrying though.

When they get there Mr Aresti has gone. 'He'll be in the staffroom,' someone says helpfully. The staffroom is between here and their classroom. They skitter back along the corridor, glance guiltily at the staffroom door and slide past, heading for the sanctuary of their home base.

A CULTURE OF UNDERACHIEVEMENT?

Tyrone could almost be described as a little diagram, with three magnets pulling him in different directions: his parents, the school, his mates. When he talks to his mum and dad about school he wants to show them he can do well. Seven Kings High School dedicates itself daily to the cause of securing his academic success. But his mates give him something that neither his parents nor his teachers can: they determine his place in his social hierarchy. They are the cool boys, and among them Tyrone is one of the coolest. The things that matter to them – clothes, music, sport, girls, their loyalty to one another – have nothing to do with passing exams.

They're not bad boys. They're cheeky, energetic and a bit irreverent but they do not, on the whole, display the characteristics of disaffection that a few of the older boys at Seven Kings do. But their attachment to one another, which is genuine and touching, is like an override button: it cancels out everything else. Why focus on the teacher when there are others in the room whose opinions matter far more?

There is nothing new about young people seeking – needing

– the endorsement of their peers. And it works both ways. While Tyrone impresses his friends with his cheery, outgoing nature and the right clothes, his sister Tamia competes with hers for academic success. There are plenty of others in this school who do the same.

Yet there is something new in the degree to which a culture of underachievement pervades the life of the children at this school, whether they subscribe to it or not. Before they even arrived here, the children in Ruhy's class understood that being 'dumb' was considered cool. They did not all agree with the notion: when asked by their teacher, Tony Lord, just over a third of the class said they thought it more desirable to be smart. Yet they all understood it.

So where does it come from, the notion that clever kids are not at the top of the social heap? It springs, ultimately, from the same source as all youth culture: the need of young people to define themselves in relation to the rest of the world. And one of the simplest ways in which to define anything is by contrasting it with something else. So Tyrone and his friends define themselves in relation to their peer group. They are the black boys, the cool boys, the up-for-a-laugh boys. They can see how they differ from the Muslim boys, the geeky boys, the girls. They can see how they differ from those to whom achievement matters more than popularity.

There are clear hierarchies, underlined in daily interactions around the school. Tyrone understands that he is 'top boy', and that really means something. While his encounters are always cheerful, outwardly friendly, they denote other people's places in the social structure. When Tyrone meets a close friend in the corridor, he greets them with a handshake. When he meets a friend from outside his group there will be a hug or an embrace for a girl and, for a boy, a hand deployed jokily as a weapon. Everything happens with a smile, but subtle messages are conveyed.

Tyrone's group defines itself by comparison with others in the school, but there is another culture against whose light all youth cultures must be silhouetted: that of adults. From its earliest days, the notion of youth culture has been tied to this idea of 'otherness', to the fact that it deviates from society's adult norms. Stanley Cohen's classic 1972 work *Folk Devils and Moral Panics*, which explored the ways in which society reacted to define and attempt to control the deviant activities of youth cultures, is still pertinent today. Where mods and rockers once stood as emblems of all that was threatening and untameable in the nation's youth, now stand rap artists, chavs and street-corner kids in hoodies.

Yet while youth culture has continued to re-create itself with each generation, the adult world has gone into retreat. It no longer fights the notion that youth has its own culture. Parents, remembering their own youthful indulgence, sanctify their children's. They pay for their CDs, they take them to the shops for Nike trainers, they try to close their ears to their telephone lingo: 'Awright. Cool. Safe. Later.' Shivanie's mother, pulling her up when she mimics one of the boys at school – 'Man? What is this, "man"?' – is the exception rather than the rule.

Paradoxically this leaves young people in something of a bind. Otherness, even deviance, has an important role to play in their lives. How can each new generation adequately define itself, how can it create a world of which it can take full possession, if the older, established order keeps blurring the boundaries by giving its youthful innovations the stamp of approval? The young, nothing if not adaptable, have sought out zones of sanctuary that their parents' generation can never storm.

The first is the belief defined by Ruhy's drama teacher, Tony Lord, that it is 'cool to be dumb': the culture of under-achievement. Within it, the modern generation finds its toehold on delinquency. While youth music, youth language, youth style have been endorsed to some extent by the adult world, adult attitudes to education have travelled away from those prevailing in the world of the young. Generations of children have located themselves mentally in relation to the class swot, the geek in the corner with the neat homework, but gradually the parents of the current generation of young people have come to prize education.

In the 1960s, most working-class children went through school expecting to emerge with little in the way of formal qualifications. They knew that the labour market did not demand them. Anthony's dad learned a skilled trade – eventually – but still lacks the certificates to prove it. Anthony will not have that luxury: in the modern world, you need qualifications. Anthony's mum has acknowledged this by embarking on a part-time degree course.

There are other reasons, too, why the adult world's attachment to the notion of formal education has grown. Schools are under increased pressure to ensure that pupils achieve the maximum number of GCSEs for reasons not directly related to the job market: school league tables, Ofsted inspections, the predominance of education at the top of the political agenda.

So, in the ever-inventive imagination of youth culture, education has become ever more strongly associated with all that is adult, all that is distinct from the notion of youth. The pre-existing notion that swottiness is undesirable has been thrown alluringly into relief. If the young are seeking a means to deviate, here is an opportunity for them to grasp.

There is a second barricade, too, behind which today's youth can gather. Unable, in these enlightened times, to kick against the prevailing culture merely by donning a parka or coveting a Harley, modern youth culture has ventured further into the world of deliberate, calculated deviance – that of the gangster. Youth culture has always been associated with random violence. Now that violence is premeditated and murderous.

This is not to say, of course, that most of the children in this book are likely to start toting guns or earning a mint through drug-dealing. The adult world – let us be clear about this – still holds enough sway to teach them right from wrong, good sense from bad, even if sometimes they ignore the lessons. Yet an element of the Seven Kings youth culture glamorizes that world.

The argument that rappers such as So Solid Crew have popularized a scene characterized by drugs and violence has been well rehearsed. But it has usually been assumed that the children attracted by it are feral youths who hang around on street corners with their hoods up; children of never-married single mothers who lack strong educational or parental role models. Tyrone and Anthony do not fit this stereotype, but there is little doubt that they are attracted to aspects of that culture.

Anthony, in particular, with his raps and his drugs, is in closer touch with it than his parents would wish. He is exposed daily to pernicious sentiments and ideas to which he would probably not otherwise subscribe. He says he does not

mind that some of the lyrics he hears are violent or misogy-
nistic. Sometimes when he is high, he says, he can listen to
them and see the pictures in his head but that does not worry
him so long as they sound good.

It is not only Anthony and Tyrone who are exposed to this
culture through their taste in music and clothes. The school
talent evening was full of it, albeit in an anodyne form. The
style of dress espoused by many of the boys, when they are
allowed to abandon their uniforms, smacks of it. It seeps into
people's lives so insidiously that some barely notice it.

Another major element defines youth culture: the market.
Youth culture has always been driven by economics. It
emerged when post Second World War prosperity gave young
people in their late teens a disposable income. Markets grew
up to help them spend it – markets for clothes, music and
magazines that perpetuated the cycle by helping them decide
what to buy.

Now it is not only post-school working youth with money
to spend: a survey in March 2006 estimated that the average
schoolchild has £800 per year to spend. The maths is simple.
With almost four million children in English primary schools,
the pocket-money market for the under-elevens is now around
£3.2 billion. Children must decide how to use their spending
power, and to do so they must define themselves: they must
associate themselves with tastes – a personal style. This, then,
is the key to that conversation between Tony Lord and Ruhy's
class.

At an ever-earlier age, children are forming closer ties with
their peers, and with distinct subcultures that have little to do
with the adult world. Ruhy, who loves fashion and bling, is
just one harmless example. Before she can make a decision on

which colours to wear in spring, she must have a notion of who she is, which style she espouses. Even though Ruhy is clever, and proud of it, her fashion mentors are not advising her on what the A-grade student is wearing this season: the A-grade student, in the popular imagination, does not have time for such fripperies. The polarization between cool and clever continues.

Perhaps we can get too hung up on some of this. Youth culture is, after all, about fun. It is worthless if it doesn't upset the older generation. Where are all the punks now? Mostly working hard and paying their mortgages, as Anthony and Tyrone will probably be doing in twenty years' time.

The cool-or-dumb divide is one to watch. The most striking thing about Ruhy's drama class was not so much the children's attitude as the way they expressed it. Most pupils, particularly at the tender age of eleven and particularly at Seven Kings, desire the approval of their teachers. On this occasion they were asked whether they wanted to be smart or dumb. Why did most of them not tell their teacher what he wanted to hear? There is only one explanation. Even so young, just a few weeks into their new life at secondary school, they were making a choice: they would rather impress their peers than their teachers.

DECEMBER

PERIN

On a bitter morning in early December Perin Patel, sunk into the passenger seat of his dad's car, is trying not to think about his Cambridge interview. As they slide up the M11, there is a cold knot inside him. He is feeling crisp in his suit, his new white shirt, his pale blue silk tie. They left home at six thirty, in darkness, but as always he found time to run some gel through his hair.

They talk about other things – even when Perin's mind is elsewhere he can usually manage a conversation about cars. Ideally, he would like a fleet. His dad knows this. It is a conversation they have had many times, comfortable, well-worn, amicable and familiar. But the list of models Perin favours is ever-changing.

'For going to work,' he muses, 'a Mercedes SL. With the family, it would be a four-by-four Range Rover. For trips out, a Bentley...' He pauses, checking them off in his mind. 'That would be an up-to-date model. I'd keep the vintage one in the garage.'

His dad takes up the baton. 'I'm not sure I agree with you about all this, Perin. You'd be wasting your money, buying all those cars. They depreciate too fast.'

'Dad, if I'm earning enough, I'll be spending it on cars. I enjoy cars. Cars will be my hobby.'

There is a lull and the interview creeps back into his mind. 'You know what, Dad?' He's casual, now. Careful. 'If I get an offer from LSE I think I'll take it.'

'Even if you get one from Cambridge?'

'Well... the thing is, we've all said we'll try to stay in London together. Ranjit, Vijay, Naresh... LSE, Imperial or UCL. Then we'd still be able to see each other.'

They have talked about it a lot at school in the past months, batting the options between them. Cambridge has taken on a mysterious, almost mythical quality. No one seems to have any firm information. Someone says they should apply to Trinity College 'because it's the best'. Someone else says they should just make an application to the university and not specify a particular college, that it shouldn't make any difference. Another says some colleges are happier than others to take state-school pupils, but no one has a definitive view on which.

Perin talked to Dr Pithia, of course. He is Perin's physics teacher, and he likes him, especially because he has his own law – Pithia's Law, about the velocity of bubbles. Dr Pithia went to Cambridge, and he was an academic before he decided he had to work with younger students to make a difference. Earlier this week he and Perin did a practice interview.

This term Cambridge has been a constant feature of his life.

It has popped up at odd points in lessons. 'This is the sort of question you might be asked at your Cambridge interview. Why is light refraction important?'

Dr Pithia says it's a lottery. He says they ask everyone the same questions, and almost everyone gives the same answers. Almost everyone is clever enough to do a degree at Cambridge. 99 per cent of the time the admissions tutors are not going to make the right choice. It's a lucky dip.

Perin is not even sure, now, why he applied to Downing College. Maybe someone said there might be more state-school students there. He was sure, in the end, that economics was the right choice. He'd thought about pharmacy, which is what his parents do. But they said, 'No. Don't go there.' The pharmacy has been good for them, but maybe that won't last. And his dad says that at the end of the day, he's a shopkeeper. They might live in a lovely house in Hornchurch with a swimming-pool, but every morning his mum and dad still have to go to Dagenham and roll up the shop's shutters. They work there six days a week, and they rush back after a snatched week's holiday to make sure everything is running OK. Perin's dad wants something more for his son.

Perin thought about IT. He is good with computers. But then he read somewhere that the IT market might be going down, and he wouldn't contemplate three years of a degree without the confidence of a good job at the end of it. Investment banking is tough, he knows, but he thinks there will always be money to be made in it.

Looking back now, he supposes his interest started when he was small and his dad would ask him to help him check the prices of his shares. He didn't understand it then – it was business – but his dad started to explain how the markets worked, and he got interested. He would like to make a lot of money and live in a big house.

And he likes the City of London. When he was younger he used to go to Great Ormond Street hospital for medical check-ups, and his mum and him used to drive through the City in a taxi to get there. He used to look up at those tall buildings and imagine himself driving into the basement car park, going up in the lift...

There are six places this year to read economics at Downing, and sixty applicants. One of the places has already gone, presumably to someone who took their A levels last year.

Coming down to earth later that day, in a big, airy, lemon-and-white-painted room where tea and coffee are on offer, he can admit that he likes it there. 'This is quite something,' he says, motioning his dad to look out at the expanse of grass, the huge neo-classical stone building opposite.

He feels more assured now. The day seems to have gone well. There was a thinking-skills test, not for the purpose of assessment but for the university, to see if the people they picked out at interview did well in the test too. There were big chunks of text, then three statements, and you had to say which most accurately represented what was in the text. That was hard.

Then there were two interviews. They asked about his personal statement, about how he'd made a film for the Disney Channel about his life, and about his disability. He'd asked about wheelchair access – they'd put up a big wood-and-scaffolding ramp for today, so he could get into the building. 'Downing will do everything in its power to make your stay as pleasant and comfortable as possible,' they had said.

Dr Pithia warned him that the interviewers would do a 'good cop, bad cop' thing, so he wasn't surprised when, in the second interview, one of them kept making strange noises, like a sort of snort or grunt, every time he started to speak. He thinks the man was trying to put him off.

He had said on his application that he read *The Economist*, so they asked him to talk about an article he had read recently. He talked about oil and the dollar. They asked, 'Do you think *The Economist* is left-wing or right-wing?'

He didn't know the answer to that – he doesn't know much about politics – so he had to guess. He said, after thinking for a bit, that it was right-wing.

'Do you think that would make it predisposed towards greater government intervention or less?'

He had to think on his feet. 'It would be against greater invervention,' he said. Fortunately, he's good at thinking quickly. All his friends say so. If he doesn't know an answer he can make one up – and it seemed he'd got this one right, which was a relief. They didn't pick up on what he had said. Which, he thinks now, might be a good sign. Or a bad one.

At the other end of the room, some candidates are sitting or standing around, drinking tea and chatting. They look a bit uncomfortable.

This morning, he had made up his mind that there was no hope. But now he feels more positive. People talk about Cambridge not taking so many students from state schools, but others say they're biased *towards* state schools. He doesn't know. He thinks you have to have all the evidence before you can make a judgement.

He weighs up the pros and cons. There is the weather. When they got out of the car this morning the wind cut right into him. And although the buildings look impressive he *is* a bit worried about access. If they offered him a place there would have to be some changes. There are a lot of stairs. There is no ramp to the toilets in this building.

But today has been a good experience. He is happy he came here. At the end of the day he had an interview at Cambridge, and how many people can say that? And if he doesn't get in he can go to LSE or UCL. He had an interview at UCL and that went well. He hasn't had an offer from them yet, but Nottingham have offered him AAB.

He thinks of what his dad said when they first talked about applying for Cambridge: that it would be better to fail than not to try. He looks at his dad, and his dad looks back with a sort of muffled pride – he doesn't have to say anything.

Why does Perin work so hard? Why does it matter so much to him that he should do well? He isn't sure. He doesn't think it's because his parents have driven him. His mum always says she has never had to do that: he has always driven himself. No one else drove him to his thirteen As and A stars at GCSE: he just wants to be the best. He can remember being like that even at primary school. His parents have assumed he will do well, and usually he has.

But he comes from a high-achieving family. His grand-parents arrived here with nothing after they were thrown out of Uganda in the 1970s. They alighted, as many new arrivals do, in inner-city Newham. Perin's dad went to secondary school in Canning Town, near London's Docklands. He did well, qualified as a pharmacist and married another. Perin's mum was born in Kenya but educated in India. The rest of the family thrived, too. One of Perin's cousins is studying medicine, another law. One is doing pharmacy. Another is reading finance and accounting. Perin knows how it pleases his grandfather to see all his grandchildren getting on.

So, he has a lot to live up to. And – he can admit it now – he has been nervous about today. But when that fear grips him, he knows what he has to do. He has to make himself feel that he is up to it. He just has to think, 'I'll do it.' He has to know he can.

DOUG HARRISON

As he makes his way back to his room, swinging his carrier-bag, he's thinking about urban redevelopment. With his year-seven class he has been looking at a painting of Greenwich in the 1960s. What words would they use to describe it? he asked.

'Pollution?'

'Sewage.'

'Rubbish.'

'Jobs, factories?'

'Dirt.'

He told them about going there before the area was redeveloped, and about the cloying smell of malt and hops that hung around the brewery. When he asked them if anyone knew what 'derelict' meant, Ruhy and her friend Waseme went for their dictionaries. Everyone else looked blank.

Yet redevelopment is a major issue. Not so long ago, Doug went to a conference about the building trades. The level of development in the Thames Corridor over the next twenty years will be phenomenal, especially with the 2012 Olympics in prospect. Yet the numbers of Seven Kings pupils who will benefit, through becoming electricians, plumbers or bricklayers, will be relatively small.

If he is honest, the problem is not only that employers no longer line up to offer Modern Apprenticeships, but that Seven Kings pupils feel those careers are not for them. It's an academic school. Its parents have academic aspirations for their pupils. Most want to do IT or business studies. Some struggle, and sometimes Seven Kings loses them.

He reminds himself that he has an appointment at Redbridge College this afternoon to see the Seven Kings pupils who have been diverted to vocational courses there. In some sense, those pupils are already 'lost'. They failed to thrive at school, and at fourteen or fifteen they have already had their first 'fresh start'.

There are three or four of them under the affectionate tutelage of Suzanne Levy, who acts as a sort of mother figure to the under-sixteens at the college. But only one, Ian, is attending regularly. He's doing a music course. Another, Damon, seems to have got a job: every time Doug rings the boy's mobile someone else answers. The background noise suggests a garage or workshop.

Suzanne does her best, he reflects. She seems to like them. 'I have very few horrible students,' she will say. 'Most of them are lovely.' Then she will pause. 'Anyway, it's this or prison for quite a few.'

Does college really help these lost children to find their way? Doug wonders. Maybe. Sometimes. Perhaps a few of them will even play a part in redeveloping the Thames Corridor, but the courses won't qualify them to a level where they can start a job. He smiles. It's not the Seven Kings way to send girls to college at fourteen to do courses in 'Nail Art'. But

maybe even that can keep pupils in the system when otherwise they would drop out completely. Perhaps they will go on
to do a hairdressing and beauty course at sixteen, and from
there to a junior job in a salon.

Sometimes, he reflects, it's not the A-grade students who
give him the greatest sense of job satisfaction. He can get
anyone through GCSE geography. If he can persuade them to
do the coursework, they'll get a G grade and pass. But what
good is that? No, the ones who make him feel it has all been
worthwhile are those who come in rude and aggressive, or
from really difficult homes, and get through. There's a lad he
sees quite often in Sainsbury's. When he first came to Seven
Kings he was isolated from the other pupils, could hardly put
two words together. Now he holds down a job. He fits in. He
has a sense of self-worth.

But it's hard work with some of them. Which reminds him:
he needs to check on Amina Simpson. He turns left off the
main corridor and pops his head into the school office. 'Has she
been in yet?' Everyone knows who he means. No, she hasn't.
But her sister has phoned to say she's had to go to A and E with
a bad back.

There's been a lot going on. Arron has been a worry. After
Angela took him to social services, he came back to school
looking chastened but calm. His dad had followed them to the
offices and, with the help of the social workers, had persuaded
him to come home. He was OK, he said. Everything would be
fine. Angela says Arron has not been in to see her since. When
Doug sees him around school he has the odd friendly word, as
he does with so many of the kids. He seems fine, but who
knows?

And there is Ruksana. It had all started last year, during the summer term, one of those situations that don't seem too serious at first. A Muslim girl in year eleven whose parents didn't approve of her having a boyfriend and who wanted the school to stop her spending time with him. Although he was a nice enough lad – a Muslim in the year below her at a neighbouring school – the staff did their best. Sometimes her brother, who was in the upper sixth, would take her out at lunchtime to stop her meeting the boyfriend, and her dad would be waiting by the school gate for her when lessons ended.

But, really, it was impossible. Such situations are not unusual. Many of the Seven Kings girls lead double lives. They come to school and spend the day in a completely Western environment. If pushed, he would say that the school promotes Western culture. All the girls' conversations are about what they've seen on television, which boys they fancy. They've had girls in the past who've kept changes of clothes at different friends' houses. One girl kept up two completely separate, parallel existences for years.

Parents often expect brothers or cousins to keep an eye on their daughters, to make sure they behave themselves at school. But as often as not the girls know that the boys are leading double lives, too. Within an extended family there can be a whole subculture of young people, all behaving in ways their parents certainly wouldn't approve of. The local library is a key meeting-place for Muslim girls and their boyfriends, because it's one of the few acceptable reasons for the girls to be out alone.

Ruksana's parents thought her brother was looking after her last year, and this year they asked a cousin three years younger to do the same. The poor child came in to see Doug earlier this term to tell him that Ruksana had put pressure on him to lie for her. 'If Ruksana asks you to do anything like that, you just come and tell me. I'll deal with it,' he told the boy. The key, for him, is in keeping open lines of communication. Keeping talking to everyone, so they don't clam up and avoid him. The best the school can do is to let everyone know they're prepared to hear all the different points of view.

And, up to a point, it worked. Like a few others before her, Ruksana came to see him to beg him not to tell her parents about some transgression. 'Please, sir. They'll send me to Pakistan to get married if they find out. They've already threatened to do it.'

In most cases, girls are just testing the boundaries. They know in the end that they'll accept their lot, marry someone their parents approve of, settle down to a family life not unlike the one in which they grew up.

But there's something about Ruksana: a sort of grim, gritty determination. A sort of steel in her eye that stayed with her even through those tortured conversations with her father. Even though she was lying: 'But, sir, I *was* in chemistry yesterday...' Even though he and her father knew she was lying, and even when the chemistry teacher was brought in to testify that she had not been in his lesson, she stuck to her story. 'Well, I *was* there.'

It was this refusal to back down that made it less of a shock when she and the boy disappeared. Both had packed bags, delivered them, as it turned out later, to a friend's house. Both were in their school clothes and started the day as usual, Ruksana waved inside the school gate by her father, the boy waved off from home by his parents.

That had been a fortnight ago. And this is where the story

gets really strange, because they have had these situations before. Usually by now they would have turned up.

The whole business has taken up a lot of time. He has had all Ruksana's friends in to see him, giving him statements, trying to piece together everything that happened. Her little cousin, in tears. Other pupils who overheard things. The whole place has been abuzz. A little voice whispers that maybe they *have* turned up but their families have dealt with them by removing them from the scene. Only time will tell.

There is a knock at the door. It is Amina Simpson. As always, she is smartly turned out, uniform ironed, hair pulled back into a neat ponytail. She is a conundrum. If you wanted to put together an identikit of the perfect pupil, it would look a lot like this: bright, good-looking, polite. Amina used to get straight As for everything and you'd have expected her to breeze through school straight into university, probably ending up as Businesswoman of the Year.

Doug is serious now. 'Amina your attendance hasn't got any better, has it? Mrs Cassidy thought she saw you yesterday, but you weren't in lessons.'

'Wednesday? I was in all my lessons.'

He knows she wasn't. But why? There were one or two problems last year – hanging around with the wrong boys outside school, that sort of thing – but nothing insoluble. Nothing like this. Ask her why she won't come to school, and she'll just say she was late getting up. Never anything more coherent, never anything that might give him a handle on the situation. 'You weren't in history. I've checked.'

'I haven't been well, sir, so I came in for the afternoon.'

'Have you signed in with Mrs Cassidy?'

'I'm going to now, sir.'

Amina's mum is due in court in a couple of weeks for failing to ensure that her daughter attends school. In days gone by, the child had usually left school or moved by the time a case came to court. Now the process has been streamlined. There'll be a fine, probably, if she turns up.

He's not sure what he feels about it. On the one hand Mrs Simpson has a duty to make sure her daughter attends school; on the other, taking her to court isn't going to solve the problem. Amina is fourteen and her mother cannot physically drag her out of bed. And she's getting further and further behind. They've tried talking to her. They've tried talking to her mum. He's monitoring her every day. Angela's monitoring her every day. Phoning Mum every day. None of it's working. But there's nothing to be done except to keep trying. With some kids it works and with others it doesn't.

'OK, then go straight to your lesson.'

And off she goes, slim but not thin, serious but not down-trodden. Something in the way she walks tells him she still feels like an A-grade student.

SHIVANIE

She is staring at her sparkly pens, with a half-frown of concentration. 'Did you know I'm colour-blind? But I don't just see black and white, I see different colours. Anyway, I've memorized them. Look.' She picks them up one by one. 'Silver. Gold. Red... Blue? No, green. This is...' she picks up the blue pen, '...purple? Blue. I'll use this one.' She picks up the silver. 'This pen is like me. Like a silver angel!'

She beams around her, comical now, and they all laugh.

Miss Adams has told them to write a Christmas speech, working in a group.

Christmas, she thinks. She'll be in Birmingham for Christmas, at her auntie's house. What is she looking forward to most? Maybe they'll go to Cadbury World. Maybe her auntie will cook egg and chips. Shivanie doesn't have egg at home because it's not really vegetarian. If they go out, they'll go to an Indian restaurant but, given the choice, she would rather go to Pizza Hut.

She has told her mum and dad she doesn't really want any presents. One year her dad put fifty pounds under the tree for her, but they give her things all the time. Her mum does all the cooking for her. They buy her food, and pay for everything for her. When she was little, her sisters told her Father Christmas was coming. Then they put footsteps on the carpet, made out of flour, so she'd believe he had been. But then she heard a story about St Nicholas and it said he'd died on a particular date. And she'd said, 'That can't be right. That means Father Christmas is dead.' So then she knew there was no Father Christmas. When her sisters were little, before she was born, they wanted to stay up to watch the radiator to see if Father Christmas came out of it because they did not have a fireplace. And when he didn't come they were upset.

She's working in a group with Stacey and Amit. She has written the first couple of lines already: 'This year has been a fabulous year, with different ups and downs. And here we are, Christmas has come already. Time flies, it really does. Now has come the time of joy, where we can forget all of the bad things that have happened.'

Stacey looks severe. 'We have to make it formal.'

Shivanie thinks. 'What about Arsenal and Chelsea?'

'It has to be formal,' she repeats.

'That's quite formal!'

'What about international affairs?'

Shivanie says, '*Weell*... We're not very happy about George Bush.' Then a thought strikes her: 'I heard on the news that there was a sandwich worth fifteen thousand pounds because it had the Virgin Mary on it, and the cheese didn't go off after ten years.'

'Did anything happen to do with religion?'

'We could say about the sandwich.'

Stacey ignores her. 'Someone smashed up the statues of David and Victoria Beckham because they were acting like Mary and Joseph.'

Amit, silent until now, says, 'That's not a joyful event.'

'Some people might say it is.' Stacey has another thought. 'What about the twenty twelve Olympic Games?'

Miss Adams says, 'We have just fifteen minutes left. Wayne, if I have to tell you one more time to sit on your chair properly, you know what will happen.'

Shivanie, excited now: 'We can go and see it! How much does it cost?'

Stacey doesn't respond. She is concentrating, staring at a list of words in her book. 'On the contrary, Great Britain has had some success with the Olympics...' She breaks off. 'Shivanie, are you sure you don't want me to push my chair in?'

Shivanie looks up at her from beneath the desk. She has slid under it to find a thesaurus, and is returning by the same route.

At break she starts walking towards the medical centre. Jas bounds up to her and they fall in together, Shivanie doing a jokey, jerky walk. Jas shakes her head. 'You're crazy!'

They have just had their reports. Shivanie got five As, five

Bs, two Cs and a D for PE. The D had really got up her nose. She told the teacher she should have been marked on how well she did on the trip to Keswick. Then she would have got an A. 'I'm so cross they gave me a D,' she says. 'They put things like "Due to poor eyesight, Shivanie cannot do this." Blah, blah, blah. Like I'm an invalid or something.'

In the medical centre they wander into one of the little side rooms. Jas has some homework to finish. They have CPHSE – Citizenship, Personal, Health and Social Education – next with Mr Webb. 'It's going to be about sex,' Jas says. 'There's going to be a lesson where the boys are separate. I hope it's today. Because they're so—' She breaks off, her face screwed up in distaste. 'Eurgh!'

Shivanie's head is down: she's doing Jas's homework. It's headed 'Decisions, Decisions'. She's speeding up now. The bell is about to go. The paper has about fifteen lines on it, the top ones neat and careful, the lower ones a hurried scrawl: 'The bottom line is that decisions are easier to make on your own.' She hands the paper back to Jas, who pops it into her bag.

Mr Webb seats the class in a ragged circle and tries to create an air of calm. 'Now,' he begins. 'Today is a lesson we've been talking about for some time. It's a lesson we were going to have last week but PC Pope came in instead. And—'

The door opens, and a tall, willowy girl walks in. Laughter bursts out.

Mr Webb begins again. 'We're going to be talking about puberty. The details of what occurs. And I also want to create an atmosphere where people feel they can ask questions and others aren't going to laugh or make them feel small.'

Three hands are up already. Someone asks a question, but no one can hear it. Probably it wasn't a serious one.

A boy with spiky hair says, 'If you ask a question people might laugh and you'll feel...'

'Bullied,' his friend finishes.

Mr Webb says: 'Where do we get our information regarding sexual health and puberty? Tahir, can you not do the things we just talked about?'

Stacey says, 'Peers, parents, TV...'

'People come from very different religions, different backgrounds, and school is one place to get the right information, because it's very important to live a happy, healthy life. You are twelve, thirteen, and this is an important junction in your life. For example, you may call a penis a willy—'

There is more laughter. Shivanie is sitting next to Mr Webb, looking hard at the floor. She does not want to smile but embarrassment is forcing the corners of her mouth upwards. She forces them down.

Now Mr Webb hands out pieces of paper with a line drawing of a woman. They have to split into groups and label the drawing to say what changes take place at puberty. Stacey says, 'It's a she-male!'

One of the boys puts up his hand. 'Sir, can a girl die if someone kicks her in the vagina?'

'I suppose if someone kicks you hard enough anywhere you can die.'

'That's what my mum says.'

'Are you relating that to the idea that if a boy was kicked in his testicles you could kill him?'

'Yes.'

Shivanie has the paper on her knee. They did this last year in science. She writes quickly. Breasts become bigger to store milk. Hairs grow. Pubic hairs. Hair gets more greasy.

Whiteheads and spots. Hips change shape. 'Why do I have to do all the work?' she asks, as she adds 'skin changes'.

'How does it change?' Stacey asks.

'It gets more wrinkly.'

Stacey frowns. 'I don't know half the stuff you're talking about, Shivanie.'

They play pass-the-parcel with the finished sheet, passing it as if it were on fire. It lands back on Shivanie's lap. Worse, Mr Webb makes her read it out. First. She gabbles, head down. When she stops a blush of relief rises from her toes to her scalp.

Mr Webb goes on. 'One of the things Shivanie picked up was that periods begin between ten and fifteen.'

A girl interrupts: 'Sixteen.'

'And this is a very normal part of life. Usually, as you know, we would split this class in two, but I think it's important that boys get to hear about periods so that they know what's going on.'

The spiky-haired boy puts up his hand. 'If you're Jordan you can get implants. We have names for those things. Tits and big boobs.'

Mr Webb puts on his calm voice again: 'This isn't the way I want this to go.'

Then someone says, 'Your hormones start to change. The scientific name for a vagina is... erm... a vagina. And it could also be a clitoris...'

'That's a very different part. Tahir, you don't have to be a silly little boy all the time, sniggering behind your hand.'

'And I think a period is when the lining in the vagina breaks down.' A boy, now, holding a piece of paper up in front of his face.

Mr Webb reads out a biological description of what happens to girls at puberty. 'Has anyone got any questions?'

Shivanie shakes her head, still looking at the floor. Someone asks a question about oral sex.

'Oh, my God!' Stacey puts her hand over her mouth.

As the bell goes, a quiet-voiced boy is asking a complicated question about how homosexuals get an erection, or maybe he means transsexuals. He trails to a halt, confused. Mr Webb says maybe they will deal with that next time.

At lunchtime they rush to the canteen. Shivanie needs a fix of waffles. 'With spaghetti hoops and chips. Yummy!'

'What did you have for tea last night, Shivanie?' Jas says.

'Chips. But I don't usually. My mum's a good cook.'

'Sometimes my mum makes something from her cookbook. One time she made Italian pasta. But usually we have Indian food because my dad likes it. Or I get a pizza out of the freezer for myself... Does your dad eat chicken?'

'No, only vegetarian.'

'Sometimes my dad has chicken, I think. I'm not sure. Maybe men are allowed to eat chicken sometimes.'

'The food here's OK, isn't it?'

'Yeah.'

After lunch they rush back to their classroom to collect their coats before afternoon lessons. They're not supposed to do this: they're meant to leave their coats in their lockers until the end of the day. But at five past three the room will be full of boys. There'll be banter and maybe a bag will be thrown. And maybe Shivanie won't see it because her peripheral vision is poor so she won't duck in time. Sometimes, just sometimes, school can make her feel a little bit vulnerable.

JANUARY

DEBBIE ADAMS

Her first year-eight lesson of the day is drawing to a close. The theme for the early weeks of the post-Christmas term has been speeches and other pieces of work designed to inspire or motivate.

Shivanie has just given an impassioned talk about the lack of facilities for disabled people: 'If you don't treat them equally it's you that's missing out. Everyone should be kind to each other. It doesn't matter that the disabled are different. Aren't we all?'

Now today's last act is about to begin: Stacey, with a talk about religion. She stands straight, sure of herself. 'Christianity. You can hear this word countless times, like Mary, Jesus and Bethlehem. But what are the meanings? I am here to tell you.

'An experience me and other Christians have shared is being saved. My friend told me she was saved at church and it was scary, whereas I have been filled with the Holy Spirit.

'You may think, "What's she going on about? She sounds like Dot off EastEnders." Zainab has a strong faith for Muslim, and Coab for Sikh. Were you told to go into the world and preach about your religion? I was.

'You may think, I'm not going out in Ilford and telling people about my belief. I did.

'I have been able to stand up in front of you and talk about my religion, and you should be able to. Telling others about Christianity and giving my life by following in the steps of Jesus. Thank you for listening to me.'

Debbie has been sitting on her desk at the side of the classroom, but now she stands. She always finds something nice to say, but it isn't hard with Staccy, who is bright and focused. 'That was *excellent*, Stacey! Very well done!'

She dismisses the class. Her year-nine group is lining up outside. They are quite different. While Stacey, Shivanie and their friends present few serious problems, there are some difficult boys among this lot. In fact, she's apprehensive. Last Friday she had her worst day with them so far and ended up calling in the head of English, Paul Lindsay-Addy, to back her up. Some of the class, two in particular, were really bad: shouting, getting out of their chairs and walking across the room to hit each other. And even when Paul came in, they were insolent. They were, like, 'We haven't done anything, sir. All we've done is trip each other up, and hit each other over the head.'

So Paul had told their year head. The two of them, a boy and a girl, were put on report. Now they're clutching their green report forms, folded and refolded to fit into their blazer pockets.

In general she has not had these problems but when she did she was grateful for reinforcements, grateful not to have been left feeling alone, or as if she had failed in some way. She has to be strict with the odd kid in year eight or nine, but mostly they're fine. The little boy with the big mouth who wouldn't shut up in her first lesson has been a different child recently.

She lets the class in, a big one, about twenty-seven kids, which doesn't help. Today, like most of her younger classes, they're making speeches, which leaves scope for trouble.

She begins by giving them a roadmap for the lesson. She doesn't mention last week, but it hangs above them all like a livid cloud. 'Right. Before we start, I expect you to listen, mature year-nine students, to each other. Have respect.' She calls Amarjit first. She needs someone to set a positive tone, and he obliges, as she knew he would.

'Do you think it is fair that people with cancer are forced to live shorter lives? Listen to the story of little Annie...' He does a straight, competent job and sits down to spontaneous applause.

The girl who is on report is next. She makes a bad start. Someone begins to heckle. 'Shuddup, Tracey!' she splutters, but she recovers. There is no disaster.

The boys shine at this sort of thing. The girls, in general, are better prepared but they hold their speeches in front of their faces and read them in toneless voices. The boys are much happier to put on a show and enjoy themselves, to really communicate with their audience.

The star, though, is Haroon, the naughtiest boy in the class. She watches with an inkling of concern as he strolls up to the front. He is only just the right side of dishevelled, his tie just a millimetre too loose, the merest hint of ruffle in his hair. He faces the class, pacing himself through a moment. Then he throws his arms wide.

'*Lay-deez* and *gen-tle-men*! I stand here before you as a minister. As a preacher! I am here to try to persuade you to support Children in Need!'

The class is almost on its feet already.

'*I* was once a child on the streets! *I* had no place to go, nothing to eat! *I* was continually beaten! I am here to tell you – to preach to you – about those children who are physically and mentally abused. They will be scarred for life!

'Tell me, is it fair? Two children die *every day* in Uganda! Me, I think it isn't right and it should be Stamped Out!'

He stamps his foot dramatically on the last word, and sits down to a cacophony of cheers and wolf-whistles.

Debbie's face is suffused with pride. Haroon can let himself down badly, but when he's in his stride he's brilliant. Actually, he's one of the brightest in the class. 'You were *so* good! All of you!' she enthuses.

As the lesson ends, she reflects. Her first term has been and gone. It was hard work, but she'd expected that – staying for hours marking, planning lessons late into the night. The tube journeys have been a bonus, in a way, a time to mull over how different groups are working, maybe consider little changes she can make to her lesson plans.

When she is marking she hands out lots of stickers and praise. Everyone gets a sticker for something. Sometimes it's hard to find something good to say, but she would hate it if all some of them ever got was criticism.

She picks up the pile of homework, and closes the classroom door behind her.

ANTHONY

As they file out of the science room Anthony flashes Miss Thaker a grin. 'You take care, Miss. There's bad things happening out there.' Somewhere in the air he hears an echo of a rap he wrote recently.

> *Having blow on the way to school when im yawning...*
> *teachers on ma case, but I got da warning...*
> *So it's cool... at the end of tha day, fuck school...*
> *fuck education, I aint making no progress...*
> *n I don't care cos marijuana causes no-stress.*

It is non-uniform day. He has on a pale blue tracksuit with white lettering on the back: 'Finest Since Day One Mecca, Victory League, The 13th Edition'. About half of his year are in jeans, half in tracksuits. In his science class a couple of girls were in *salwar kameez* and little pointy slippers with silver and gold embroidery.

His next lesson is just for boys. There are twenty of them in this IT class and they are taught by Mr Rosewell and Mr Hayes, both deputy heads. Some people call them the 'naughty boys group', or say they're thick. Mr Rosewell says not. But whatever the reason, they get special treatment. They're doing a vocational exam, and if he passes, it will be worth four good GCSE grades.

They have Mr Rosewell today. He's OK, they get on all right. As always, though, he's in a hurry. His sentences are short and clipped – he's a ball of energy.

'Jack! Tie! On, please. Right! First thing to set down. We've got loads to do. By half-term we have to finish the coursework. Four weeks! Donal, if you left Tariq alone you'd be more likely to pass.'

Everything is broken down into small parts so there's never time to let your mind wander. Anthony has a sheet to fill in with details of his project, a financial plan for a football club. He is writing, head down, when Mr Rosewell plonks his coursework on his desk. He's got nine out of sixteen. One mark short of a merit. Pinned to the back is a list of the things he needs to do to reach merit standard. Deadlines are written on the board. Everything is urgent.

'Anthony!' Mr Rosewell barks.

He raises his head, blurry. Too late. His teacher has moved on. 'Why do we have testing?'

A pale, skinny boy starts to speak but Mr Rosewell stops him dead with a sharp 'Sssh!' and a hand gesture, palm out, fingers splayed, then turns to the boy next to him instead. 'Tariq! You haven't answered yet. Why do we have testing?'

Now they have to move to the computers to do some work. Anthony gets up. Walks a few paces. Stops in the middle of the room, feeling blank.

'Anthony!'

Mr Rosewell's bark again. He comes to, sits down, stares at the screen. Types in a few words, then goes to Google, loads Word Shark and watches as his screen fills with brightly coloured fish. Then he goes back and finishes what he needs to do.

He leans back in his chair. Waqar, sitting next to him, gives him a nudge. He looks round. Mr Steer is standing by the door. Anthony touches his clipped beard, and smiles a secret smile.

He knows that if the headmaster sees it he will be in trouble: it infringes the uniform rules. Rahul gets up and comes to stand between Anthony and the door. Anthony puts his head down, and focuses hard on the keyboard.

Afterwards he wanders towards Miss Handley's office, just for a chat. Nothing serious. This year he hasn't seen much of his year head. Last year she used to pull him up sometimes, about his hair being almost shaved, about him using his 'Blaze King' tag in school, stuff like that. Anyway, he thinks his coursework is up to date, mostly, though to tell the truth he isn't quite sure. He waits outside her office till she arrives, hurrying. Somehow he manages to insert his big frame inside the room. There are books and papers everywhere.

She produces a computer printout of his target grades, mostly Bs and Cs. A couple of As, for art and drama. 'At the moment, you're fractionally under these. It's maybe not a question of effort, but of how you're working.'

Anthony is quiet for a minute. 'Why is science so low?' Everyone seems to be predicted a B or a C for science.

She smiles. 'I'm a fount of knowledge, Anthony, but not the fount of all knowledge...' She waits. He has nothing to add. She goes on: 'What I can tell you is that when you first came here, you were getting an average of two for effort, on a scale of one to five with one at the top. At the end of last year, it was 2.18. It's now 1.91.'

'So, basically, I'm improving.'

'Yes. You haven't just arrived here and stayed, you've improved. But you've got to learn to work wisely. You need to go to your teachers and say, "What do I have to do to get this D up to a B?"'

Anthony is looking at the floor.

'But the difference I've seen with you is in communication skills,' Miss Handley continues. 'I don't think you used to see teachers as people you could communicate with. It was "them" and "us".'

'In my old school, it was different. They didn't really care. They cared about themselves.'

'Do we hound you more?'

He smiles, rueful. 'Yeah. Here, there's only two members of staff I don't get along with.'

'Maybe it's about maturing. It's also about the way you deal with staff. It changes the way staff deal with you. And I think your parents are supportive. Even if you're at loggerheads with them, you can stand back and see they want the best for you.'

'Before, I had problems. But I've sorted it out.'

'When I first interviewed you with Mr Steer, you were trying to be so street cred. I couldn't hear what you were saying because all your letters and all your words ran together. It was very street wise. You were coming into a new place. You were setting out, "Don't mess with me." I would have wanted to protect myself, too, coming into year ten.'

'I was lucky I settled in how I did. Most new people get picked on and stuff.'

'That's down to you.'

'At first they tried it, they said I was racist to Muslims. But they've stopped now.' Now he's thinking about what happens next. 'I'm looking into going to sixth form, but when I'm looking in detail there's not a lot there. I've been offered a place, but I think loads of people are just doing that because they can't be bothered going to college. Half my life will be trying to sort out my music, my rap. Other people are saying I can make it. But...' This is the hard part. This is where reality comes in. He ploughs on: 'Most of my life is going to be about trying to get an apprenticeship with JTL, for an electrician. I've got an application form and they, like, help you to get a place.'

Miss Handley looks encouraging, but her words have an edge they both understand. JTL is a training company that finds apprenticeship places for teenagers. But she knows its places are oversubscribed. 'It's quite hard to get in there. A lot of students end up going to college instead. The criteria aren't just academic. It's behaviour. Are they people who're going to work with us?'

She gives him a hard look. He blushes. Earlier this week she pulled him up after lunch one day. His eyes were red and bloodshot, his pupils huge and dark. She doesn't speak now but he knows she is waiting.

'I must have had a cold, Miss. I weren't smoking or nothing.'

He's on his feet before she has dismissed him. It's lunchtime. There are places to go and people to see. Delroy greets him with an understated touch of the hand. They slope down the corridor and out of the gate.

JEMMA

Jemma drops her bag, bangs over to the side of the room to fetch a stool and clangs it on to the floor. Electronics is not her favourite lesson.

It's mid-January – less than six months till the GCSEs – and her teacher has been ill for six weeks so a cover teacher has been in charge. Worse, it turns out that the circuit board she is making is the wrong way round and will have to be done again. But her normal teacher has the acetate, so she can't make progress. She feels aimless. She needs something to do. She wanders to the cupboard, gets out a drill and makes a few tiny holes in her circuit board.

'Jemma! Goggles!'

She gets up again, wanders back to the cupboard and picks out a pair of goggles and an apron. Wanders back again, tying the apron round her light blue short-sleeved blouse and dark trousers. Sits down. But the goggles aren't comfortable so yet again she gets up, goes back to the cupboard, changes them. Really, what's the point? This lesson is a mess.

By now the cover teacher is eyeing her with some irritation. 'You've got loads to do Jemma. Start practising your soldering.'

This time she doesn't return to her stool. Instead she pushes through the swing door into Mr Pugh's class.

'Miss,' she says, swinging back a couple of minutes later, 'Mr Pugh says I don't have to practise my soldering.'

The cover teacher is getting cross. 'Jemma! When I tell you to do something, you have to do it!'

'OK, Miss. I'm going.' The minute the teacher turns away the encounter is forgotten. As she walks back to her seat again she begins to sing inarticulately and to do a little dance. 'Do-doo-doo-*dooo*, der-der-de-*der*...' Her hands splay out.

But as she fiddles with the drill frustration wells up again. Then she throws the circuit board down with a staged 'Aaaargh!'

'Keep *calm*, Jemma.'

'I *am* calm!' She is shouting now, hands above her head as she flounces towards the door again. Before she gets there she stops. Turns on the kitten heel of her slip-on shoe and walks back with a wide smile on her face.

The teacher isn't smiling. 'Jemma. Look at me. Do you understand what I've told you? You have eight LEDs to solder. You don't need your acetate. You have loads to do. Now do it!'

Reluctantly, slowly, Jemma picks up the soldering iron and starts work on the LEDs. A minute later she is singing to herself again.

Jemma knows that mostly she is a good student, but sometimes she gets frustrated and angry. And sometimes she has been in trouble. She was talking about this with her parents the other day, in the warm kitchen that is the heart of their house. It was about four thirty and she was just in from school. Her dad works shifts, in the fire service, and he was at home that day – he has been promoted recently so now he has a car with a flashing light on top. Her little sister Lydia calls it the nee-naw car.

Jemma had been crouched on the kitchen floor, pulling brightly coloured plates from the dishwasher, which she calls the 'wishdosher'. That is one of her jobs. Her godmother was there, and she was helping her. She was trying to do it quietly, because her mum had complained that she was crashing about and making a lot of noise, saying she'd always been like that. Very outspoken – 'Not backward in coming forward.' That made Jemma laugh. It seemed to her a strange expression because she is very literal in the way she thinks. But her mum and dad have never discouraged her from having opinions.

'But there does come a point where there is no more argument. And that is what you don't take very kindly to. You just had to learn to live with it,' her mum said.

At school sometimes this is a problem. For Jemma, 'Because I say so,' is not an answer. She wants a proper 'because'. And even then, if she's honest, it isn't always good enough for her.

Her dad liked Seven Kings when they came to the open day five years ago; everyone confirmed what a good school it was. But he has some concerns about it now: 'It is really how controlling they are, I suppose. Like when you had that bad run with your science teacher.'

'Yes... But she wasn't a very good teacher. She wasn't the normal teacher. And the normal teacher knew she wasn't a very good teacher. And she knew we knew... And she was trying to teach us something about how the earth's core was formed. And I was sure that wasn't right. Because really they don't know. So I said that. And...'

Her dad looked at her then with a mixed expression on his face, which she understood. Her parents don't approve of her arguing with the teachers. They say she doesn't always listen to other people, or understand how they are feeling, and that there comes a point when she has to do as she is told. But they also agree with her that she has to make up her own mind.

Her mum agreed. 'You do need to learn how to express yourself, and to listen to others. But if you manage to control the way you argue and to be a little more subtle, that quality could be a huge asset to you in life. Your strong, opinionated nature could take you a long way. But I don't think Seven Kings has really channelled your confrontational way of being. They've only ever seen it as negative.'

'I know often I can be wrong, and I can be rude, but it isn't just a random thing. There is usually a reason. And they never say, "What is your point of view?" The attitude is "Because I'm a teacher, you must do this."'

That is one reason why she has to work hard for her GCSEs.

It is still not certain that they will give her a place in the sixth form. They might take it away if her behaviour does not become more 'appropriate'. Last year they threatened to stop her going on work experience at a nursery because she had got into a pickle with her DT coursework while the teacher was away.

'I think it's quite sad,' her dad said, 'that you won't be given that opportunity unless you conform. Work experience is a valuable part of your education. It shouldn't be a privilege they can take away...' Then he went on, 'But the focus of the school is good. In some schools, they discourage competition. But at Seven Kings they use their high-achievers as role models. There's competition in life, why not at school?'

Jemma knows she's clever. She took a GCSE in statistics last year and got an A; she will do eleven more this summer. But sometimes the teachers get a bit tired of her: 'Because I always put my hand up, the teacher will say, "Everybody – apart from Jemma!"'

Her dad says as long as all of his four daughters achieve their potential, it doesn't matter what they do. He says if they do their studying now, their life will be a lot easier. Neither her mum nor her dad felt they'd achieved what they were capable of at school. They met in the sixth form in Ilford, although Jemma's dad was born in India and her mum is half South African. Now her dad is working full time in a demanding job, bringing up the four of them and finishing a masters' degree at the same time.

'I look back and think, why was I so stupid?' he says. 'I had the time when I was young, and all my resources could have been put into studying. If you haven't got the education, you get overlooked for promotion. But that doesn't mean I see academic qualifications as any measure of intelligence or capability. I want my children to have rounded lives.'

Jemma agrees with that. She will go to university, maybe to do something like child psychiatry, and she thinks Seven Kings will help to get her there.

'Ilford isn't the best place. But I do know I'm quite privileged to go to that school. The catchment area is the best thing about it, in a way. We might get beaten by the grammar schools and the private schools. But, hey, we're ordinary people! We get in there because we live here. And we try our best. It's real.'

ALAN STEER

Through the narrow glass in the door of his office he can see Anthony sitting outside in the lobby next door, to which pupils are sent when they are in trouble. He is hunched, as usual, as if embarrassed by his height. Today he is clean-shaven.

Alan sighs inwardly. They are playing a game, he and Anthony. Both know they are playing it, but neither can acknowledge the fact openly. And perhaps they are playing slightly different games. Anthony's game is about display, revealing himself to the world. Before, he says sometimes, he was just small. Then he got to be a big person. But even when he was a big person, he still had to wear the uniform that small people wear. Now he can see the time coming when he will no longer wear that uniform, when he will not be Anthony, Seven Kings schoolboy, but some other Anthony. He wants the world to meet that person, the person he thinks he is going to be.

Alan's game is about stopping something bigger happening.

What if he were to allow the chrysalis to open and the new Anthony emerged in all his prickle-faced, shirt-tailed, diamond-studded glory? Maybe dozens of Anthonys would burst out all over the school. And maybe that crucial frontier-post between school and the street would lose its potency. Maybe they would begin to wonder who they are.

The importance of the uniform is not that it makes every-one the same because it does not. Sikh boys are allowed to wear beards, Christians wear crucifixes, Muslim girls wear scarves. Sixth-formers wear whatever they like, within reason. Those are not concessions: they are part of the school's core. And that is the point. Because that is the core, it cannot speak with its own voice. It cannot be used by the pupils to proclaim their individual differences. It cannot make a rent in the fabric of the school.

Every day at Seven Kings you will hear someone say: 'This is what we are. This is the Seven Kings way of doing things. At Seven Kings, we work hard. At Seven Kings, we all know where we're going. At Seven Kings, we support each other. We like each other. At Seven Kings, we are like the herrings: we must always keep swimming, and preferably in the same direction.'

So after Alan saw that big Sikh boy trying to hide Anthony's beard as he leaned forward over his keyboard, he had acted to preserve the school's ethos. Anthony's mother was telephoned, and Anthony was told to report to the headmaster's lobby with a shaven face. He followed up the order with a second, sterner command after Anthony had failed to respond to the first. Maybe it would sound pompous to say so but he was under-pinning the foundations of the school. Seven Kings High School will always turn a unified face to the world. And if the

112

rules say that faces should be clean-shaven, it is his job to ensure that they are.

So Anthony's in double trouble now, for growing his beard and evading his punishment. Alan goes over to the lobby door and opens it. 'I'm glad to see you've had a shave, Anthony.'

Anthony does not speak, but he looks up at him. He is not exactly smiling but there is a hint of an offering on his face. They both know that the points for this round have been awarded to the headmaster, and they both know the joust is not over.

'Where were you on Monday? I said you should come to see me.'

'Sorry, sir. I forgot.'

It is his turn not to respond. Like hell he forgot. But he will not labour the point. He dispatches Anthony to his lesson.

The truth is, he likes the boy, who has a quiet, laid-back charm. There is no front, very little open defiance. And – if his desk were wood rather than laminate he would probably touch it – he thinks he will be one of Seven Kings' success stories.

When he had agreed to interview Anthony with his parents after he was excluded from his old school, he knew he had some strong cards in his hand. Anthony would be made to understand the gravity of the situation. He would be made to feel that the decision to grant him a place at Seven Kings would be a hard one, to be made only after Alan Steer had been assured of Anthony's deep and heartfelt contrition.

If Anthony had been caught smoking cannabis with his mates on the Seven Kings school field, it is likely that he would not have been permanently excluded. He would have been severely disciplined, of course. Sent home, parents called in, steps taken to ensure it could not happen again. But Anthony does not know that.

The boy's crime had not been, in Alan's eyes, a capital offence. And he was a bright, promising boy in some respects. He had only just failed the eleven plus. In the right surroundings, with the kind of constant, chivvying, muscular support that Seven Kings gives, he could do well. Maybe sixth form, maybe even university. At the very least, a clutch of good GCSEs. There is no reason on earth why Anthony should not leave with his five or more A–C grades, he thinks. In fact, he's not sure that anyone has to. Well. Not most people. This, he would be happy to acknowledge, is a recent departure in his thinking. And it is an area to which he has been devoting some thought.

Last summer, 85 per cent of the school's sixteen-year-olds jumped that bar. If you had asked him a decade ago whether such a thing might be possible he would have said, no, it was not. He would have said they could go further than they were going, but not that far.

Now, though, he thinks that if they took certain decisions they could get virtually everyone through. They could offer more vocational courses, for example. Beauty, perhaps. Those courses can be worth four good GCSEs on their own. They could push kids into subjects where the pass rate is high – drama, art. He can think of schools where most of the kids are getting their five good grades, but not in maths or English.

But that is not what he wants to do. He wants to target the 15 per cent who do not make it by trying to change the way they think about themselves. He was at a Treasury seminar recently where a man was talking about the Tories' policy on council-house sales and how it made people think differently about themselves, made them more aspirational. He wants to use that here.

Some of the kids arrive here knowing they're failures. They have failed at primary school and they are destined to fail here. He would like to divert resources to them. He would really like to know which ones really have the capacity to improve. But how can you tell? Some will fail, whatever you do. Look at Amina Simpson, who won't come to school. Is she going to leave without qualifications and drift into some unskilled job on the fringes of society? Or worse? She might. What about the Ambrose kids, with their chaotic family life? Possibly they will all end up in court, whatever Alan does. But he doesn't know that.

If he were a business he would take Robbie Ambrose and Amina Simpson off the shelf and pulp them, but he is not running a business. A school must have humane values. A school must put the Robbies and the Aminas – and the Anthonys – on the best shelf near the door where they can be cherished and polished every day. Where they can be pushed and primped, tweaked and harried until they know they are worthy of the Seven Kings brand. Until they can hold up their heads as they walk out of those gates on to the street with a piece of paper that proclaims them fit for the world.

PERIN

Perin is sitting in the dark drama studio, assiduously reading a set of borrowed biology notes. Around him, other students are engaged in similar activities. A few have brought books. One girl has an Alice Walker novel; a boy is reading *Moby Dick*. Someone else has a book called *The Witching Hour*, which has a lurid green cover with big drippy letters.

Perin has no recollection of being told there was a 'whole school read' this morning. If he had known, he would have brought *Lord of the Rings*, which he has read four times. So he is staring at the biology notes, which mean nothing to him. His A-level subjects are physics, maths, further maths and economics. Several others are doing the same. One girl has a UCAS magazine. No one is complaining. They are doing their best to comply.

There is plenty to do at the moment, with exams in just a few months. But alongside the doing is also the waiting. He must continue to wait to know what his future might be. Cambridge was a disappointment: he expected to hear something during the Christmas holidays but by the time he returned to school there had still been no letter. When he saw Miss Jones, the head of the sixth form, her face wore an expression of sympathy. She was sorry, she said, to hear his news.

That was how he had found out. He had had nothing from the college. When he phoned up to ask, they said they supposed the letter must have got lost in the post. And that was the end of the matter, really. He would have liked to know why: he felt he had performed well at the interview.

He felt quite down for a few days. He asked himself if he could have done something differently. But now he has put it away because he can't change it. If someone else got the place ahead of him it must have been because they were better. Or because there were so many good candidates it was impossible to choose. Either way, what can he do?

None of his friends got in. Vijay was rejected, and the boy in his physics class who asks the perceptive questions. They had all known from day one that it would be a lottery – and that has helped, in a way.

No one here can tell him why. He went to all his teachers and checked whether the answers he had given were the right ones. He asked Dr Pithia; he asked Miss Jones. He asked other students who had interviews last year. And the outcome of his research was that the reason he didn't get in remains unclear. No one can say for sure what Cambridge wants. So now he must wait till March to see if LSE will offer him a place. They have told him he is shortlisted. He has an offer from UCL, though – three As and a B.

His dad voiced a few tiny concerns about Cambridge and how temporary that wheelchair ramp was, with its big sheets of board and its scaffolding poles, and the steps down to the toilets. 'I was saying to myself, if Perin does come here he's going to find it difficult,' he said. 'If they'd accepted you, they would have had to make a lot of changes.'

But thinking like that is the easy way out. He won't do it. He's glad he applied. No one can take that away from him. His dad says lots of clever people don't get on in life because they don't push themselves forward, they don't think they're good enough. He had an interview at Cambridge. How can he complain about that?

Complaining does not come naturally to him. Once, a couple of years ago, he went to a computer-games convention at Earls Court with a friend. When they got on the tube at Ilford they asked if there was a lift at Earls Court, and the station staff said there was, but they didn't say it wasn't working. So they had to get back on the tube to the next station, and it took them twenty minutes to get back to Earls Court. But he didn't feel he needed to waste his time complaining. It's been done: nothing has been achieved.

Anyway, he likes to take in a number of different

perspectives before he makes up his mind. He likes to see the whole picture. He doesn't get angry much. And neither do most of the other sixth formers at Seven Kings because they're too busy studying. Maybe at other schools they get excited about the environment, or about the war in Iraq, but not at Seven Kings. You don't get to be a doctor or a lawyer or a merchant banker by standing on the street with a banner.

His first lesson is cancelled. 'If that teacher dies we're screwed,' Vijay jokes, as they head for the sixth-form block. They spread their economics graphs on one of the aluminium café tables in the canteen area and chat as they pore over them, the conversations swinging without warning or artifice between last weekend's football and the task in hand. 'No, it was definitely a foul... If you add in the running profit there, it changes the end result.'

They talk about where they will be this time next year. They both expect to be in London, at LSE, UCL or Imperial. A good college of London University is now their aim. And where will they be in five years, or ten? Of that they are less sure. Perin hopes, though, that wherever he is he will be making good money. Maybe, he thinks, he will be living in a big mansion somewhere outside London. A country estate, even, with a big garage for all his cars.

And how will he live in his big house? Will he be alone? He hopes not. He likes to think that he will be married, with children, maybe. He wants to have a decent family and live a decent life, and to be totally himself. Then he will be happy. 'But that will depend on finding the right person, of course,' he says quickly.

Maybe there will be a little temple like the one they have at home. He goes in there sometimes to pray. He would like always to be able to do that. You can take your troubles to the gods and they will help to bring you solace and guidance, he says. But you have to remember them when you aren't troubled, too.

Vijay says God is within yourself. 'You have to remember God is going to give you peace in the afterlife,' he says. 'My mum says if you can't do anything good for a person, don't do anything at all.'

Perin thinks if you're not good then maybe you will be reincarnated as someone with a poor quality of life. But what you need most is a good family background, strong family values and the will to succeed. That, he thinks, is what helped his family to climb, in a single generation, to where they are today.

He thinks anything is possible, with hard work and the right values. But he has learned that success is not just a question of hard work. He will also have to be lucky.

SUCCESS STORIES

In the end, though, Perin will not have to rely on luck. Whatever setbacks life throws at him, he will weather them and plough on. In the end he will succeed, because he will not be deterred from his steady path.

Perin's teachers say what a lovely lad he is, how decent, how charming, how hard-working. And he is. Perin is an embodiment of everything Seven Kings High School stands for. He is serious yet friendly, he is hard-working, never rebellious, flashy or loud. After seven years at the school he has absorbed its values.

But while the school has played a big part in making Perin

what he is, it has not been his only influence. There are children at Seven Kings who drift, or struggle to conform. So, there must be something else about Perin and those who succeed without struggling that differentiates them from the few who do not. Perin has roughly the same experience – certainly the same opportunities – at school as Anthony, Tyrone and Jemma. The difference, then, must come from within their homes, their communities and themselves as individuals.

Research shows that family background and parental attitudes to education are crucial in determining how a child will get on at school. Yet all the parents of the young people in this book seem to hold strikingly similar views about their children's education and the role they play in it. They believe that ultimately it is up to their children to grasp that hard work will be rewarded. They all say things like, 'So long as they do their best, that's OK.' The reasons for the differences in our seven teenagers' attitudes towards their education, then, are harder to unpick than we might at first assume.

In some cases, it has to be said, the mould has long been set. Seven Kings is an aspirational school in an aspirational area. It has a large and all-important group of pupils who are almost predestined to climb the social ladder, the 'critical mass' that academics say, sets the tone for a school. In many cases these children's families are richer educationally than they are financially. Shivanie's parents' education was curtailed by circumstance but they have a tradition of academic achievement. Jemma, too, has grown up in a house where the notion of achievement and expectation is writ large. It would be hard to express in bald terms of social class, but many of these children have grown up with a strong expectation that they will succeed.

Perin's grandfather, who came to London with nothing thirty years ago, is proud when he sees his grandchildren training to be lawyers, accountants and pharmacists. Yet he is probably not surprised: he might always have believed they could do it. Perin's mother and father say they didn't have to push him because he just got on with it. But they must have had a quiet sense of expectation, based on experience, optimism and aspiration. If Shivanie achieves her potential, that will be enough, her mum says. She believes her daughters will do well, and Shivanie's older sisters are already showing signs that their high aspirations will be fulfilled.

It seems such a small thing, this implied, sometimes almost unspoken assumption, that it's hard to believe it is really the main factor in determining whether a child will pass or fail. If the message is delivered from parent to child, how does it travel? Surely something more specific, more fundamental, is happening in these homes. Sometimes, certainly, there is open exhortation. Jemma's mum says she has to push her daughter sometimes. Kessie's dad reminds her, if she flags, not to give up.

But something else helps some of the highest achievers. It is hard to define but there is often a particular structure to their home lives, which may relieve some of the stress of school work: dinner at eight thirty in Perin's house, prayers before school in Kessie's, a space made in the day for homework. No one factor will make a pupil succeed, but all of these are important: a tradition of educational success, a structured, safe home environment, parents who have high expectations and who, when it proves necessary, are prepared to tackle their children's underachievement head-on.

There is something bigger and harder to grasp, too, which

must play a key part in determining which children succeed. It is a sense of the inevitability of progress, the unshakeable belief in each generation of a family that the next will be more successful, more prosperous, than the last. These are not the archetypal middle-class 'pushy parents', who are much talked about in other parts of North London. They hesitate before questioning the way the school teaches their children, and in general they trust its staff to do the right thing. But they have a strong belief that their children will succeed, and that the school will help them to do so.

MARCH

JEMMA

'Let's talk about electronics,' Mr Rosewell says.

'Do we have to?'

'Your mock result was a C. Tell me about it.'

There is no aggression in Jemma's posture as she sits on the low, padded chair in the deputy head's office. As March has crept in and the time left before GCSEs can be measured in weeks rather than months, a subtle change has come about. It seems right, somehow, that they should be having this rather adult conversation about her grades.

'Lots of stress! Lots of the teacher not being there. Which is a major issue for you, actually, because we're doing everything we can and you're failing to give us a teacher.'

'Yes, it has been difficult. But let's throw it back to you. The effort grade is three. You've got to push yourself more than that. We need to think about the situation you're in as a mature young person.'

'Well, it won't help in the exam. I can't say, like, "My teacher wasn't there." They'll be, like, "Do we care?"'

He is looking at his laptop. 'You're predicted a D in your actual exam, but I don't think you'll get a D.'

She smiles. 'If I do, Mr Rosewell will be knocking on my door!'

'Now. What about your other mocks?'

'Academically... My marks are terrible. The mocks were really bad.'

He looks up, surprised. 'But based on your marks... you would get ten A to Cs.'

'It isn't good enough.'

'Even within that, you have starred As in maths, business and science. You're being too critical of yourself. If you do as your teachers think and hope, everything will be C and above.' He fiddles with his laptop again. 'Let's look at this... Business. Miss Malik says you're predicted an A star in the exam, but your effort is only two. And English, you got a D in your mock.'

'I really should be A, A star. My weakness is in my writing. And I'm practising. Science. That was fair. I got a B. And I didn't put any effort in... Can I talk to you about subjects for next year?'

'I'm coming on to that. Last time we talked about maths, physics and English.'

'Well, what Miss Bourke was saying – it's kind of brilliant, actually – she was saying, "You're a bright student. You could cope with two sciences and maths. You could even do medicine."'

'That's good advice. I'll put you down for chemistry as well, then. You're not stuck with it.' He looks up now. 'So. Keep positive. Keep on track.'

'What happens now? Do my mum and dad get a letter or anything?'

'Right. What will happen in terms of a sixth-form place? It remains conditional on you being good until the end of the year. To be fair I haven't had any moans from anyone. Provided you don't do anything stupid. It's the things we talked about last time. Inappropriate or silly behaviour.'

She is a little taken aback. There were one or two incidents last year, but she had thought they were in the past. 'Oh. I thought it would have, like, changed by now.'

'If you'd got worse I would say you should be looking elsewhere. I'm not saying that. We had a long chat about it last time. Have you been keeping your nose clean? No silly games?'

She sidesteps the question: 'I thought... So how come it stays on there?' She isn't angry or aggressive: this is just something she wants to know.

'Don't be too hung up on it, Jemma. I don't think it'll be an issue. If there was a ridiculous incident we'd review the place. But I want a reminder in the back of your head.'

She bounces off the chair and makes for the door, smiling, swinging her cloth school bag over her shoulder. There is a cartoon face on it, and underneath it says, 'Boys are So Dumb, they can't even chew gum.'

In the warm fug of the changing rooms they seem to take longer than usual to change for football. Although spring is on its way, London is muffled by a cold, sour mist. Outside, the scene is unwelcoming. As Jemma and her classmates trail round the side of the school, carrying football paraphernalia, they can see the bones of the trees, the scuffed earth showing through winter-trodden grass.

She dumps the kit bag on the ground and glances back towards the school, with its old clock fixed at a quarter to nine. Clumps of daffodils with purple and white crocuses are framed against the dark brick building. But she has no time to reflect, or even to shiver, in the bitter cold. She begins to jump around, punching the air with a boxer's jabs.

Miss Marshall looks up from sorting the kit. 'You really are a footballer, aren't you, Jemma?'

She grins. 'Am I a captain, Miss? Am I a captain?' Like most of the group she is in a thin white polo shirt and black track-suit bottoms.

Miss Marshall ignores her. She is looking with some distaste at one of the green bibs she has pulled out of the battered bag. 'One of the disadvantages of girls' football is that you take over the boys' bibs,' she says.

'When I leave,' Jemma says, 'I'm going to buy this school some girls' bibs.'

A girl with long blonde hair says, 'Maybe I could wash them!'

Miss Marshall looks up now, irritated. 'Jemma, if you were taking one of your trampolining classes and someone was talking, what would you do?'

Jemma stops talking. Miss Marshall counts out the teams, and makes Jemma a captain. She kicks off, sideways.

'Jemma! Football rules? Which way does the ball go at the beginning?'

'Forwards, Miss!' She runs for the ball, and as her back recedes across the pitch, the chill, damp air is pierced by her laughter. Someone shoots.

'Goal!'

Jemma yells, 'It didn't go in!'

'It was a *goal*!'

She shrugs, sticks out her tongue, conceding.

They are passing it back down the pitch now. Jemma is screaming, 'Go on! Go *on*!' Then the ball rolls over the touch-line and she laughs again. 'You're fired!' She is jumping up and down. 'Goal kick! Goal kick!'

'It is not a goal kick, Jemma!'

'It's a corner!'

'Goal kick!'

'Corner!'

The discussion is becoming a pantomime. She explodes: 'Oh!' she cries. 'Who cares? We're only having fun!'

By the time they change ends it's 3–0 to the opposition. The pitch is alive now, warmed by the running and the screaming. Jemma captures the ball and shoots. Razia deflects her shot. Jemma shrieks with laughter. Two of her team mates have fallen on to the ground, helpless with mirth. She runs over, picks them up and hugs them.

They troop indoors for a PE GCSE lesson. The room is full of noise and clatter, with the energy of the pitch. The boys, fresh from their own football game, bring their own quotient of static. In front of Jemma, the blonde girl is brushing out her hair down to her knees. 'Look at my split ends,' she says. Jemma pulls forward her own shorter, darker ponytail and holds it alongside for comparison.

Miss Abbott is scanning the room. 'Who's missing?'

'Delroy's gone,' someone offers.

'What? Gone from the school?'

'Suspended,' Jemma says.

Delroy's OK, Jemma thinks. He's not one of her particular friends but she gets on with him. He's often in trouble, but this time he went over the top and swore at a teacher. She thinks he won't be back until at least next week.

Today they're learning first aid. There's a drill they must know: danger, response, airway, breathing, circulation.

'Samir,' Miss Abbott says, 'I asked you to stop talking. Now. Move it!'

Samir is defiant. 'I didn't talk to him, man!'

'Move, Samir,' she says, pointing at a seat on the other side of the room.

He gets up, but as he shoves back his chair it falls over. He doesn't pick it up, just walks slowly, deliberately, to the other seat. Miss Abbott carries on talking to the rest of the class. A few minutes later he is writing, along with the rest.

TYRONE

He strolls in at 8.33 a.m. and looks about. The classroom is in uproar. A clot of girls at the front is huddled round something. A birthday cake, with candles, for Spencer. Spencer is loving it, of course. Running out of the room. Having to be dragged back, yelling.

Tyrone saunters past the front desk to the window, then back again. He slaps Spencer on the back, then wanders back to where Jerome is sitting and carefully removes his new Adidas hat. It is Peruvian-style, grey wool with white patterns and bobbles that dangle on strings from the earflaps. But he will not pull it over his ears. He balances it, carefully, on the front of his head. March winds or none, he would rather have cold ears than messed-up braids.

He's on a bit of a flier today, so far as uniform goes. He has a problem: he has new white socks and the standard black school shoes mess them up so he has put on his white trainers. The bell goes and he follows Jerome into the corridor. He sees two girls from his class in front of him, runs, jumps, slaps each one simultaneously on the shoulder with the flats of his hands. They squeal, laugh, then carry on together in a little knot, with Jerome alongside.

Nowadays they do not need to fill the corridor with their energy, like they used to. They are cool, confident. When they pass Wesley in the corridor he and Tyrone touch fingertips quietly. 'See you at break, man.'

Standing in line outside the geography room Tyrone takes a foot out of a trainer to show his sock to someone. Just at that moment Mr Mortiboys comes past. Tyrone slips his foot back in. Mr Mortiboys spots the expression on his face and understands the substance of it, though not the specific. 'Tyrone, tuck your shirt in.'

Tyrone does so and laughs. Distraction is a good tactic. Then Mr Rosewell comes past and points at his foot. 'Tyrone, what's that?'

'Er, trainers, sir.'

'Where are your shoes?'

'In my bag, sir.'

'Well, change them. Now.'

'Yes, sir.'

Mr Paterson arrives and they tumble into the classroom. Soon it is quiet and Mr Paterson is talking about the weather. He walks over to the window. 'You can see the nimbus stratus. It's a high. We're going to have nice weather again.' Tyrone leans down, pulls off his trainers, slips his shoes out of his bag and puts them on. Everyone else is busy with coloured pens.

'Come on, Tyrone. You always seem a bit sleepy on a Friday morning. It's all that Thursday-night partying.'

Tyrone starts underlining the key words on the printed sheet. 'Warm front. Cold front.' He hasn't quite finished when they all move on again. Filling in a chart now. He isn't sure what he has to do. It's complicated. And the girl sitting next to him is fiddling with his braids, pulling out a stray hair, motherly.

A few more minutes pass. 'Sir? What are you supposed to do with this one?'

'It's all there, Tyrone, on the worksheet.' He is kindly, not angry. Tyrone looks at the sheet again. You have to put down what happens when a weather system passes over. 'Warm front. Temperature rises. Pressure goes down.' This is OK. He can do it. Actually, things have been going much better recently. He even got 64 per cent in a maths test.

The girl next to him has finished. 'Sir, can you come and see if this is right?'

By the time they get to drama, everyone else is already sitting on the floor in a circle with their legs crossed. Miss Bonsall looks grim. 'I'm waiting for you to sit down.' She has *Macbeth* open on her knee. Tyrone settles next to Jerome, reclining on one elbow.

The door opens again and two more boys troop in. She snaps the book shut, exasperated. 'Go to Miss Pereira, please. It isn't good enough.'

A little undercurrent of discontent ripples round the circle.

'They're going to Miss Pereira to explain why they're walking in five minutes late to my lesson. Anyone else want to join them?'

The murmur subsides.

'We are three lessons behind. We should have done this before, but we haven't because of your behaviour. Who still has to do an essay on *Macbeth* for homework?'

Tyrone looks around, unsure. A few hands go up.

'*All* of you. What happens in Act Three, Scene Four?'

Jerome says, 'Banquo's ghost appears.'

'How do you think you would direct that scene? Do you remember what we said last week?'

'No,' Spencer says.

Tyrone holds up two fingers towards Spencer, like a gun: 'Pfff.' Then he slouches back on his elbow.

'Tyrone, could you sit up, please?' He sits up, and listens for a minute while the girl who sits next to him in geography is talking about Macbeth, and how he isn't looking at the others during the banquet because he is talking to Banquo. 'That's really good,' Miss Bonsall says. 'You're thinking about ways you might stage this scene.'

'So,' she says, 'today we're going to improvise Act Two, Scene Two. I'm going to put you into groups of three. Macbeth. Lady Macbeth. Director.' She puts Tyrone in a group with Amit and Gulika. They have to act out the scene where Macbeth comes back after he has killed Duncan to find Lady Macbeth.

Tyrone, lying down now, says, 'I want to be the director.'

'Tyrone, you're Macbeth.'

'I want to be the director,' he repeats.

Tyrone, what have I just said?' She is standing in front of him.

'All right, Miss.'

'No! Not all right!' She sighs. 'OK, Tyrone. You're the director.'

He is sitting up straight now. 'Yeah! Great! Thanks, Miss!'

'OK. I'm giving you ten minutes. I want you to improvise this scene where Macbeth has just killed the king. How is he feeling? What state is he in?'

Tyrone gets to his feet. 'Miss? What are they supposed to be doing?' He trots over to where she is talking to another group on the other side of the room, then comes back. 'Right. Amit, you're like this, right?' He's on his knees, now, hands in front of his face. Then he puts his hands on Amit's shoulders and pushes him into position.

'You're loving this, aren't you?' Gulika says.

'So go on,' he says, 'do it! "What are you, Macbeth? Are you a man, or a mouse?"' He turns Gulika round, showing her how to walk. 'Like this. Right! One. Two. Three. Action!'

Then he plays out the scene himself, animated now. 'Have you done it? Haveyoudoneit? Haveyoudoneit?' His energy is up and he is all bounce and spark. 'You're like, "Aaaargh! I can't believe it!" And he's like, er...' He trails off. 'Miss? What happens after that?'

'You pull out the dagger, Tyrone.'

He puts them back into position. Stands over them. 'Right!' He is pointing to Gulika. 'Are you *stuu*-pid? What is your *pro*blem?' He is twirling from one to the other, his arms punctuating his performance.

'OK! Everyone freeze!' Miss Bonsall says.

They sit down to watch each other's improvisations. The first team's performance is lively, passionate, even. When they stop, everyone claps. Tyrone sits back, not quite joining in but wanting to.

'So, why was that good?' Miss Bonsall asks.

Tyrone is feeling more confident now. 'Because they can both act.'

'Good, so we believed in the emotions they put into it. They really got it together, really clear and focused.'

One of the groups has a narrator, like they do in *Scary Movie* where the director appears in the middle of the scene. Another's Lady Macbeth gets so worked up that she shouts, 'What are you? A man or a *cow*?'

They all laugh so much they have to stop. Even Miss Bonsall cracks up. 'Right,' she says. 'One more. A volunteer?'

'Tyrone!' everyone choruses.

She smiles. 'I said, "volunteer", not "volunteer Tyrone".'

But he is up already. 'Gulika, don't laugh. She always laughs.'

And they do it. Amit forgets to kneel, but it isn't bad. At the end Tyrone shouts, 'Cut!' then sits down, beaming.

'I've really enjoyed today's lesson,' Miss Bonsall says. 'You put in a lot of effort and energy. Why couldn't you have done that three weeks ago?'

'Can we get a merit?' someone says.

Tyrone looks stupefied. A thought has struck him. 'I've already got one,' he says. He pulls the pink sheet from his blazer pocket and looks at it with bafflement.

ALAN STEER

The door from his lobby opens and Sanjay comes in, a tall boy, with a hint of adolescent acne on his face. Alan taps a few of the keys on his laptop and looks round with a cheerful expression. 'So, Sanjay, how were your mocks?'

'Yeah, sir, my mocks went good.'

'You're happy?'

'Yeah. I'm all right with it, sir. I'm really pleased with my business studies cos I got an A for that.'

'Do you know why it went well?'

'Yeah, because I was revising properly. I got my mates together and we were asking each other questions. I didn't leave it till the last minute. You know, some people have been spending five hours revising. That's impossible.'

Alan looks at the laptop again. 'So there's just the one area where you got less than that B...'

'Yeah, but I've got this strategy. I'm not good at the theory but I'm really good at the coursework. So if I get A for my coursework I automatically walk in.'

Alan pauses. 'Everything you're saying to me is really good. Yet when I look at what your teachers are saying about you going into the sixth form, there's a C by your name. That means "conditional".' He waits for an answer.

'Well. Sir. I've got. Myself into some trouble. Previously.'

Alan Steer is still smiling, but the tone of the conversation has changed: Sanjay has started to deflate. 'They're saying they're concerned about attitude and effort. You're coming across really positive and that's good but...'

'Sir, if I was to talk about last year and the year before...'

'You were a bit of a lazy toad, were you?'

'Erm.' He smiles now. 'Maybe mischievous, sir.'

'This is an adult conversation. What on earth is the point in us enrolling you on a two-year course to do A levels and you going back to where you were before and wasting two years? Everything you're saying is great, but you know what *I'm* going to say. It has flaming well got to continue. What subjects do you want to do?'

'I want to take English language, economics, because it's

similar to business studies, psychology – and media, because it complements psychology.'

Sanjay gets the talk now, about how hard A levels are, how he will have to raise his game. How Alan Steer raised three sons and how at the end of the first term of the sixth form they were all asking, 'Can I do it? Can I cope?'

'What's the dream, again?'

Sanjay has reflated, and is making full use of the extra air in his system. 'If I do economics, and do well, I could become an investment banker. Good money, sir. Or if psychology goes well, a psychiatrist or something.'

Alan pauses, again. Will he kick the boy's feet from under him? 'It's a fairly broad choice. Do you actually know what you need? For economics, you need maths A level. If you want to be a psychiatrist don't you want to go to medical school?'

Sanjay shrugs, admitting defeat.

'Well, I'm fairly sure of it. What you're doing is OK, probably, for banking, but not for psychiatry. You aren't choosing subjects that would enable you to do psychiatry. You would need to be much more science-oriented, and I'm not convinced that's your strength.'

They both laugh, Sanjay sheepishly. 'No, it isn't, sir.' He is fiddling with his chunky silver bracelet.

'We're happy to offer you a place in the sixth form but it would initially be conditional. We won't go into what you did in the past, but your teachers obviously think it's a bit more important than you might. The key thing is getting the right courses. It will be as much about thinking as about sweat.'

Sanjay gets up, looking relieved. 'Thank you, sir.' He shakes Alan's hand awkwardly.

That's the first of today's year-eleven interviews over. Several more to go, and yet more later in the week. Everyone has these sessions with senior members of staff before and after their GCSE mocks. It helps to reinforce the messages the school needs to get across: that students should work smart, use brains not brawn in their study. An hour working constructively is better than three hours' staring blankly at your book. It is also about gently challenging the idea that so many Seven Kings pupils share: that there are only two good careers – merchant banking and medicine. And, of course, it is about handing out a few witches' warnings, keeping them on their toes.

ANTHONY

When Doug Harrison comes for Anthony, one day in late March, he is in a sociology lesson, looking at an essay that has just been handed back to him: 'How Far are Differences in Educational Achievement between Individuals the Result of Differences in Home Background?' Miss Lomax has pinned a slip of paper to the back. 'Five out of seven. Excellent effort, Anthony, and a good range of factors discussed. When looking at alternative arguments, show an example.' Underneath that he has put his tag: Blaze King. He yawns. He is the tallest in the class but he is slumped in his chair so his shoulders are lower than the others'. The door opens. He looks up and sees Mr Harrison beckoning to him, asking him to bring his bag as he may not be back before the lesson ends. He experiences a moment of concern. Things have not been too good.

Fortunately, though, he has had a shave. Mr Steer had

another go at him the other day. Now there is just a little patch of bristle on his chin, and two tiny squiggles down his cheeks. He is quite pleased with the effect.

He sits down in Mr Harrison's office, feeling awkward. Even on these big, armless padded chairs his legs seem somehow too long. His school uniform is hanging off him as if it wants to be somewhere else. His black slip-on shoes are polished, his blazer and trousers clean and pressed, but nothing feels right.

'OK, Anthony, this is obviously to firm up what's going to happen next year.'

He waits, knowing what will come next.

'You know we won't be offering you a place in the sixth form because of what happened.'

He nods. It has not been a happy time. His year head, Miss Handley, had pulled him up once or twice, for having blood-shot eyes, dilated pupils. He had refused to admit anything, but on one particular day there had been a reason why he'd needed a smoke. There was stuff going on at home, and he was wound up about it. He had been uncharacteristically aggressive with his mum. When she had bought him this new coat he didn't like, he'd shouted at her and made her upset.

The next morning he could see he had been wrong to react like that, so he apologized, expecting to make everything all right. But she had still been angry with him. He had kicked his way to school with a miserable, furious knot in his stomach. That was why he'd needed to blaze such a big cone at lunchtime, and had returned to class bleary-eyed, vague and quiet. That was when Miss Handley had made him go and talk to Mrs Cassidy in the medical centre.

She had wound him up, too, going on about how stupid he was being, how he couldn't expect people to ignore what he was doing just because he was good-looking and charming. Going on about how he was frying his brain and about the crack addicts who used to come into the hospital where she worked, looking for methadone.

'I'd never do that.'

'Anthony, you're on the first rung of the ladder. They would have said that when they were doing what you're doing now.'

'Yeah, I suppose. But the thing is, right, I've just given up cigarettes. And I really wanted a smoke.'

And they chatted, and when he felt a bit better he told her about his mood swings. She said that was probably because of his abusing drugs. By then he was dejected, flat and low again. She said she would have to phone his mum to ask her to take him home. And he begged her not to, because he knew how upset his mum would be. Later he wrote a rap:

I don't give a fuck, don't give a damn
I got a Big foot n bare tall like jap stam
Rollin a joint, bare flips like jean Claude van-damme
I don't take crack like a strict vegetarian and ham
But I especially like Mary-Jane ma girl
the only important shit that exists to me in this world
Yeh when I blaze
I blaze big cones, blunts and Ls...

He hated all that trouble because he knew how his mum would be. Normally they get on – they talk about stuff. She can tell him her troubles, and he can tell her things too. So he felt bad, knowing how she would feel.

She took him home, and later she had to come back and see

Miss Handley. And when she came home she'd been crying. She said she didn't mean to, she was just shocked, really, and then Miss Handley was all nice and sympathetic to her, and suddenly there were tears streaming down her face. And Miss Handley was filling up too, because she felt sorry for his mum. For what he'd put her through.

So he knows, now, what Mr Harrison is saying to him. He will not be invited into the sixth form at Seven Kings. He will not be going to university. He is not a person that they want in the Seven Kings' sixth form, even if his grades are good, because he is not a good influence. He doesn't care. He is vague and uncertain about so many things but not this, not now. They don't want him? Fine. Because he doesn't want them either.

> *Its old unit, the sixth form unit*
> *I never wanted to choose it*
> *Fuk da A-S and A2*
> *Bare hard work plus sixth form's gay too*
> *Seeing the same old faces*
> *Walking and educating in the same old places*
> *My exams no As no Bs or ticks*
> *Just crosses, Cs, Ds, and in brackets (Anthony*
> *You are shit.)*

He doesn't look at Mr Harrison. He nods.
'Let's start off with your mocks.'
'Some of them I done OK. But the rest weren't so good.'
'You know why you didn't do very well? Because—'
'It wasn't cos of that. It was revision. Because of that, probably.'

'In the end if you'd revised a bit more your grades would have been a bit better.'

'My predicted grades were good...' He is clapping his hands in front of him.

'Were you a long way off your predicted grades?'

'Some of them were, yes... I've got a maths tutor now. My mum got me this tutor. If people give me questions and I watch them do it I can do it myself. Then I've learned it.'

'I would say, "Have fun over Easter." But for the next month or two it won't be any fun. You'll make the difference between getting good grades and not in that period of time. Then you'll have all summer. Did we talk about what you were going to do?'

'I've been offered a place at Havering College. And I applied for Barking but they said, "Find an employer and come back to us."'

'It's very hard to get into Barking. What have you got to do to get a place at Havering?'

'There's two courses. The foundation one – if I don't do so well I can go on that. Or if I do good in my GCSEs, C or above, there's no problem.'

'So that's the intermediate? Part one? Two years?'

He nods. Actually, he's not quite clear about this level of detail.

They talk about his application for an apprenticeship. He took a test at the JTL training centre and passed. But they can only get him an apprenticeship if there's an employer they can put him with. He wrote a CV and a letter, and his mum has been posting copies to addresses she has written down from electricians' vans, but so far nobody seems to have a job for him. So he thinks he will be going to college.

'And is it construction, or specifically electrician?'

'It's *spec-if-ically* electrician.' He marks the word out to pronounce it. 'So if I do OK now, that'll be my whole life, sorted. For ever.' He says it with a strange mixture of relief and resignation.

He gets up to leave, uncertain now. He is on an edge, one foot in each of two worlds, pulled one way, pushed another. He is not sure what he wants, and sometimes not sure if he even cares.

Sometimes truth hurts
And fiction gets scary
Fuck fire, earth, wind and water, weed's my element.
With blaze and drink I think
God's already given me the symptom
A warning,
An indication.

THE TROUBLE WITH BOYS

It seems strange to say it now, but thirty years ago it might have been Jemma's level of achievement that was causing a headache, or Shivanie's. In the early 1970s there was growing concern that girls were underachieving, particularly in subjects such as science and maths. Now it is pupils like Tyrone and Anthony who are the focus of the school's efforts to raise standards.

Much has been said and written about this phenomenon. Some commentators believe the enthusiasm of boys for their lessons is being dampened by a system that is increasingly catering to the needs of girls. Some say education has become more feminine, with more female teachers and increased amounts of coursework that favour the more focused, compliant approach of girls. Some say the rise of women in the workplace has led to a male backlash, to boys feeling that there is little point in working hard because the rewards for doing so will be too few.

Educational research on this subject tends to focus on the micro-management of classrooms and schools. It shows that boys indeed respond differently to different styles of teaching. They respond better, for example, to structured lessons, clear presentation of facts, clear expectations of them in terms of what they need to do. It points to why Seven Kings seems to have had some success in closing the gap between the achievements of boys and girls, for its approach is nothing if not structured. Lessons here usually follow a similar pattern: an introduction, some independent working by the pupils, a plenary at the end to sum up. 'Learning objectives' are set out in advance, homework flagged up at the start of the lesson. No one is allowed to drift or to flounder unnoticed.

But other, bigger factors are at work here. A major one – and it is immutable – is the simple fact that boys tend to mature later than girls. For all of us, key education takes place while we are still children and while some of us are not ready to value what we are offered. In terms of self-confidence, too, the contrasts can be stark. Look at Anthony, and then at Jemma. As far as we know, their natural ability is similar. Jemma is stronger in maths and science, Anthony in English and art. But when Jemma has to meet the deputy head to talk about her sixth-form place, she looks him in the eye and fights her corner. She is articulate, forthright and positive. Anthony, on the other hand, often seems unsure of himself. Although on paper he is good with words, he often seems diffident when speaking. He does not present himself as a high achiever. It would be easy for a teacher to assume that a boy like Anthony is less bright than he is, especially if he tends not to try very hard.

While Jemma, Shivanie and Ruhy – and Perin, for not all boys struggle – talk with enthusiasm about their future careers, Anthony and Tyrone seem to lack focus. Talking with their parents or their teachers, they seem to want to please but not to have given the matter much thought. Anthony talked in the early part of the year about going to university, becoming a rapper or working at Sainsbury's. When Tyrone's dad suggested he might go to university, he responded with impressed surprise: 'Am I smart enough?' Neither boy sees himself as particularly able. Meanwhile Sanjay, the boy Alan Steer met for his year-eleven interview, spouted cheerfully about becoming either a banker or a psychiatrist, without any very clear notion of what either career might entail.

So what will become of these wandering boys? There are some good portents. Both Anthony and Tyrone have supportive parents who will nudge them – shove them, if necessary – in the right direction. Yet the world has become a different place since they had the same decisions to face, which points to a much more fundamental reason for the boys' confusion.

It was not a change in the school curriculum or in the examination system that spurred girls on to do better. That had begun to happen before GCSEs and the National Curriculum – with their more 'child-focused' individual approach to learning – arrived in the late 1980s. The schools inspectorate, Ofsted, reported on this in a study of the relative performance of boys and girls in the mid-1990s. So if not that, then what?

In the end it is not the world in the classroom but the world outside that spurs girls on to greater things and leaves some boys floundering. The decline of traditional male employment has been much talked about, yet in this area, at least, there is no shortage of unskilled jobs. Anthony was told within a few days of starting work experience at Sainsbury's that they would be happy to offer him a job once he had left school. Other parents talk about McDonald's as a last resort, or even as a threat: 'If you don't work harder, you'll end up at McDonald's.' The old sources of unskilled labour – London's docks, for example – have been replaced not by the dole queue but by shelf-stacking and burger-flipping.

The problem lies more in young men's concept of what might be suitable for them. These back-stop jobs are far removed from the old male preserve of manual work. The workplace has become feminized, not because of the increased presence of women but because of the nature of the employment available: it is about service and caring. The big growth areas in recent decades include childcare, healthcare and education support, such as classroom assistants. There is no reason why more boys might not aspire to such work, but while Jemma talks about going into child psychiatry, for she loves children, the idea seems unlikely to occur to Tyrone or Anthony.

While the jobs market has changed, then, the mindset of those applying for the jobs has not. Girls have not had to change their view of the world so much in order to see attractive career possibilities in the modern world.

Boys will never again grow up in a world where their future

is clearly marked out for them in advance. Some, like Perin, will have the focus they need to make a path for themselves, whether it leads to university or in some other direction. Some will have the confidence, even at a relatively early age, to face the world with a smile. But many more will not. The shift that needs to take place in the young male mind of Britain – of the whole Western world – seems almost too huge to contemplate.

RUHY

The Easter holidays find Ruhy in the Exchange shopping centre, scanning the racks of clothes. The colours for spring are pale green and pale yellow. Maybe she would like a pale green skirt and a pale yellow top. Or something with sparkle in it. Bling is good.

Her mum catches her eye and she trots cheerfully behind her out of the open shop-front, the Muzak trailing gently in their wake.

As they ride down the escalator with their carrier-bags, Ruhy remembers the top she bought from Wallis for her mum. It was a Mother's Day present. 'That top cost forty-five pounds, Mum. Two months' pocket money.'

Her mum laughs. 'And how much did I spend on you? My whole life!'

Today Ruhy is wearing her black jacket: skimpy, fitted at the waist. And flared jeans. A pink T-shirt top with thin black gauze over the top. Black slip-on shoes. She got them at her favourite shop, Linzi's.

'Mum, can we go to Linzi's? I want to look at those pink court shoes again.' They push through the glass doors and out into the street, cross the road and go into the Chinese buffet restaurant. 'Don't take too many spare ribs!' her mum exhorts. Tomorrow Ruhy will go to the kids' gym at East Ham leisure centre with Gita. Last time she did twenty minutes on a steppy thing. Gita has asked Waseme to come. And Waseme was like, fine, but don't tell Ruhy because it'll be a laugh. But Gita told Ruhy anyway. So she knows Waseme is coming, but Waseme doesn't know Ruhy knows. So when she sees Waseme she'll be like, 'Hi! *You*'re late.'

It is Persian New Year. Her dad bought her a watch, with a wide, white strap. On the television they saw pictures from Iran on the news of protesters, just before New Year, on the night when they have the bonfires. And in their living room they made up a table, like they always do, with seven things beginning in Farsi with S. They include a live fish in a bowl, special food such as garlic, vinegar, spices and an apple, a mirror, some candles, the Koran. And you have to have some wheat growing. That causes trouble. Her mum says in Iran you can buy wheat and it sprouts. But here it doesn't. Last year she even went and bought some special stuff from Holland & Barrett but that wouldn't sprout either.

On New Year's Day her mum spends hours in the kitchen, making a special lunch. Rice, vegetables and fish. Rice in all different colours, green, yellow and white, in a pattern.

She laughs, remembering something funny. Her auntie rang up to tell her mum off. 'Why haven't you called me yet?' Because at New Year younger people are meant to phone older people to wish them well. But that was a joke, because her auntie isn't much older than her mum.

What is it all about? She's not quite sure. All the things on the table are symbolic. New life, hope and renewal, she thinks.

And on the thirteenth day after New Year, you have to go out and throw the wheat into some running water. That signifies throwing away all your bad luck so your next year will be a happy one. Usually they go to Valentine's Park and throw the wheat into the lake. Last year when they did it, there were other patches of wheat floating on the water. Like a message, from some other Iranians living somewhere near.

Now she thinks about it she can remember a New Year once in Iran. She must have been two or three and had received two chicks as a present. One was yellow, and the other was dyed pink. When she let them out, the dog chased them. Funny how she remembers stuff like that. Sometimes things just pop into her head.

They went to Iran last year – the first time since they left seven years ago. She wonders, a bit, about what school would have been like there. More homework, fewer holidays. Never having Saturday or Sunday off, just Friday. Her mum says they would not encourage you in the same way that they do here. When her mum went to school she was just given the text-book, and if she didn't get to the end of it that was her problem, not theirs.

Her family have always believed in getting a good education, her mum says. At the moment her cousin is doing a PhD in Iran. Another cousin is doing one in Holland. And when they came here they would go to the library every day. Even before she went to primary school, she had read all the library books.

She thinks she will probably go to university even though she would also like to be a fashion designer. When she talked to her mum about it she said, 'Which is the best university in England?'

'There are two universities you could go to: Oxford or Cambridge,' her mum said.

When they went to Iran all they ate was rice and kebabs. But her mum cooks all sorts of different things, which take a very long time. Sometimes she watches her as she potters about the neat kitchen in their flat, which is down the road from school. Sometimes she makes things for herself. Cheese snacks, or soya mince with tomatoes.

Ruhy makes a list of her favourite foods:

1. Spare ribs
2. Chocolate
3. Crisps
4. Chips
5. Water, from the tap or from a bottle
6. Soya beans from Iran which are salted and dried
7. Salted pumpkin seeds – sometimes her mum roasts these for a snack
8. Spaghetti Bolognese
9. *Bagali polo*, which is made from rice and butter beans
10. Chicken Cup-a-soup

Oh, and pizza.

How else will she spend her holiday? Maybe tomorrow her dad will take them to Romford, to the shops. Maybe later to-day she will play some music. She plays four instruments, and in the summer she will go on a school music trip to Belgium.

'If you have this to occupy you,' her mum says, 'you won't want to go out drinking with other teenagers when you get older. You'll have better things to do.'

Ruhy thinks about it. 'You know, I don't think that's fair. Just because my friends might do that, it doesn't mean I will.' Then she thinks some more. She decides to voice the thought, tentatively: 'I *might* do those things. Everyone goes through that phase when they go drinking and smoking.'

Her mum smiles. 'If it's once, it doesn't matter.'

Ruhy knows there are lines she cannot cross. Even if she is late at school, she has to phone. At home in the quiet flat, her mum is always waiting for her.

Her mum is still smiling. 'I worry about you,' she says. 'You are all I have.'

JEMMA

Cranbrook Baptist Church sits just down the road from the Exchange shopping centre, behind Somerfield and opposite McDonald's. Its modern brick face is unassuming but welcoming. Today Ivan is standing at the door, greeting the worshippers as they arrive: 'Happy Easter! Welcome!'

Inside they are practising the Easter hymn one last time. Jemma's mum is singing, too, and her dad is playing the guitar. The words flash up behind them on an electronic whiteboard, white on a purple background, and they turn their necks to read: '*Thine* is the *glo*-ree...' Even though it is grey outside, light is streaming through the big, high, clear glass windows. The walls are painted in plain magnolia and there is a blue banner: 'The Real Story. Emmanuel. God With Us.'

As she sings Jemma can watch the people filing through the back doors of the big, open church and taking their seats. Some of the older ladies are wearing hats to match their outfits but she, like the other younger members, is not. She is in a pair of baggy cotton khaki trousers with a vest top and her hair, often tied back, is hanging in loose curls.

There are only about fifty people so far. The clocks went back last night and some of the congregation are missing. Jemma's twelve-year-old sister Louise is fluttering around, willowy in a big T-shirt. It is Louise's baptism today and her friend Stacey has already arrived with some others from school to help her celebrate it. Waiting for the service to start, Jemma shadow-boxes with her dad, Sanjay.

Then Ivan comes to the mic: 'The Lord is risen! He is risen, indeed! Do you get that feeling? This morning? That the Lord is risen?'

Jemma joins in with the answer: 'He is risen indeed.'

'We particularly welcome family and friends of Louise and Tom as they follow Jesus into baptism. Looking around, I'm guessing some people probably didn't adjust their clocks, so they'll be here for coffee and bagels a little later.'

Her mum takes over then, to lead the singing. The first hymn is one Louise has chosen. 'This is to prepare our hearts for what Jesus wants to say to us today...' More people are coming in all the time. There must be a couple of hundred here now. As she sings, Jemma raises her right arm and a sort of quiet joy spreads across her face. She has a different kind of confidence here, which is calmer and softer. She isn't conscious of how others may see her.

Her mum says, 'Those of you who are members, if you would like to give any prayers of thanks today... I thank you for the tiny things, a nice day, friends and family, and all the love we have in our hearts for you...' Others join in. Some Jemma knows as well as she knows her family; others she does not know at all – an African man with a carrier-bag of shopping at his feet, a stout lady in her best clothes.

Ivan gets up again. 'We've got two lovely people who are going to be baptized because they want to follow Jesus. There is nothing holy about this water. It's Essex and Suffolk water, out of the tap, and we've put some hot in to warm it up for you. What is special is that Jesus is here and he's so pleased to see what they're going to do. Sanjay and Ruth are going to perform the baptism.'

Jemma's dad gets into the pool now with Ruth. Ivan invites the younger children to the front, to sit near the baptismal pool. Tom is first. He stands in the water with his back to the two adults. Jemma's dad, Sanjay, says, 'Tom, do you profess Jesus Christ as your Lord and Saviour?'

'I do.'

'I baptize you in the name of the Father, the Son and the Holy Spirit.'

Tom falls backwards into the water and their waiting arms. They're all singing: 'Lord, reign in me. Reign in your power. So won't you reign in me again?' Jemma is dancing. Then there is a moment of silent prayer during which a baby makes a small, definite sound.

Louise is sitting in the front row with her long fingers grasped round her knees, which are pulled up under her chin. Now she stands up and moves slowly to the mic. 'A month ago a friend asked me if I wanted to go on a Christian weekend with her church. The preacher talked about baptism, and said if you're serious about God you should go through with it. I felt very moved and felt God was saying something to me. I'd been thinking about baptism for a while. So here I am. Dunk me!' She walks to the pool.

Her dad is there still, with a huge grin on his face. 'Do you profess Jesus Christ as your Lord and Saviour? Do you seek to live within the fellowship of the Church?' She falls backwards into the water and everyone claps.

Jemma closes her eyes. Her mum and dad wouldn't make her go to church if she didn't want to come. But she thinks she's becoming more religious as she grows up. Church is important, central to her life, even though most of her friends at school are from different religions. They talk about it a lot. Her best friend is Jewish and he teaches at the synagogue on Saturdays. Her other best friend is Christian, but she isn't really religious. She's Church of England. Jemma's dad was brought up as a Hindu. And some of her friends are Muslim, but she isn't sure what that means to them. Once they talked about Ramadan and fasting, and she asked them what it meant. They talked about showing devotion to God, giving up everything to Him. Then she talked about Lent, and about Jesus going out into the desert and the temptations to which he was subjected. She explained that to her this abstinence was about driving out your demons. It made her wonder because, for her, religion is about knowing why everything is as it is, having something to believe in. The Bible says He sent His son to die for everything she will do wrong in her life. But she wonders if for some other people religion is really about duty, obedience and tradition.

She thinks that when she goes away she will take all this with her. Wherever she is, wherever she goes, she will try to create it afresh. The constant company, the bustle, the companionship of her extended church family.

There are six of them at home – herself, her mum and dad, Louise, Thea, who is ten and Lydia who is six. The house is always full. Ruth is there a lot, with her little girl Nicole. Other people from church pop in. Her friends, her sisters' friends. She has people in her life. Her friends from school say to her, 'Jemma, is there anyone you don't know?' She can't go to the shops without meeting someone, and she loves that.

They all get along well, though they have their moments, which is inevitable, really. Jemma is feisty, outspoken, flares up. The other Sunday, for example, she hadn't stuck to the revision timetable she had agreed with her mum: a forty-five-minute session every night, two each day at the weekend. She's slipping behind. She has a busy life. Trumpet lesson on Monday, choir practice Wednesday, church music group Friday, trampolining Saturday – she coaches the younger ones now. And she gets involved in stuff. At the moment she's on the school yearbook committee; in July she will go on the music trip to Belgium.

Anyway, the other Sunday after church they were all going out to lunch for her uncle's birthday, and her mum pointed out that if she came with them, she'd get even further behind with her revision. She argued. She sulked. Then she went home and did some work. That's the way they do things in her family. She has to decide for herself.

APRIL

PERIN

While Jemma waits to learn whether her Seven Kings years will continue, Perin is nearing the end of his. He waits in the car park at the back of the school, eyeing the gate for sight of his mother's car nosing through. It is a grey, windy day early in the summer term, a Friday, nothing unusual planned for the weekend. Work, of course.

There is a pattern to his life. He can see clearly how it will be. Tonight it will be around five when they crunch to a halt on the parking area at the front of the house. It will be quiet, on the wide tree-lined street, but there will be the residual sounds of builders packing up after their days' work somewhere nearby.

He will get out of the car, his sister already heading down the wide hallway. He will greet his grandparents and accept a cup of tea. Tea punctuates his life. It is one of his many constants. Then two hours' work in the airy downstairs study just inside the front door. Childhood pictures of himself and his sister will look down from the glass-fronted cabinet and the window-sill with rather serious expressions. Six weeks till the first exam. He knows now how many days. Tonight, as always, he will mark out a block of time and spend it getting his head round something. Light refraction, maybe, or astro-physics.

Then at seven thirty he will take a break and lounge on one of the sofas in the living room while he watches *Coronation Street*, then *EastEnders*. He will tease his sister gently. 'Get me a drink.'

'No. Get it yourself.'

'Please.'

'Don't be so lazy. Get it yourself.'

He's lazy, of that he's sure. Sometimes he'll just veg out. Sometimes at lunchtime his friend Vijay will want to go down to the shops in Ilford, and Perin will go with him rather than staying and working. He knows it's all right to do this because his work is up to date. His dad worries: is he doing enough? But he just says, 'Calm down, Dad. Everything's under control.'

His dad does not push him because he does not have time. He works six days a week until seven o'clock, and when he comes home he's tired. Anyway, he does not have to push him because he believes in him. He knows Perin has common sense and is intelligent. 'You can go a long way with those qualities,' he always says, 'so long as you also have an ability to speak well.'

Sometimes his dad pulls him up about the way he speaks. Maybe Perin ums and ahs a bit too much when they're practising interview questions in the car, he says. But Perin says that's because he's talking to his dad. Or because he's speaking like a teenager.

His dad worries about these things. He got A grades in all his O levels apart from one, even though he had only been in Britain for three years. His English language let him down and he failed it. He thinks that that must have been the reason why only one medical school wanted to interview him, and why he didn't get a place. It was why he went to Sunderland to study pharmacy. Perin's mum did her pharmacy degree in India, then came here.

His dad says if he had had a television at home when he was a teenager he would have learned to speak English in the way that the English speak it. His English teachers in Uganda were all Indian so they had a different accent.

So, it's OK for Perin to watch *Coronation Street* and *EastEnders*. After that they will all sit down together to eat supper. His grandmother will have made Indian food but she will produce a baked potato and baked beans for Perin. He does not choose, usually, to eat Indian food. He thinks that when he goes to university he'll eat fast food. He'll apply for catered accommodation, although he can cook fish fingers, eggs and toast. After a while he thinks he'll enjoy coming home to eat his grandmother's Indian food.

His grandparents have a house in Gujerat, now, and they go there every winter. Perhaps next Christmas he will go too, to visit them. He's bilingual in Gujerati but he doesn't know what India is like, still less Uganda. At some time in the past his ancestors emigrated from India to Uganda but he doesn't know why. He has no relatives there now, of course.

What does he know about India? He knows there's a lot of poverty, and he thinks that's sad. He knows its economy is booming. Maybe one day he might be able to make use of his links with India, but business there is conducted in Hindi, which he speaks about as well as he speaks French. When he watches a Bollywood movie he reads the subtitles, and when he tries to speak Hindi people look at him strangely. He thinks it would be really useful to learn Mandarin while he is at university.

After supper he will watch television again till eleven, then go back to his study and mess around on the computer, maybe do a bit more work, till about two. Tomorrow he will work from ten till one, take a break for an hour, work again from two till three. From four till five he will watch the football on Sky Sports. He has supported Arsenal since junior school; his dad supports West Ham. West Ham are not playing Arsenal this season but when they do it will be a grudge match.

On Sunday he will do more work; they will have family over for dinner. His cousins will be supportive and sympathetic about his recent rejection from the London School of Economics. They are good like that. They wish each other well; they don't compete.

The rejection letter was a kick in the teeth, he can't say otherwise. He doesn't know what to think about it, really. There is so much competition, and they have to choose from a long list of people who are estimated to get four straight As at A level. All people who probably got thirteen As and starred As at GCSE, like him. And they didn't choose him. He has to think that the other people must have been better than him. Or maybe their personal statements were better than his – but those are just pieces of paper, lies to make you look better. It must be like picking names out of a hat.

So next year, he now hopes, he will go to University College, London, to study maths with economics. A degree from UCL is a good degree and he will be proud of it. All he has to do now is get three As and a B in his A levels. But he will get them. He has to believe it. Otherwise he'll mess up.

He is ready for university, ready for new friends and living independently. He can still remember his first day at primary school, and how the teacher was shocked when he arrived in his callipers. He was the only boy at that school with special needs, and the head had forgotten to tell his class teacher about him.

He does not remember ever having a conversation about why he hadn't learned to walk in the same way as other children. His mum says he did ask, when he was little. Was he going to learn to walk too? And she had to tell him that he was not. Even now she struggles to contain her emotion when she talks about the day – he was two months old – when she went to his cot and he was not moving his legs. They rushed him to the hospital and the doctors used an angiogram to stop the bleeding on his spinal cord. After that he spent two months in Great Ormond Street. He still goes back for regular check-ups, even now.

It used to frustrate him, but not any more. He has dealt with it, and after all, he thinks, he leads a pretty normal life. If he didn't have the wheelchair, the only thing that might be different would be doing more sports. He used to play basketball but he gave it up. He stopped enjoying it. Maybe he'll take up golf.

But if he didn't have the wheelchair he wouldn't have made the friends he has, because he wouldn't have gone to Seven Kings. He would have taken the eleven plus, and would almost certainly have gone to the local grammar school.

When he was eleven his mum prepared him for the exam but then she went to an open day at the school and there were no lifts, so they didn't put him in for the exam. And he was happy, really, because he didn't have to sit an exam.

When he came to Seven Kings he still had his callipers but they slowed him down. And there were such great distances to go between lessons that it took him ages to get about. He really wanted that wheelchair, and he felt so liberated when he got it.

The teachers said it took him a while to settle in and make friends but he didn't feel that. He felt he'd made friends quite easily. He soon got to know Vijay and Ranjit. He knew they were OK, because they didn't see only his disability when they talked to him.

He got off to a flying start, he thinks, and then he had to maintain standards. So he carried on. His dad reminds him, sometimes, of when he went to the open day at Seven Kings and there was a particular piece of work on display in the IT room, clearly marked out for special attention. It was really stunning. And he said to Perin's mum that he wondered if Perin could ever do anything like that. Five years later, they were there again, and Perin's work was in that position. It had made them all so proud.

ANGELA CASSIDY

It is a few weeks after the Easter holidays, and Angela is kneeling on the floor of the medical centre with a needle and thread, sewing a button on to a shirt. Jarvis's mother has not been well, which is becoming increasingly obvious. His trousers are too short. His shirt has not been ironed. His blazer looks as if it has not been acquainted with the inside of a dry cleaner's for some time.

'What did you have for breakfast, Jarvis?'

'Oh, I got something on the way to school, Miss.'

'What sort of something?'

'An Egg McMuffin.'

'OK. What lesson have you got now?'

'Maths.'

'Have I still got your history book or have you got it?'

He looks blank. 'Erm. I'll call in at break for it.' He picks up his bag and makes for the door.

She watches him go then sits down and resumes glaring at her computer terminal. 'What's wrong with the bloody thing? Why won't it start up?' She needs to print out the attendance data. The Education Welfare officer will be in later, and will expect to be updated on various cases. Amina Simpson. Robbie Ambrose. No great news to relate there. Amina's mum has missed her court date. They have had endless meetings, made countless phone calls, filled in ridiculous quantities of forms. And what's happened? Nothing much: the hearing has been put back to another day; Amina has realized nothing much is going to happen. If her mum was the type to respond to threats of prison, she wouldn't need threatening in the first place. Ironic, Angela supposes. The ones who respond to threats are the ones who go on holiday for a month in term time but otherwise send their kids to school every day.

Amina's attendance record is no longer taped to the side of her computer monitor. She was wasting her time, chasing that girl around the place. When she does see her, Amina always seems cheerful, not a care in the world. Angela knows there are no consequences to this game. If it was down to her she would take away their child allowance. That would shake them.

Robbie Ambrose isn't much better. His big sister was in school the other day – not a welcome visitor, considering her record: excluded for bullying other girls; prostitution; drugs; a spell in a young offender's institution. She was looking for another girl she had some beef with. Had to be escorted from the premises.

She gives the computer a shake. 'Oh, come on. How long can it take to load personal settings?' They've been promising her a new one. 'Windows cannot update your roaming profile. Possible causes include network problems or insufficient security rights.'

She picks up the phone. 'Diane? Why do I need a roaming profile? Oh. OK. It's doing something now.' She replaces the receiver.

Anyway, she won't have to worry about any of this for much longer. She is leaving. Thirteen years is long enough. It is time, though, with the kids nearly grown-up. She and her husband are moving but haven't decided where to go yet. This weekend they'll take a look around Kent. They're planning a trip to Ireland. She's half excited, half scared. But she does not want to be here when she is sixty-five.

She goes next door to clear out the medical room, sends a couple of pupils back to class and is about to do the same with the third when something makes her look at him again: a rather small year-seven boy, Talib. She has seen him a few times recently, usually complaining about stomach-ache. She calls him through to her office. 'Another stomach-ache, Talib? That's the second this week.'

He doesn't answer.

She thinks for a minute. 'What do you usually have for breakfast, Talib?'

'Well, it depends...'

She waits.

'Sometimes if my mum's there she gives me some break-fast.'

'And if she isn't?'

'Normally I don't bother.'

'And do you have anything at break?'

'Not usually. Unless I have some money.'

Angela is concerned. 'It isn't good enough, Talib. You're harming yourself by not eating.'

He looks miserable, uncomfortable on his chair. 'Well, last week my dad said he was going to give me five pounds...'

She phones Talib's mother and asks her to collect him. She has a stiff word with her about the dangers of a child not eating or drinking all day. There is little more she can do. It's not a case Social Services are likely to get involved with: they are always looking for extremes.

So much of what she sees falls into a grey area: a child who is withdrawn for no obvious reason, who cannot make relationships. Social services will react if there is a suggestion of sexual abuse, but not this kind of thing. Sometimes she thinks that by the time the children come here it's too late. By now they've learned that this is their life. The school can footle about on the margins, offer a bit of counselling. It can be kind and caring. It can sew buttons on. But that will never be enough. If only there was an army of mature women who could go into these children's homes from birth, do the washing, cook a decent meal, sort them out.

One day she might write a little *Play for Today*. She daydreams about it. In it, someone like her would be able to see what was really happening inside those houses. Maybe she would be in their gardens at night. And she would phone them. Maybe three of them – anonymously, of course. She would tell them she knew everything, that when they shouted at their kids she could see them. Then she might make threats about what would happen if they didn't stop. In her play, two out of the three would probably change. They'd sort themselves out because they're cowardly and scared. And the third? Maybe the third would need to be pushed a little more. But they wouldn't know who was watching them.

It is frustration, she supposes, that makes her think like this, because she can't call the parents in and shout at them. It's all 'Can I help you with this?' and 'Is there some support I can give you with that?' It sticks in her gullet. Sometimes she can almost hear the sharp intake of breath from other professionals in meetings when she says so. But it makes her feel better.

DEBBIE ADAMS

Debbie Adams is in her classroom, writing her learning objectives on the board. 'To look closely at the techniques used in a poem. Homework: to complete Haiku.'

'Now,' she says, beaming at her year-seven class, 'today we're going to look closely at the techniques in a poem. Timothy Winters...'

The door opens and Adil walks in.

'Hello, Mister!' Debbie says. 'Long time no see! Did you have a good holiday?'

'Yes, Miss Adams.'

'Right. You're next to Tahir.'

She hands out a sheet of words that are easily confused.

Its, it's.
Their, they're, there.
Of, off.

'Now,' she says, 'you've got two minutes to finish that sheet while I take the register. So you've got to be Speedy Gonzalez. There's lots of paper action going on today, I'm afraid...'

All of her lessons follow the same format: starter activity, fifteen–twenty-minute introduction, twenty minutes' working in pairs, groups or individually, ten-minute plenary at the end.

'OK! Absolute silence, please! Right. On your desk there's another sheet for your delight. It's a poem called "Timothy Winters" by Charles Causley. I'm going to be asking questions about the techniques it uses.' She begins to read, her delivery straight and clear:

> *'Timothy Winters comes to school*
> *With eyes as wide as a football-pool*
> *Ears like bombs and teeth like splinters*
> *A blitz of a boy is Timothy Winters.'*

'What's this poem about?'
'A boy, Miss.'
'A boy called...?'
'Timothy Winters, Miss.'
She reads on:

> *'His belly is white, his neck is dark*
> *And his hair is an exclamation mark.*

His clothes are enough to scare a crow
And through his britches the blue winds blow.

When teacher talks he won't hear a word
And he shoots down dead the arithmetic bird.'

'And?' she asked.
   'It's about the welfare state, Miss.'
   'Good. So what does the welfare state do for children?'
   'It looks after them.'
   'He lives very poorly...'
   'OK,' she says.

   'Old Man Winters likes a beer,
   And his missus ran off with a bombardier...'

'That's someone who was in the war,' she explained.
   'So his mum ran off and his dad's a drunk,' someone
says.
   'He might be upset because his wife ran off.'
   She goes on: 'It says:

   'Grandma sits in the grate with a gin
   And Timothy's dosed with an aspirin.'

'What does that show us?'
   'He's a druggie?'
   'Ye-es. Or maybe Grandma gives him the pills because she's
drinking and doesn't want to be bothered.'
   They settle down to fill in the question sheets she has given
them, picking out metaphors and similes, alliteration and

assonance. The words and phrases of the poem murmur slowly, sadly, round the room.

'"Law's as tricky as a ten-foot snake..." That's a simile, isn't it? Miss, what does assonance mean again?'

She's fond of this class, comfortable with them. Her babies, she calls them. Her year-nines are much better, too. They had their parents' evening last week. She had Haroon, the naughty boy who raised the roof with his speech, with his parents and she told them straight how he had behaved. They were visibly shocked and told her to write in his homework planner if she had any more trouble so that they could deal with him. Then they made him shake her hand. He has not given her a moment's bother since.

A plump, round-faced boy has his hand up. 'Miss, what if you just don't find the words interesting?'

'Well,' she says, 'you *will* find them interesting, because, you remember, we had that chat about being positive and not negative.'

The boy puts his head down again.

'OK!' she says. 'We have just over two minutes to complete the work. So move it, move it, move it!'

'But, Miss, I'm still stuck on question four.'

She gives Adil a new exercise book. He has been away for a month, visiting relatives in Pakistan. 'This is a new book. A new start for us,' she says. She gives him a smile.

He looks back, somehow chastened. He is not a difficult boy but he's all over the place. He's disorganized, can't seem to get it together, doesn't seem focused on school. He might become a problem.

'Right!' she says. 'Who can give me an example of assonance in these verses?'

'At Morning prayers the Master helves
For children less fortunate than ourselves,
And the loudest response in the room is when
Timothy Winters roars "Amen!"'

DOUG HARRISON

He looks up as his office door opens. Lindsay's face peeps round, cheerful as ever. Her straight, reddish-blonde hair is tucked behind one ear, her slight pallor mitigated by a hint of blusher and blue eyeshadow. The usual array of badges: the diamanté-studded teddy bear, the enamelled breast-cancer bow with a diamanté L hanging from it. On one wrist she wears a cluster of coloured string and plastic bracelets, on the other a silver one. Her necklace, with a big fake diamond in it, should be hidden under her uniform but it isn't. She looks at him and understands. She pastes a serious expression on her face and takes out her big hoop earrings. 'I know these aren't appropriate for school, sir, so I'm not going to wear them.'

He studies her sceptically. 'Have you just realized that?'

But she's here, which is a breakthrough. The past few weeks, the early part of the summer term, have been a soap opera. Lindsay's life is like that. Sometimes he wants to laugh, but only sometimes.

A couple of weeks ago there were tears. Lindsay was saying goodbye for ever. Her family were moving house, about a mile away on the other side of the A12. She was going to a new school. She hugged all her friends, one by one, and slipped the farewell presents into her bag with mascara streaking her face.

Doug witnessed this scene with mixed emotions. He was

sorry to see Lindsay go – he had become fond of her over the years, despite the poor attendance, the frequent lateness, the endless discussions with Education Welfare. And he had not been sure that Lindsay's last day was the end of the story. There was a problem about her move to Oaks Park School, which had never heard of her. Indeed, neither had the local authority received a request for her transfer, despite her assertions that her mother had been to the council office to sort it out.

The week after she left, he made some phone calls. It took a few days to track her down. Eventually he caught up with her, still on the old number. 'Are you going to Oaks Park? Because as far as we know, you aren't.'

'I'm on the list. But I thought I'd leave it for this week so we could do the decorating.'

'I'm afraid decorating isn't on the agenda. You need to be back here tomorrow.'

She didn't arrive. The next day he rang Mum, who works long hours as a cleaning supervisor and isn't always home to make sure that Lindsay goes to school. The day after that she was back, looking worried. The move, it seemed, had been postponed. 'I don't know what to say to my friends, sir. Do you think you could make an announcement in assembly?' By lunchtime she was wandering down the corridor, arm-linking two of them as if she had never been away. Since then, she's not been in much. Her attendance has dropped to 72 per cent for this term. But she's here now.

'Can I have a word with you, sir?'

'Of course, Lindsay. Come in. Sit down.'

'Sir, I think it might be better if I went to Redbridge College. I just can't settle.'

He cannot think of any good educational reason why she should stop coming to school. She is an average student. If she's struggling with the work, it's only because her attendance is so poor. Lindsay has a novel take on education. She can see the point of it, but only when it seems relevant to her and her particular life plans. There are some things she feels she does not need to do.

They have had these conversations before. About geography, for example. Lindsay wants to work in the travel industry, so she recognizes the need to do geography – but you don't necessarily need to know everything you learn in geography, she says. 'Like rivers and things. I didn't take geography to learn about rivers. I took it to learn about different holiday destinations. Not about hills and lakes and how they developed. In life, are you going to go up to someone on the street and say, "I know how rivers and lakes are formed?" I can't see the point. Why learn it? Maybe if I was going to work as a sailor, or something, I'd say, "Don't go too close to the edge because that river's been formed that way..." but otherwise I can't see the point.' And PE. Lindsay walks to and from school and she thinks that's enough exercise for her. And she doesn't get on very well with her PE teacher, so she prefers not to go to the lessons.

Work experience has been a problem, too. The year-ten students can organize their own work experience for the beginning of year eleven, though there is a company that finds placements for them. And Lindsay did make an effort: she called in at Going Places in Ilford, and they were very welcoming. They offered to let her help in the foreign-exchange section, or just to show customers the brochures. But when she thought about it, she wondered if they wouldn't just be using her? She wouldn't be very happy if they wanted her to make tea and coffee, stuff like that.

Then she went to her old primary school, and they said she could help out in the nursery. But then she thought, no, maybe that would be a bit stressy. And she might shout at the kids. Because sometimes she gets like that. So now they're thinking maybe the local community centre will take her to work with the pensioners. She quite likes that idea. Old people are quiet, quiet, quiet. But she would not want to empty bedpans.

If she goes to Redbridge College, enrols on one of the courses they run for under-sixteens who have become disaffected, at least the problem will go away. But Doug is not keen.

'I do enjoy school,' she admits. 'It's a time that I can mix with my friends. And some learning can be fun. I don't want to sound like a geek or nothing, but it can be fun. When it comes to essays and stuff like that, it's quite difficult. In some things I've got left behind.'

'Lindsay, you're bright enough to do GCSEs. I just can't see how sending you to Redbridge would be justified. Your only problem is that you don't attend school regularly enough. Which means you're behind with your coursework.'

'That's the thing. I don't feel like I'm achieving in the school. If I was in Redbridge, they'd make me match up.'

He sighs. He doesn't think Redbridge College is the right place for her. He thinks she needs the disciplined approach that school offers. If she can't get herself into school on more than seven days out of ten, what will happen if she goes to college? College courses are meant for disaffected students, but Lindsay is not disaffected with school. The problem is that the lack of structure in her life impacts on her school attendance.

He's not going to give in – not yet, anyway. But it will have to be considered if her attendance doesn't improve. And Amina Simpson's another. She is still not attending school. And there has been a worrying development in that quarter.

Last year there was some hint that Amina was hanging around with rather unsuitable boys, but that worry seemed to have gone away. Now it has come back with a vengeance. It seems she's been going out with a member of one of the local street gangs, BIG. And BIG is having some sort of war with another street gang, the West Side Boys. Amina has been threatened. Her mum is terrified. Men have been round to the house looking for her. Again, Amina would be better off at school where they can keep an eye on her. She's a bright girl who should be walking away from here next year with a clutch of starred As at GCSE. But the way she's going she won't get any. Redbridge College would be so inappropriate for her.

In one respect Amina is like Lindsay: they're both lazy. Can't get up in the morning. But Amina comes across as so reasonable, so comprehending. Yes, she understands she needs to come to school regularly. Yes, she understands that if she falls behind she will not be able to take her GCSEs.

After missing several court appearances, Mrs Simpson was fined in her absence. It made no difference to Amina's school attendance. Doug's guess is that real parenting skills are lacking. Mrs Simpson is always pleasant and sensible, always says the right things, but what parents say and what they do can be quite different. At this point, he thinks, she needs to have a battle with her daughter. Not to give up. Not to take the easy way out. His guess is that the easy way has been taken. At school, at least, that won't happen.

There are some wayward girls, though, who go beyond their reach. Ruksana, the girl who went missing after her parents tried to stop her seeing her boyfriend, turned up last week but there was nothing the school or anyone else could do to change anything. The suspicion that she had been spirited away to Pakistan was wrong. She really had been with her boyfriend, in Scotland. They had managed to find work, apparently. Her parents could not make her come home because she's over sixteen. Although legally she was in their care and custody it was unlikely that the courts would order her to return home if she didn't want to go. And she didn't.

He does not know where she is now. She has disappeared again, and he has heard that the boyfriend – who is not sixteen – has gone too. But one thing is certain: Ruksana will not be taking any exams this summer. She is no longer on the school roll. There is nothing more that Seven Kings High School can do for her.

MAY

ALAN STEER

It is eight o'clock on a Tuesday morning, and the senior management team is having its regular weekly meeting in his office. His three deputies, Dave Hayes, Clive Rosewell and Tracy Smith, are sitting in low-slung chairs. As always, Doug Harrison is there too. On the coffee-table there are coffee cups, a bag of Italian biscuits and a box of chocolates. Papers are stacked on every surface of his office, including the floor. The year-nine option booklet. *The Times School Report*. An estimate from a flooring company. The annual league tables...

They're talking about staffing. More and more staff – including men – have been asking to go part time so they can spend more time with their own children. And there are several pregnancies, which have to be covered for. He sighs. 'Do you think we could have a policy of employing only nuns in the future?' They laugh.

They move on to the monitoring work they're doing with

years ten and eleven, which is crucial if they are going to keep pushing the exam results up. With 85 per cent getting five A–Cs last year, it is going to be hard to get much further. A few staff have started a 90 Per Cent Club for this year, but few people really believe it can happen.

Year eleven are a good year, but there are still those worrisome groups of pupils who are not achieving. It can be so time-consuming, keeping on their backs. Sometimes Doug or one of the other year heads can be chasing a kid all week for a piece of coursework, and at the end of the day they will produce something that took twenty minutes. It isn't an effective use of an assistant head's time, but it has to be done.

Alan wants to focus on specific intervention projects with particular groups of pupils: black boys, borderline students, the gifted and talented, those in danger of dropping out. 'I don't want your job reduced to dealing with naughty boys, Doug.'

'Yes,' Doug muses. 'But we've got to bear in mind that my role is coming to an end.'

Alan groans inwardly. 'Don't remind me.' Doug's retirement, when it comes in a couple of years' time, will leave a huge gap.

Later Alan has lunch duty. Leaving his office for the canteen, he checks his lobby. Should Anthony be in there? He will ask his year head, Helena Handley, to check up on him. He enjoys the lunchtime interludes. They make a refreshing change from the policy formation and decision-making that take up most of his time. It's a performance and he's a ham. 'Gogogo!' he cries, moving the queue along rapidly, then: 'HALT! Did you just push in? No? OK, well... I believe you... Young lady, where are you going?... No! To the back of the queue, please!' It's a show. But it keeps him visible, along with the rest of the senior management team.

'How are *you*? Did you have a nice half-term?'

Two bashful year-seven girls in headscarves. 'Good, sir. Yes, sir.'

'What did you do?'

'My dad got a new car. And we went to the fair in Seven Kings Park.'

'Arthur. Did you do a lot of work? That four-letter word?'

'Yes, sir. I've done lots of revision.'

'I'm impressed! And I'm sure the girls will be impressed, too. And they'll be impressed by your haircut! The old jokes are always the best, aren't they?'

Arthur is a pasty-faced lad whose hair is spiked up on top. 'I hear that one every year, sir.'

Only a few of the staff eat in the canteen. There is a staff table in the far corner, and Doug is there with Duncan Paterson and Colin Gratrix. Most teachers prefer to eat sandwiches in the staffroom. The range of food here is pretty dire. Burgers. Chips, of course. Potato waffles. Nuggets. More burgers. An occasional slice of quiche so bursting with high-cholesterol, low-flavour cheese that it could hardly be considered a healthy alternative.

Walking back to his office he wonders about this, as he has done many times recently. Jamie Oliver has been making a big noise about school dinners, and the Seven Kings meals, provided by Scolarest, are certainly no exception to the general rule. He has wondered if they could look at alternatives when the contract with Scolarest ends in a couple of years' time. But, frankly, it probably won't happen. He has enough to do without the stress of in-house catering. Who will ring round for a stand-in when the kitchen manager goes sick? Who will deal with the hiring and firing of staff? And, in any case, can the kitchen take the strain? The school's catering facilities are not geared up for cooking. They can cope with heating and serving several hundred pre-prepared meals each day, but home cooking? Not a chance.

The problem is, you cannot get kids to eat healthy food unless you offer them nothing else. That would mean asking Scolarest to change the whole menu – no more chips – and banning years ten and eleven from leaving the site at lunchtime, as they do at the moment. Then there would be knock-on problems. Outside space is at a premium, and at lunchtime the school field is already a patchwork of inter-twining, competing, often clashing football matches. Forcing two more year groups into the mix wouldn't be an option. So, they would have to keep the gates open and the main beneficiaries of a healthier menu for Seven Kings would prob-ably be McDonald's, who do quite well enough out of the school already. They have opened at the top of the road in a converted pub and the queues of uniformed kids run out of the door most lunchtimes. Then again, if parents gave their children a healthy breakfast and a nourishing evening meal the problem wouldn't exist. A fatty snack in the middle of the day wouldn't do them much harm. But that isn't the way it is.

As he walks along the corridor, he spots Tyrone coming the other way.

On your way to Homework Club, Tyrone?'

'Yes, sir! Working hard.' There's a glint in his eye.

TYRONE

It's raining, a fine, soft, early-summer rain that coats the asphalt with a thin, oily slick. He didn't really want to get out of bed – it is Saturday – but here he is. The under-eights are waiting for him. His mum has already gone ahead, brandishing a sheaf of instructions for the young footballers about a forthcoming change of venue for their weekly session.

He swings the big bag of footballs over his shoulder, grabs the shirts with the other hand and shambles through the park gates to where the little ones are kicking a ball about. On the sideline an improbably tiny boy in a too-large T-shirt is clinging to his mother's leg, looking tearful. He's had a fall but he'll be fine in a moment.

Tyrone lands the balls on the ground with a thump and starts handing round shirts. Luminous greeny-yellow shirts for one team, which hang off their shoulders and drape round their knees, and McDonald's ones for the others, with big yellow arches printed on the front. He wades into the middle of the diminutive crowd and blows his whistle. 'Right! Let's go!'

It has been six weeks now since he started referee training. The parents used to referee the matches, but with all the child-protection regulations it's not as easy as it used to be, so the Football Association started this scheme and his mum put him down for it. He could earn sixteen pounds an hour when he's qualified. And he'll get an official black uniform.

'Jamie, this way. That's right. Pass to Warren.' Warren is hovering on the outside of the game, trying to find a painless way in. Tyrone makes one for him. They play for ten minutes each way. He likes the little kids, and they seem to like him. This is something he can do well. When the game finishes, the coach lines them up for some ball exercises. Tyrone wanders to the side of the pitch, inserts himself under the low front post of the mini-goal and pokes his head up through the middle. He leans over the bar, and after a minute his hands come up to his head in an expression of boredom rather than of despair.

In the next few weeks he has a lot to do with SATs looming. But he has less than Tamia, who has her GCSEs. She doesn't want to join in with the football any more, even though she likes sport. She is in the car now, maybe reading her books, maybe texting her friends or listening to music. She went out this morning with their mum to buy a prom dress, the full, flouncy, traditional article. With the shoes, the bag, all the other stuff, it will probably cost about two hundred pounds. There will be a limo to take a crowd of them out on the town afterwards.

Tyrone looks at his feet. The greyish water from the asphalt is starting to soak up from the bottom of his white sweatpants. He ducks back under the goalpost and goes to his mum, his hands in the pockets of his big red Chicago Bulls jacket. 'Mum, look at this! You told me to put these on.'

'Tyrone, I was just trying to get you out of bed.'

'They'll have to be washed,' he says. She gives him a look. He grins. Maybe the thing that happened a few weeks ago has changed the way she thinks about him a bit.

It had started as a laugh. Looking back, he can see it wasn't funny. A crowd of them were hanging out in the boys' toilet, joking and larking around. And Jaz came in. He had been mugged not long before. They all heard about it. Some guy robbed him. It happens a lot. They started to tease him: 'Why did you give him your money, Jaz? Are you gay or something? Are you pussy?'

Jaz was laughing at first. He was trying to make it all right, trying to join in, but feeling a bit off balance, probably. It was not a happy laugh.

Then someone slapped him. Not hard. Just joking. And suddenly they were re-enacting the mugging. Something about the group around him said they were having fun. Something about Jaz's face said, 'No, I'm not laughing any more.'

Tyrone was in the thick of it. He did not start it, but he's not a boy who stands and watches. If his friends are up to some business or another, he will be part of it. He and his close friends are a unit; they're not separable. He grabbed Jaz, one arm round his neck, in his usual style. He does it every day to some boy or girl as he ambles along the corridor with Jerome or Wesley. Cuddly, he likes to think. And he started to walk him towards the door, laughing. Saying something to him, he cannot remember precisely what. 'Did he take your money?' or maybe, 'Give me your money.'

By then they could all see Jaz was upset, and the next thing they knew there was trouble. Jaz told a teacher he'd been bullied: Tyrone had got him in a neck-lock and demanded his money. Which, Tyrone supposes, was kind of true. But in another way it was kind of not true because he never wanted to take Jaz's money. He would not do that. It was all a big joke. Jaz is a mate. Not a close mate, like Jerome, but still a mate. He would not do that to him.

So then he was in detention. And a letter arrived saying he'd been involved in a 'bullying incident'. Usually if his mum gets a letter from school she will say; 'Tyrone, what have you done now?' But she wouldn't believe he was a bully, and neither would his dad. They know him better than that.

When it mattered, they stood up for him. They went into battle for him. They ceased, for a brief moment, to be part of the adult establishment that always says, 'No, Tyrone. You must not, Tyrone.'

Mind you, his mum was not entirely happy. She gave him a talking-to. The school had to take this seriously. This boy was obviously upset. What would his parents have said if the school had not dealt with it? But she didn't believe he was a bully. She had faith in him.

She went up to the school and spoke to his year head. She said she didn't want this word 'bullying' on his school record. She didn't want some file mouldering away there, year after year, with that stain on it. And the school wrote another letter, putting it differently, saying what he had done might have been 'interpreted as bullying'.

In the past his mum has given him those looks when he's come home with some tale of woe.

'Mum, you've got to talk to my teacher. She keeps saying things to me and I have to say things back. She should show me more respect.'

'No, Tyrone. You are the one who must show respect. If your teacher tells you to do something, you must do it.'

She is smiling at him now. Maybe, she has said since that incident, he is not really a Seven Kings kind of boy. Seven Kings is about being quiet, studious and respectful. Tyrone is big, loud and bouncy. He is physical. How often does she have to fight him off when she's having a sit-down and he lands on her with a big, sweaty thump, smothering her with one of his animal embraces?

Right now, in fact, he's wrapping his arms around her neck, smiling soppily. 'Can we go to Lakeside this afternoon, Mum? Can we? Can I have some new trainers? Some new Nike trainers? Some new *good* Nike trainers?'

She doesn't stop smiling, just bats him off, feigning weariness. 'Get *off* me, Tyrone,' she says.

He has a feeling that means yes.

RUHY

On the sports field on Thursday morning, with a thin, early-summer sun struggling to appear, the year-seven girls are skippy, fawn-like. When the teacher calls them up for a team-talk, Ruhy practises a little catwalk shimmy. She's developing curves. Some of the other girls are skinny, though not in an Atkins Diet way. They're just unformed wraiths.

They start a warm-up exercise, running from one end of the pitch to the other, touching the white lines at each end with a finger.

'Miss, do we *have* to touch the grass?'

'Yes, Ruhy, you do.'

When Ruhy has to pick up the ball, she hesitates. It's covered with mud. She uses the tips of her fingers, then examines the smears and shows them to her friend. She makes a run for it, slips and lands on her backside. She squeals and giggles. Miss Marshall blows the whistle. 'Girls, you're going to have to get muddy! It's what happens. You have a whole week to clean your kit!'

They all laugh ruefully.

She's a reluctant runner on the games field yet nowadays

she often arrives at her lessons running, laughing, a few minutes behind the rest of the class.

Today she rushes into the library and flings her bag on to the rack by the door. There's a comic expression on her face that says, 'Yes! I'm late! Am I in trouble?'

All the boys sit at one big table, the girls at another. It's the way they like to arrange themselves. She sits at one end with Waseme, Ayesha and Sarah. Gita is at the other. They have fallen out. Things got so bad they had to go and see their year head, Mr Paterson. He made them write down everything that had happened. And then he did this thing with his hands. She giggles when she thinks about it now. He did this big mime as if he was tearing all the pieces of paper to bits. And then he pretended he was digging a hole. And he said, 'What are we going to do? We are going to *dig* this hole and we are going to *put* it all into it. And *bury* it!' But she and Gita are still not speaking.

Miss Rood is clapping her hands. 'Who's got a good memory? What is the focus of this lesson?'

Two hands go up.

Miss Rood waits. 'I've got five hands, now... OK. So it's four–three to the boys.' Ruhy slowly puts her hand up now, and another girl follows suit. 'I'm going to stop now. The girls are winning.'

Miss Rood looks at the boys' table, and elicits an answer: 'We're going to look at what religion we want to study.'

'And why are we going to do that? Ruhy?'

'Some of us may be whatever religion we are, but we don't know much about it.'

Another boy now: 'Maybe our friends are strongly religious. We might want to understand them better.'

Miss Rood stops them. 'Can I just remind you about active listening? That means not fiddling with stuff in your hands. OK. Show of hands. Who is doing Christianity?... That's seven. Hinduism? No one?'

Ayesha says, 'I could do it, Miss.'

'OK. Islam? Nine. Good. Sikhism? Gita. I think Taoism would be a problem. You wouldn't have enough resources.'

Everyone rushes for the bookshelves. They have to find out enough information to fill in a printed sheet they've been given. Ruhy has chosen Islam. She settles down at a table with Waseme, Sarah and Ayesha, and starts reading a bit out from an encyclopedia: '"China. The Philippines. Le—" How do you say this? Le-ba-non. "There is hardly a country that does not have Muslims among its population."'

'Sarah, are you Jewish?' Waseme says.

'No, I'm not. But my surname is Jewish. My great-granddad was Jewish.'

'Ayesha, what is the date and place of birth of Muhammad?' Ruhy says.

'Saudi Arabia,' she says, not looking up. She is reading from her book on Hinduism. '"Hinduism is the world's oldest living faith." Well, that's not true. When was Christianity created?'

'Two thousand years ago.'

'Jewish is probably the oldest,' Waseme says. It's from the time that we began.'

Ruhy has put back the encyclopedia and picked up a thin book with *Islam* on the cover.

'I'm sort of Jewish,' Waseme says, 'but Christian. My church is way down in South London and I go on Saturday.'

'What's it called?'

'I don't know. Just... Church.' She thinks for a bit. 'It's

Seventh Day Adventist. We believe the seventh day was Saturday, not Sunday.'

'My religion is boring,' Sarah says. 'Why do we have to worship God with long faces? I'd like to be a Pentecostalist. They do gospel and that. They always seem happy.'

Waseme nods. 'There are lots of teenagers who come to my church and say all these things, God loves you and all that. Then they go and do bad things. Getting pregnant and stuff. If you want to do drama, come to my church.' She turns to Ayesha again. 'Do you believe Jesus was the son of God?'

'No. He was a prophet. In Islam we don't have Before Christ and After Christ. We have AH. After Hijra. That was when the prophet Muhammad – peace be upon him – emigrated from Mecca to Medina.'

The two other girls sitting at the table with them, both in headscarves, look up briefly, then return to their work. They sit quietly filling in their worksheets in neat, close writing. They barely need to use books because they have chosen Islam and they know the answers already.

Ruhy is looking at her book. 'OK. So Muhammad was born in Mecca about 570 AD.' She holds up her sheet so that everyone can see she has filled in the top two boxes. 'I know nothing about my own religion. And I learned one thing.' Sometimes she thinks people are racist against her because she is Muslim. But actually, although she is Muslim, she is not really Muslim. No. She *is* Muslim. But she's not a *religious* Muslim.

The other week they were looking at newspaper cuttings about Iraq. There was this story, 'I begged my killer for my life.' It was about this woman and she was begging a soldier not to kill her. She said, 'Don't kill me. I'm a Muslim.' And the soldier said, 'You're not a Muslim.' He pointed to a terrorist, and he said, 'That's what a Muslim is.' She talked about it with the boy sitting next to her, and they both agreed that that soldier was a racist. Her mum says after nine/eleven people started thinking all Muslims were terrorists.

When she gets home she tells her mum about her RE lesson. 'Mum, I learned something. That Muhammad was born in 570 AD. I already knew he was born in Mecca. And seven days after a child is born they kill a goat. You did that for me, didn't you?'

'A sheep,' her mum says. 'Then we got them to give it to the poor people to say thank you for God giving us this precious gift.' She laughs, teasingly.

'Some of the other people in my class have had that, too.'

'It is especially for boys. But as there is no difference between boy and girl, we wanted to prove that.'

'I think that's wrong,' Ruhy says, 'only having it for boys.' She thinks for a minute. Sometimes she doesn't like what she hears about religion. Some people's parents teach them that, if they are bad, on Judgement Day Allah will save all the good people and then He will bring the sun five miles from the earth and burn everyone else up. She doesn't want to believe that. 'The only reason I picked Islam was because it's my religion and I wanted to learn about it. But I don't really, like, believe in it. I don't believe in religion at all.'

KESSIE

'I'll tell you something,' Mr Gratrix says. 'I can see some right old rubbish being written down here. Amit, "What type of compounds?" Not "Name the compound".'

The exams are just a few weeks away, and Kessie's chemistry group are practising A-level questions. She is sitting at the front with her parka on, staring hard at the question sheet in front of her. She's on the third question out of four. Some of the boys have finished and are putting their hands up, eager with questions. She picks up her red pen to write down an answer. Mr Gratrix is looking over her shoulder. She needs to get this right.

'It's fifteen marks, which means in the exam you would have to complete it in fifteen minutes, roughly. You're moving into an error there, Kessie. Perhaps I should move on.

'Right,' he says, drawing their attention back to the whiteboard. 'As long as you've seen what's going on it doesn't matter whether you've got the answers right or wrong. Kessie, how do you know it's this type, not that type?'

She frowns. Pauses.

He smiles. 'Well, don't worry. I'm checking, Kessie. You're my marker for the class. I always know if we finish something, you'll let me know if you haven't got it. And then I'll know no one else has got it either.'

She smiles, just a little one. Then she casts her eyes down again and gives the question paper another hard, interrogative stare.

'Hang on a minute,' he says. 'She just might get it. Which of these fragments, that's forty-three, twenty-nine, fifteen, can I not get if I fragment this one?'

Now she's grinning. She has the answer.

'Yessss!' He's not quite punching the air. But she's looking up at him, serious now. She got the answer right, but she didn't write down her reasons. Would she still get the marks?

'No, Kessie,' he says. 'You wouldn't.'

Later she catches the bus home to Stratford. With the strange, modernistic bus station behind her she picks her way past posters and banners about the Olympics. She steps carefully around the debris on the pavements as she walks down West Ham Lane and to the parking area at the back of the low-rise flats. She lets herself in, her eyes adjusting to the darkness of the hallway. She greets her brothers and sister, goes into the bedroom she shares with her sister and puts her school things away. She doesn't like mess or clutter. She changes her blouse for a green T-shirt with pink and white writing on the front, and a black shawl. She tidies her hair and ties back her plaits in a looser, softer style. She changes her parka for a fitted tweed coat. Then she is ready.

The Elim Church of Pentecost's Fountain Gate Tabernacle stands on Green Lane, Dagenham, between Panascope Training and Cash Concepts: The Shop With Options. It is a former cinema, its arch freshly painted and decorated with a dove. Outside, a notice advertises services in English and in the Ghanaian Akan language. Inside, it is clean, neat, painted freshly in welcoming shades of lilac, pale green and pink. In a room at the back, a prayer meeting is already in progress. She is a little late tonight. The others are standing in a circle at the front of the wide auditorium in front of the stage where amps, keyboards and drums are waiting. She takes off her coat and silently slips in, two of the others moving aside to make way for her. The first sound is barely audible. Then it begins to rise, a thin, gentle, toneful, melodious song. 'Oh, come let us adore him, Chri-ist is the Lord.'

After a few minutes the singing dies away and the choir leader, Joe, begins to speak. 'We should never worry because you love and keep us… we praise you. Hallelujah.' His eyes are closed. He sways gently as he leads the prayer. 'Blessed be the name of the Lord.' Other voices are joining his now, together but separate. 'Blessed be your name. Stand up. Stand up for Jesus.' Their voices are drifting up like single flames into the clear space above them.

Joe is in the centre of the circle, now, walking slowly, his arms outstretched. His voice rises above theirs: 'Because Christ is our Saviour, we are standing with Jesus Christ.'

The circle breaks up and Kessie flops on to one of the front-row seats to drink from her bottle of water. Then she sashays over to a group of girls who are chatting and laughing nearby. She sits on a random knee, grinning. One of the boys is jumping around, larking about somewhere in the crowd. She throws her head back and her laughter floats towards the high, blue-etched ceiling rose.

Grace is waving a piece of paper. 'Excuse me! He-llo!' She is trying to read a letter about a conference the church youth choir is to attend, but she is struggling to be heard over the drums and keyboards starting up behind her.

Joe is trying to talk, too. 'Ssssh!' he calls, exasperated. The clattering and chattering stop and they can hear praying again, from the room at the back. 'Come on, guys! *Please* be quiet! Aaaargh!'

Now they are silent.

A boy in a baseball cap and a grey hoodie takes the mic. 'OK. We'll kick off with "Days of Elijah".' They arrange themselves on the stage, messily at first. There's no hurry, nothing regimented. They begin to sing, altos first, then sopranos and tenors joining in. They break off, then begin again.

Soon, the melody fills the huge room: 'Hallelujah for the

God I love and your Mi-*tee* Ray...' Kessie is dancing now, clapping along with everyone else. The boy in the hoodie is still at the mic, trying to harmonize over them but it's hard for him to compete. One of the boys at the back is jumping on the spot, one arm in the air, exaggerated: look at me! But no one is really noticing. It's safe here, happy, close and relaxed.

They stop again. It's Kessie's turn at the mic. A slower one: 'I would give everything to you... and I'm getting the feeling you would too.' The choir answers, 'Yes, Lord, yes.' Her voice is a rich alto, and she does not have to strain to be heard. She stops with a little arms-out gesture, momentarily uncertain. They break for a minute.

She wanders over to Grace. They embrace, a long, friendly hug. Then they turn and chat to the others, their arms draped round each other's shoulders.

She supposes, when she thinks about church, that it's a sort of second family. There is nothing heavy about it: it's just there. People from different backgrounds, all there for one purpose, relaxing, chilling out, getting away from stuff. You can fit thousands into this church, if you want to, and sometimes they do. On Easter Sunday it was packed to the roof.

Church is her social life, her fun. Last Sunday there was a party after the service for someone's birthday, so that was how they spent Sunday afternoon. Eating joloffe rice, rice and beans, chicken and kebabs. And kenkey. Kenkey is corn, ground together with some other stuff and made into a ball. Actually, she's not sure how you make it. She really needs to learn to cook before she goes to uni. Otherwise she'll end up at McDonald's every day. Soon she'll miss that heavy, filling Ghanaian food. Grace says the same. They both laugh, sometimes, at how similar they are. They both like maths and science. They both want to be pharmacists. They both want to study at Aston, because it would be nice to have a friend there.

At the party last weekend most of the drinks were soft, but they have both tasted wine. On Kessie's eighteeth birthday her auntie brought her champagne. She had said she would like to go for an Italian meal, because she had never tasted Italian food. She thought her auntie would arrive in her car, but when Kessie went out to the car park at the back of the flats, she was there in a limo with the champagne and flowers. She hadn't expected that. She had already been for a Chinese meal with her friends from church, and to Pizza Hut with her dad, her brothers and sister. There was a cake, and everything. She felt, 'All this? For me?'

But when she and Grace talk about going out with their friends, they would never think of going for a drink. They look at each other and burst out laughing. Why would they do that? Anyway, they're often at church in the evening. Choir practice goes on till ten or eleven. Sometimes, on special occasions, there are all-night services.

The other week in a maths lesson some boy was complaining that all he seemed to do was work. Some of the others were saying to him, 'You have to keep at it. The exams are so important. Work now, relax later.'

But Kessie said no. She said there had to be a balance. If you do too much of anything, she thinks, it will pull you down. There will come a point when you snap. There's a time to learn, and a time to take a break. This is her break time.

JEMMA

It's sunny for their last PE lesson, and the air is joyful. They
are ticking the last things off, one by one. The classrooms and
the corridors are full of pale blue school shirts, passed from one
to another for signing. Most belong to the boys. The girls have
little autograph books. Jemma's has a clear blue plastic cover.
Inside, Naila has written the first message:

> Hey Jem wow i'm the 1st person
> 2 syn dis! lol i know u 4
> 5 yrs n u bin reali nyc n sweet
> 2 me! U alwys stik up 4 me wen
> miss used 2 annoy me! lol ur
> a luvly person n I wish u al d
> best 4 d future n evrytin u do!
> Lots of luv
> xx Naila xx

Her friend Naomi has written:

> Thnx 4 ben such a lurrrvly ms
> Over the years, and always bein'
> There 4 me
> See u in September
> Love and hugs
> NaomiXXX

On the rounders pitch they play a last game, against the boys. They all have shirts with their names on the back. Delroy's says 'Trigga'. Lily's says 'Lily Da Pink'. As if to underline the point, she's wearing shiny pink trainers. Jemma's says 'Tigger'.

'Come on, girls!' Jemma calls, laughing. 'Motivation!' She's waiting to bat, jumping about to confuse the bowler. 'Miss! That was a rounder!' When Lily comes running across the pitch towards her she drops the bat and gives her a big hug. When her turn comes she swings her bat with brio, hits the ball behind her and runs, head slightly down in a theatrical style, yelling, 'Wheeagh!' They all laugh. Everyone is relaxed. The rest of her team are sitting in the sun waiting to bat, enjoying the sun on their faces.

'Ameena, are you wearing your makeup to the prom?'

'No...'

'Nine to beat!' Miss Airey shouts.

'Go on, Kelly! You can do it, girlie! It's all about you!'

Some of the girls hit the ball hard, then stand there dithering. The boys' team are different. They hit it hard across the field, then run mock-casual, with one eye on the fielders. When Delroy runs he shouts, 'Black boooy runniiiing!' He raises his arms, wrists vertical, fingers pointing forward.

Lily produces her camera and they all pose for a picture. Ameena says; 'Watch out for me. I'm going to be on *MTV Babes*.'

Delroy says, 'I don't do none of that, man.' But he does it, arranging his face into a studied nonchalance. 'You wanna see me when the picture comes out, man.'

Today they are a unit, bonded by the prospect of the outside world encroaching on their safe, sealed-in school life and by the ordeal of the exams, which now loom. And yet the years have divided them in so many ways. They have grown up, and apart. Their differences have become more pronounced.

It is easy now to divide them into groups. It is a brutal truth that they can be separated by race. Not neatly, not in strict, self-contained groups. They mingle happily. Yet the years have made them distinct. There are groups of black boys and girls. There are the Muslim girls who always wear their scarves and are quiet and studious. And there are the other Muslim girls who go a bit mad, Jemma thinks. Because, she thinks, Islam is so strong on making sure they're protected. When they get away from home they break the rules. In her class there's a group of Muslim boys who all hang out together. But then again, a white boy hangs out with them too, and he doesn't have a religion. Jemma herself, being mixed race, doesn't fit easily into any of these groups, yet she has her own circle of friends from all kinds of backgrounds.

They are divided, too, by the way they live. In school uniform they all look the same, give or take, but they're different. They're not united by this mythical youth culture, Jemma thinks. She thinks there are lots of different youth cultures.

Her own culture is a rather wholesome one. An active culture with sport, walks in the country and church. Yet these other, more edgy cultures do not pass her by. She doesn't ignore them: she confronts them. The culture of drink and drugs, for instance. She has never been drunk. She has been out to bars and she has had a drink, but she has not been drunk. She cannot understand the pleasure of losing control, doing things she would regret, throwing up. She has talked to Anthony about this, in English lessons. She would be, like, 'Why do you get drunk?'

And he would be, 'Well – to have a good time.'

'What's it for? You're not getting anything out of it.'

And he would say, 'It's just a way to relax.'

Surely you should rethink your life if you need to get faceless.

And then there is sex. For her, because of her religion, it would have to be an act of love, yet no one she knows who has got pregnant has done it because of love. It is just because of sex, she thinks. She knows of two girls in her year who have been pregnant. One had an abortion, the other miscarried.

Some people blame schools for not making students aware enough of the risks, but she does not agree. A few weeks ago there was a story in the paper about a woman with three teenage daughters, who all had babies at the same time. The mother blamed the school. But every year at school they have it drummed into them. Be careful. Be healthy. But it's the morals she has learned at home that matter to her. There is a culture that makes everything OK. It's not the culture she is part of, but another culture. Songs that are about nothing else. Films. Some of them are at it from the age of twelve. But it just makes her think, What's wrong with you? It isn't spoken but it's made OK. Because other people do it, barriers come down.

Some of her friends' parents know they're having sex and they are OK with that. But then again, what can they do? It depends where you look at it from. Her closest friends think it's not desirable at such a young age. There are some people she knows who could never talk to their parents about anything like that. It would be taboo. But in her family they talk about stuff. Her mum will always say, 'You want to know? Fair enough. I'll tell you.'

Now they have CPHSE: Citizenship, Personal, Health

and Social Education. Today that officially means revision. Unofficially it means chatting about tomorrow night's prom. They sit in their classroom in little huddles. She is at the back with Naomi. She can hear little snatches from around the room: 'Where did you get your dress? No! How much?' Even the boys want to know what the girls will be wearing. One has spent three hundred and ninety-five pounds on his suit.

Jemma has a prom dress, but not too prommy, she thinks. She has not worn a dress for five years, not since she was a bridesmaid at a wedding. Her shoes are pointy, with two-inch heels. She never, ever wears high heels. She has been practising. The other night her sister Louise came in and found her coming down the stairs dressed in track pants, a T-shirt and these pointy shoes. She was, like, 'Nice look, Jemma!'

She has organized the limo. One of the boys was meant to do it but the quotes he got were about thirty pounds a head. She managed to get a limo for sixteen people at eighteen pounds a head. It will pick them all up from her friend's house and bring them to school for seven o'clock. Afterwards they will be driven around for an hour and dropped back at her friend's at eleven thirty.

'The only thing you've ever organized, Jemma,' Naomi jokes. Actually it isn't true. As her mum says, she's never backward about coming forward. Last year on sports day she met a new teacher, Mr Bracken, and she asked him why he had a number six tattooed on his ankle. He said it was because he used to play rugby for Ireland. And she was, like, 'Great! Because I'm trying to get a rugby team going. Can you teach us?' And he said he would if she could get a team together.

In the end there were about eight of them. Not really enough. And when the exams came it sort of fizzled out. But they enjoyed it. He taught them to tackle and stuff. He said he'd never seen kids so enthusiastic about it. They don't do girls' rugby at Seven Kings. There is a lot of stuff about safety. Maybe if enough people are interested they can get it going again in the sixth form.

And she pushes herself forward about other things, too. The school canteen, for instance. She's boycotted it this year. Well, actually, she lost the key you have to use to pay for the food – up a mountain in Wales. Her family have a house in Wales and go there for holidays. But she didn't want another key anyway, because the food is horrible and the prices are extortionate. You used to have to pay ninety-five pence for a tiny bottle of water. And they took away the baguette bar, so there was nothing to eat but nuggets and chips and waffles. They've brought it back now.

One day she was walking down the corridor and she started talking to a man who was visiting. And it turned out he came from the catering company and he was here to check how it was going. So she was, like, 'Right. Can I talk to you, please?' So they went to the canteen and they sat there for half an hour or more. And he listened. About the prices, and the food, and how her white friend used her black friend's key and how no one noticed even though they're supposed to see your photo when they put the key in the till.

Naomi is anti-prom. She says she can't see the point in all that Americanized nonsense. 'I only care about the twenty or thirty people I really like, and I can say goodbye to them any time,' she says. 'It's a trend. Anyway, I'm anti-trend.'

Jemma thinks about this. Is she anti-trend? She is certainly anti-materialism. But mostly she just does her own thing. She doesn't worry much about trends.

'Jemma,' Naomi says, 'do you remember that time when we were in year eight and we were doing PE and it started to pour with rain?'

Jemma grins. 'Yeah! I love doing PE in the rain!'

'And we got completely soaked through, and then you and me took our shoes and socks off and we were dancing in the rain?'

They both laugh.

WORSHIP

There has been a tendency, in recent years, for the popular imagination to see the inner cities as places where religion is polarized. We assume that in areas like Ilford the population can generally be split between practising Muslims and non-practising Christians, with a few Hindus and Sikhs thrown in.

In East London the big mosques throng with people on any Friday in the year, yet the nineteenth-century Christian churches stand marooned and blackened like the hulks of so many abandoned, rusting ships. This is not the case in Seven Kings, and surely not in other diverse urban areas. Among our seven young people, four – Perin, Kessie, Shivanie and Jemma – profess heartfelt religious belief, two Christian and two Hindu. Our two Christians are Baptist and Pentecostalist, and many more in their school come from those churches. Stacey, a classmate of Shivanie's, talked about how she had gone out on to the streets of Ilford to tell people about her faith. When Jemma's sister Louise – in Shivanie's class at Seven Kings – was baptized, Stacey and several of her other schoolfriends came to support her. They say their religion guides their lives and will continue to do so.

In fact Christianity is thriving in urban Britain. As our cities become more diverse they also become more religious. The Christianity that was once one of Britain's biggest exports to the developing world is now being imported, most recently by migrants from Africa.

These churches are not as visible as the older ones. Their founders lack the funds that were available to those who brought religion to Britain's cities in the late nineteenth century. These churches are to be found nestling amid rows of shops, or occupying former cinemas, like Kessie's. Unlike their older brethren, they are freshly painted and well attended.

Hard evidence of this phenomenon is difficult to come by. The 2001 census gathered information on religious affiliation for the first time, but even that does not really tell us what we need to know. The question is not to which religious group Britons are affiliated, but to what extent their religion influences their lives. There is some evidence though, which makes fascinating reading. The Aston Charities, based in Newham, along with Barnardo's in Hackney and Tower Hamlets, have built up a remarkable picture of worship in East London. They have found a total of seven hundred different religious groups, three hundred of which are non-Christian, with an average weekly attendance of 165 people. The proliferation of small Christian churches is remarkable: there are African Aladura churches, Seventh Day Adventists, Christadelphians, Moravians, Mormons, Spiritual Baptists and more.

There have been two major periods of religious expansion in this area, the charities say: in the late nineteenth century, and in the recent past. During the 1970s and 1980s, forty new religious groups started in Newham. In the 1990s, there were fifty and the trend looks set to continue for as long as London's ethnic diversity grows. There are now three times as many Pentecostalist churches in the borough as there are Anglican. And, they say, the commitment of their members may be much stronger:

> For black people in Newham, 'Christian' as a term of affiliation may well represent much higher levels of commitment and religious practice [than for the white community]... The overall pattern is of increased attendance, especially for evangelicals, Baptists and Pentecostalists, with a reported decline for the Roman Catholics. Only a handful of Christian congregations, all Anglican or Free Church, are numerically dominated by the over-50s.

So Jemma, a Baptist, and Kessie, a Pentecostalist, are not exceptional. Seven Kings is just a few miles up the road from Newham and many of its sixth-formers, including Kessie, commute from there. And while Seven Kings is not quite such a diverse area as Newham, it is very diverse and is becoming more so. This wave of religious belief, then, is spreading outwards around London. The most recent census shows that around half the people in these three boroughs are white, but the proportion of white children at Seven Kings High School is much smaller than that. About a third are Muslim, a third Hindu. A significant proportion of the rest are practising Christians, Sikhs or Jews.

Does it matter? Maybe. Seven Kings High School is not just one big melting pot. Religion is something that pupils are aware of and talk about. Doug Harrison observes that while the pupils tend to mix together in the early years, they form loose but distinct ethnic and religious groups as they get older. Our seven pupils have friends from all backgrounds, but they seek out others with whom they have things in common. Two of Perin's best friends are studious Hindu boys like himself. There are distinct groups of Muslim pupils in the school, less so of white pupils because there are fewer of them.

If there is tension under the surface, it involves relationships between the school's Muslim pupils and their classmates. Ruhy remarks that she sometimes feels discriminated against because she is Muslim, even though she is not religious. Anthony, arriving aged fourteen, was accused of being 'racist against Muslims'.

There is cultural tension, too, between the values of parents or grandparents who travelled to Britain from overseas, and those of children who have grown up here. Ruksana ran away with her boyfriend and she was not the only Seven Kings teenager living a double life, flitting between traditional homes and teenage gatherings at which alcohol is drunk and miniskirts are worn. But it would be easy to make too much of this. For the most part these children move seamlessly between the different cultures they encounter, for they are adaptable. There is much more to unite than divide them. They walk the same streets and they bump into each other at the weekend in the Exchange shopping centre; they like the same films, the same music, the same restaurants. They live side by side in the same kind of housing. Indeed, sometimes the level of their cultural assimilation is nothing less than depressing: huge numbers support Manchester United; their favourite food, almost without exception, is pizza.

In general, the young people growing up here benefit from contact with others from different backgrounds, different faiths. It is a rare day at Seven Kings when a teacher has to pull up a child for making an offensive remark about religion or race. This school will never be like those in divided towns in the north, such as Oldham, where some schools recently set up an 'exchange' programme because the lives of children from different communities were so segregated that they never had a chance to meet and understand what they had in common. Here, families living and educating their children together, have struggled to understand one another better. It may be an imperfect process, but most pupils are at ease in their mixed environment. As Jemma puts it: 'We are in this place together for so many hours each day. What is the point of *not* getting on?'

THE PROM

At seven-thirty on this warmish May evening Jemma is standing on the pavement outside the school gate in twilight, suddenly ten years older in a long black satin dress whose skirt is slashed to show white satin underneath. It has a plain, strapless top. Towering over her is a huge, overslicked man with a ponytail and a thin moustache. Even in her pointy shoes she is at a disadvantage by several inches and many kilos. The man is standing too close, making sure she understands.

Her friends have gathered a few yards away, an odd assembly of overexcitement and concern. They have tumbled out of their limo in a cascade of black and red satin, and now, between worried glances in Jemma's direction, they have joined the gateside mêlée of shrieking delight and mutual admiration.

'But I *told* you it was for sixteen people!' Her tone has all its usual vehemence, but her upturned face spells stress.

He is making it clear that a substantial payment will ease the overcrowding problem. The sixteen-seater limousine is not a sixteen-seater, he now says it is a fourteen-seater.

'I don't know about that... I just filled in the form and sent it back,' she's saying. She has not got any more money. They have spent enough. She is at a loss. She has nothing in her armoury but her ability to cling to an argument. She puts years of practice into effect and they pay off.

Finally, defeated, the man gives up and lets her go. She rushes over to the others. 'Jack, I'm *so* sorry!' she keeps repeating.

By the time they all reach the front entrance of the school she is bubbling over with excitement.

Behind them, more and more limos are stopping outside the gate. There are cars the size of buses, some big enough to take more than twenty people. There is loud Bhangra music; there is a stretched Humvee.

As each vehicle pulls up the girls get out warily, arranging their frocks. Virtually all are in huge, layered, full-length strapless dresses in silk, satin or taffeta. Most are in pastel shades, pale green or pink. Their hair is bedecked, makeup carefully applied. Months of planning have gone into this moment. Once arranged, they surrender to a barrage of photography and laughter.

The boys favour a gangster style: sharp suits, black shirts, ties in a range of pinks and purples. Anthony, unfolding himself carefully at the rear of a roaring gale of boys, is keeping cool. He looks as incongruous tonight in his suit as he did this afternoon in his school uniform. His favoured style is casual, more street, but he would not have missed this. He has even shaved off his beard. There were threats that if he didn't he would not be allowed in.

A long line of cars is building up in the street. The school's neighbours are standing outside their houses, taking pictures on their mobile phones. The gesture is not entirely friendly. One particular family always complains about limos driving across their concrete. Doug Harrison and Clive Rosewell are standing by the gate, greeting the arrivals but also keeping an eye on the situation.

Inside, the entrance hall has been transformed. A photographer is waiting with a huge umbrella and film-set props. Next to him is a clapperboard, which proclaims:

Date: 20 May
Location: Seven Kings High School
Production: Hollywood Prom
Director: Miss Handley
Producer: Miss Ranson
Scene 1: 7 till 10 p.m.

A red carpet extends down the corridor to the school hall, sprinkled with glittery stars. Miss Handley is flitting around in a red chiffon dress, checking that the DJ is ready. He looks out of place in his hoodie and shades.

In the hall the constant flashing of cameras adds to the atmosphere. A huge net of balloons hangs from the ceiling. They mill about. The awards start. Miss Top Flirt. Prom Queen. Best Dressed Girl. Best Dressed Boy.

A boy with a black suit, black shirt, red tie and trilby gets up to sing 'Hollywood', and everyone cheers.

PERIN

The next morning Perin's class gathers in the drama studio. Some of the girls are laughing at a little cluster of red balloons clinging limply to the black-painted ceiling. It must have drifted in last night from the hall. For some reason, gentle sitar music is playing. Everyone is tired.

The year-thirteen prom took place last night too but at the Prince Regent Hotel, a couple of miles up the road. There were limos, of course. Perin's had twenty boys in it. He had a smart suit and a new tie. One group even arrived in a fire engine. There was a buffet; the awards went on for ages. Best Dressed Girl. Best Dressed Boy. Best at Being Little Miss Perfect in Absolutely Everything.

One or two people drank too much. While the awards went on and on, Miss Jones and Mr Hayes had to take turns to keep an eye on a paralytic boy slumped on a table at the back. Perin paced himself, although he did have a whisky and Coke when they got back into the limo. That was at about eleven fifteen, and the driver took them all to Leicester Square. It was full of people in prom dresses and suits. On the way down there they kept passing other limos full of school-leavers, all heading in the same direction, like some lumbering, disorganized migration.

Leicester Square was a bit of an anticlimax. They got out of the limo and said goodbye to the driver, who was leaving them there. They milled about for a bit, wondering what to do next. Then they tried to get into a nightclub or two, but some were not eighteen and the doormen wouldn't let them in. So they went to McDonald's, then got a taxi home. It cost sixty-eight pounds. Perin got in about two thirty or three. Things are never quite what you expect them to be, he thinks now.

Still, it was a change of scene. In recent weeks his study at home, with its glass-fronted cabinets, its little sofa, its framed pictures of himself and his sister, has become his constant habitat. He no longer watches television in the evenings after dinner, or not for long. Instead he goes back in there for an extra couple of hours before bed. Writing things down to remember them better, highlighting things, practising questions. Just one or two marks can make the difference. Gradually the work-surfaces around his computer have disappeared under silting drifts of paper.

He must be focused, he must be calm. Sometimes he has a moment of doubt in which he wonders if he can really get the three As and a B he needs. But then he tells himself, If all those other people can do it, you can do it. If your teachers think you can do it, you can definitely do it. In the exams his heartrate will go up and he will feel nervous. Afterwards, he will think he could have done better. But then it will be too late.

Today there will be morning lessons, a gathering in the sixth-form common room at break, and then they will go. Nobody is in a state for serious work. Normally they keep at it right until the very end. No slacking: that's the Seven Kings way. But today they will not achieve much and their teachers know it. After break, they will leave, wander down to the Exchange shopping centre, have lunch, hang out a bit.

He will look at the young men in there and wonder about them. He will even recognize some, either sixth-formers or from the University of East London or somewhere else local. Yet they spend their time hanging around the shopping centre. If they have money, they will spend it on alcohol to drink on a street corner. They have been allowed to get into bad habits, he thinks, yobbish behaviour. The Americans wouldn't allow that sort of thing and neither would he. He likes to look at the world as if it were a business. Three strikes and you're out; zero tolerance.

In physics they don't work today. They chat about last night and about the exams. There are three in this class who want to be doctors, one lawyer, one dentist, four engineers. They don't need to be told to work hard. Dr Pithia tells Perin he should have a very good chance, so long as he maintains his momentum. He would be disappointed if he didn't get an A. They've had some good discussions this year. The other day they were talking about waves and curves, and Perin was trying to see how you might use them to predict the way the stock market works. He was trying to visualize how you could model it to make money.

They talk about their lives at Seven Kings. The high point for Perin was when he made the film about his life for the Disney Channel in year nine. They asked for a disabled pupil to make a documentary, and he was chosen. He was proud of that. And the low points? He can't think of any off hand. At exam times, he's stressed. Getting rejected by Cambridge and the LSE was bad, but it wasn't the end of the world. University College, London, is a prestigious institution.

'I wouldn't worry about it, Perin,' Dr Pithia says. 'At the end of the day you want to get a good degree. If you work hard, it will pay off.'

The school has a strange, not-quite-itself feeling today.

Some year-thirteen boys are still in their suits from last night, their eyes bleary. A few haven't been home; one group booked a room in the Travelodge. They look wasted. Some are still drunk. And in the midst of this there's a television van outside the front entrance. Mr Steer, it seems, has just been made head of a government advisory group on discipline and is giving interviews to the media.

The sixth-form block is even more packed than usual. Everyone is there. Perin may be tired, but he has made time to gel his hair, smarten himself up. Others are crying and hugging each other, but he is calm. It's sad, he feels, but he is ready to go, ready for the independence university will bring. In the end, you have to keep moving on.

Miss Jones is trying to contain herself for long enough to address the throng. 'I'm not going to make a long speech,' she says, 'but every time I say goodbye to one of you, the tears start to come. If I don't do this now, I won't get through it.' Already she's looking upset again. 'You lot have been such a special group of people to me. I'm not the only person who feels like that. We're all going to miss you. We know you're going to go on to achieve greatness. I'm confident that, in years to come, some of the people in this room today will be in high positions in government, in medicine. I hope you'll remember us fondly.'

The tears are flowing now all around the room, but she ploughs on: 'I just love you all so much,' she says.

Amid the cheering and whistling, someone shouts, 'We love you too, Miss.'

DOUG HARRISON

There are times in Doug Harrison's working life when he is forced to question himself, to wonder whether things might have been different. Sometimes nothing good can come from a particular situation: it just has to be dealt with and the best possible bad outcome has to be processed. The permanent exclusion of a pupil is just such a time. It doesn't happen often at Seven Kings. They started the year hoping it wouldn't happen at all. They targeted, as they always do, those pupils who were at risk. Pupils like Delroy, for example. They checked the state of his temper every day, tried to keep him calm and worked endlessly to keep him at school, to give him the chance to leave with a clean record and a clutch of GCSEs. It had worked.

But now, at the end of May, this happens: two boys facing permanent exclusion. And although neither has been a perfect pupil, no one predicted it. Wesley. Always a worry. Behaviour issues, certainly, but they contained them. And Tyrone.

Tyrone is irrepressible. If you had asked Doug a few weeks ago about Tyrone, he would have said he was a nice boy at heart. He would say so now, if you pushed him. Yet it looks unlikely that either Tyrone or Wesley will come back to Seven Kings. Everyone is desperately sad about it, but increasingly he feels sure that it is the right decision.

With hindsight he can say now there were warning signs. He wouldn't say they should have handled things differently at an earlier stage, though maybe Tyrone's parents would. There had been one or two incidents. There had been little spats in the corridor. 'Sir, I tripped. Someone pushed me.' Then there was that business in the toilets when Tyrone was accused of bullying. If he had been suspended earlier, would it have checked him? He doesn't think so. But he has to ask.

Tyrone's parents' view is that he's not a bully: these allegations that have since emerged related to Tyrone doing what Tyrone does. But Doug thinks it's to do with power.

It took a major investigation to uncover the extent of the problem. It started when one pupil complained of intimidation by Wesley. They started to ask questions. More pupils came forward, and then this whole story began to unravel. Repeated incidents in which other pupils had felt threatened or uncomfortable.

Tyrone's role soon became clear. Perhaps he had been led on by Wesley, but he had certainly been involved. Some of the pupils who said now that the boys had made them feel uncomfortable were actually quite friendly with them. And despite everything, they still wanted to be friendly with them. It wasn't a simple situation.

There was this strange thing going on. 'I want it to stop, but I don't want Tyrone or Wesley to be in trouble. I don't want this to happen to me any more, yet I still want Tyrone to be my friend.' It was almost as if they were saying they felt they had to accept the situation. That this was what went on. It was not a message the school could accept. The best thing for those other pupils, he's sure, would be not to see Tyrone or Wesley every day.

A major part of the problem has been the group culture. It is something they see a lot with black pupils. There is a street culture to which many of them subscribe. Some of the white boys do, too. It's an Americanized culture linked to rap music. And it says you put your friends first, always.

When they questioned Wesley he responded with aggression: 'You're picking on me because I'm black. Prove it. Get witnesses. I didn't do nothing.' He even said that he would lie for his friends. For one of his little group of close mates – Tyrone, Jerome, Calvin, Spencer – he would do anything. Tyrone is not so much into that but it rubs off. The day Wesley was sent home Tyrone, who had not yet been questioned, came to Doug's office. He tried to spread the blame, to own up to some of the things of which Wesley had been accused.

When Tyrone was questioned about his behaviour, his response was very different from Wesley's. He was distraught. He sat in Doug's office with his hands over his face. Owned up to everything. Apologized. Once, just once, in that long interview they had, one of his fingers moved a little, to let Tyrone peer out from one eye. Doug's two eyes met Tyrone's exposed pupil. Just for a second. Then the fingers moved back together again.

He has learned through many years of experience that you have to be very clear about your facts in these circumstances. Statements are taken from a wide range of pupils; they are examined and cross-referenced. Advice is sought from Education Welfare. The accused pupils are spoken to, along with their parents.

Now Alan will take the statements and read them through. He will think about it: he will not make a snap decision. If he feels it necessary he will take the final decisions to exclude, and he will use the statements to compile a full report. Then there will be hearings before a panel of governors. Tyrone's parents will have a chance to put their point of view, and at a separate hearing so will Wesley's.

The school has to be careful, at every step of the way. A police officer might say they should not take statements from pupils. If there were a criminal investigation – an allegation of assault, for example – they might say the evidence had been contaminated. And yet the school has to be sure of its facts, and it cannot do so without taking full statements from every-one concerned.

Having spoken to Tyrone's parents and Wesley's, he is sure they will argue that their sons should not be permanently excluded. In all his thirty years of teaching he has never come across a case where a parent said they *did* believe their child should be excluded.

Tyrone's parents will say, as they have said all along, that this is Tyrone. They accept that he did much of what the other pupils said he did. Yet they do not accept that he should be permanently excluded. They will say that this is what boys do. Some of the complainants are still friendly with Tyrone so they could not have been very upset. And yet intellectually Doug cannot accept this. It comes down to this in the end: are children allowed to behave in a way that upsets other children or are they not? Put it that way, and there is no argument. There are certain things a school cannot be seen to accept.

JUNE

KESSIE

On the other side of the main school building from Doug Harrison's office there is another room, even smaller and without natural light. And while Doug's office is full of comings and goings, this room is calm and quiet. This is where Colin Gratrix, Kessie's chemistry teacher, has his base. It is here that Kessie and Grace now spend their days: they have found a refuge where they can work. They are together yet separate, silent most of the time.

Now and again one will get stuck. If it is on a matter to do with chemistry or maths, which they both take, she will lift her head from her papers and look at the other for guidance. They will talk over the problem, turning it around and probing it. Sometimes this is enough. But if still no answer comes they will emerge, together or separately, into the light and bustle of the school corridor to seek out one or another of their teachers for help. Sometimes they will pass an acquaintance going in a different direction on a similar mission.

Kessie feels better now that she has this place to work. She did not want to stay at home to do her revision. It's not that there's nowhere for her to work, it's just that she can't concentrate properly at home. There are distractions. She might find herself wandering into the living room and staring at the television. So, from the beginning, she and Grace have continued to get the bus to school each morning, just as they did before the exams started. Yet her place in the private study area, her little booth opposite the supervisor's desk, has lost its magic. There came a time when she realized things were not going well.

She had already taken some of her exams, psychology and maths, mainly. They were OK. There were hard parts but she tried to remind herself there was no point in stressing. The hardest thing, for her, was keeping track of the time because she concentrates so hard on getting every question right, and she will not let go.

Towards the middle of the exams it all started to slip away. She was going over and over past papers, putting in the hours, up there in her little booth. Yet when she marked her answers they did not come out right. Funny how you get those days when it looks as if you've been sitting there doing a lot, but at the end of the day you haven't learned anything very much. At that stage she knew she didn't have time to waste and then it all caught her up.

That was when she had gone to see Mr Gratrix. She was making silly mistakes, she was tired, she felt it was all going wrong. He was so calm and reassuring, and he told her all these nice things about herself. How she was a hard-working student, and not to worry so much because it would all come together in the end. Then they talked about ways she could maybe work differently, to give her brain a break. And then he suggested she and Grace should have his little office to work in.

What will she do, once this is all over and she goes away to university? she wonders. Will she have a teacher who is also her friend? She wishes she could take Mr Gratrix with her when she goes.

She needs an A and two Bs for Aston. She and Grace are hoping to go there together. But her bottom line is the private target she has set for herself – three As. She has something to prove to herself. It is not a competitive thing. She has certain expectations of herself. Three As would be like a miracle.

The last exam will be chemistry, and afterwards they will go out to the Coco noodle bar in Ilford with a few friends. Someone from her maths set is organizing a trip to Alton Towers but she doesn't think they'll go. It isn't that they don't like funfairs: when they go to the beach with church, to Brighton or Hastings, they always go to the funfair. But she wasn't keen on this particular trip. She probably won't keep in touch with anyone from Seven Kings, except her two closest friends, and she knew them already because she went to Sarah Bonnell School in Stratford with them till she was sixteen.

She would like to keep in touch with some of the staff. Mr Gratrix, of course, and Miss Jones. But other pupils? No. Her two years at Seven Kings was not a time for making new friends. It was a time for studying.

JULY

ALAN STEER

As the pupils pour out of the school on this muggy early-July evening, Alan Steer has a grim task to perform. He is standing inside the entrance of the building with Doug Harrison, waiting for Tyrone's parents to arrive for their exclusion hearing.

He loses sleep over these things, he really does. It's terribly sad for Tyrone's family. He likes Tyrone, and feels a great affection for him. He likes his family. He likes his sister Tamia, who will go into the sixth form this autumn. He is genuinely sorry that they have lost Tyrone. But that is what has happened.

Heads can get these things wrong. He spent a lot of time thinking. He saw Tyrone's parents, then thought again. He had to be sure that the offences merited permanent exclusion, on their own, and of that he is now sure. Tyrone and Wesley had intimidated people who were lower in the social pecking order than they were to establish their own higher place.

The culture of that group of boys was always to say that everything was just a joke. But in the end he thinks that that will not do. It's too easy a get-out: 'I must be forgiven, I am happy-go-lucky Tyrone.' No. You are a fourteen-year-old boy who is responsible for his own behaviour and you have got to learn that. It is an absolute. Seven Kings High School must hold its pupils responsible for their actions.

It would be wrong, he thinks, to say that Tyrone's exclusion has been affected by this factor, this need to make a statement about the values of the school, but it is there. A message must be sent to the other pupils, and – crucially – to the other boys among Tyrone's friends who were on the fringes of these incidents. Intimidating behaviour is not acceptable at Seven Kings High School. Not excluding Tyrone would be like saying, 'You can get away with it.'

Among that particular group, there was a clear rule that said loyalty to your friends was more important than the feelings of other people around you. Lack of respect for other pupils, he feels, cannot be ignored.

That is the essential difference between these boys and the others who have teetered on the brink of exclusion this year. Delroy's problem, for example, was his temper. He would lose it and insult Alan, or insult Doug. He did not have to be permanently excluded for that, although his behaviour had to be taken seriously. If a kid with a temper hits another kid with a brick, he will be permanently excluded.

But staff have broad shoulders. Their job is to deal with children, and they should never forget that they *are* children. Children are not always rational, they are not always mature, so it is part of a teacher's daily task to work with that, and to counter it. That doesn't mean teachers have to put up with bad behaviour; far from it. They can teach children to behave better.

But there are times, and this is one of them, when other children have been made to feel uncomfortable by the behaviour of one or more of their peers. Times when those peers' continued presence in the school could lead to them continuing to feel uncomfortable. And all pupils have a right to feel safe when they come to school.

So now he has a job to do. He must employ all the weight of his professional skills to argue a case against Tyrone's parents, whom he likes, and to remove their son from the school that, in so many ways, has been good for him.

He has compiled a report that runs to about twenty-five pages. It spells out the full extent of Tyrone's misdemeanours, and Wesley's too. Now he must present it to the panel, which consists of the chair of governors, two parent governors and a teacher governor. He will answer questions, from the governors and from Tyrone's parents. Then Tyrone's father will present the opposing case. It's not the Old Bailey, but it is quite formal.

It's hard to know how long they will be here. Wesley's hearing took place last week, and was quite short. He attended with his mum, but she didn't have a great deal to say. He was still holding on to his attitude, saying he'd do anything for his mates, even lie for them, and that the school was just picking on him because he was black. The decision was not a hard one to take. Wesley's offences were more serious than Tyrone's. There is a chance he will not go to a mainstream school at all next year.

Tyrone, on the whole, has not caused the school huge grief until now. Who knows? Maybe the sum total of all this will be more grief, not less, for there is a *quid pro quo*. The local authority has just asked them to take on a boy who has been excluded from another school. Maybe he will be far more trouble than Tyrone, or even Wesley. Whatever the governors' decision, there will be no sense of victory.

TYRONE

It is mid-July and Tyrone is sitting on the big, squelchy sofa at his dad's house, reflecting on the strangeness of the past six weeks. He is deflated, bewildered and sad. His braids are coming loose. He doesn't fully understand how his life could so have unravelled.

His last lesson at Seven Kings was on a Thursday, after break. It was PE. Then they came and got him and took him to Mr Steer's lobby. They said all these different pupils were making statements about him, saying they felt intimidated by the way he behaved in the corridors and around the school.

He spent two days sitting there, in that little room, staring at the old-fashioned sign on the wall that says, 'This Child Does Not Know Her Tables', being walked to the canteen at lunchtime by Mr Harrison to get his food. Internally suspended. If he had known he was going to be excluded he would not have stayed in Mr Steer's lobby. He would have gone out for a little while, to his friends. People don't get kicked out for messing around and having a laugh. People get kicked out for beating other people up. Once a boy brought a knife to school and pretended he was going to stab someone. Tyrone didn't do anything like that. He was just larking about.

After two days they sent him home. Mr Steer said this might be his last day at Seven Kings, and that he had a very difficult decision to make. It all happened so quickly, no warning. When he was in trouble for that incident with Jaz in the toilets, they didn't say he was in danger of exclusion. Even Delroy wasn't permanently excluded, and he was always in trouble. He was suspended so many times, and they always let him come back. They must think this is so serious that he doesn't deserve a final chance.

He misses his friends. He would give anything to be back there with them now. He didn't say, as Wesley had, that he'd do anything for his friends, even lie for them. But actually he would do a lot for them. He can't believe he won't be going back to them, even though his parents have had a letter saying that the governors have decided he will be permanently excluded. Surely, he thinks, there must still be some hope. Just a glimmer?

He didn't say, as Wesley had, that all this was just prejudice, that he had been singled out because he was black. He doesn't see it that way. But he does think people make a thing about them being the black boys, the black group. When there's trouble someone will say, 'Oh, it's the black group.' If there's some trouble and they don't have any information about who caused it, the person they go to first is Wesley. But is that prejudice, or fact? Wesley did get into trouble a lot.

Tyrone never got up one morning and decided to make friends with the other black boys in the school. It just gradually happened. He was friends with Jerome, and of course they hung around with Calvin because he is Tyrone's cousin. They would see Wesley around, and Spencer. They were into the same clothes, the same music. There were others who wanted to hang about with them because they were popular. They always had a laugh. Being one of the popular ones is good, sometimes, but it can be bad, too, because it means you stand out, and people notice you.

He used to think maybe he could get out of going to school by acting like he was sick or something. Now if they would let him go he would be so grateful. He would be so good they wouldn't know him. His sister got through the whole school thing, so why can't he?

He didn't go to the exclusion hearing with the governors. His mum and dad both took time off work to go; his dad had read the report over and over, and worked out what he needed to say. But his dad said he felt there was so much evidence he couldn't question. In a criminal trial he could have cross-examined Tyrone's accusers, the other pupils who wrote these statements. He came back sad and frustrated, not holding out much hope.

The report Mr Steer wrote, his dad says now, was like a book. 'It was... it was like Tony Blair and the Iraq dossier. Forty-five minutes and the bombs are here... But when you delve deeper, you find there's not a lot there. 50 per cent or more of it was about Wesley. It was very serious, with regard to Wesley, but not so serious with regard to Tyrone.

'If you give someone a book and say, "It's about your behaviour," they're going to think it *is* about them. But if you took out the part that was about Wesley, there would only have been a couple of pages left.'

He said this to Mr Steer, who replied that he didn't want to cut and paste, he wanted to give the full picture. But it seemed to him it meant Tyrone was treated as if he and Wesley were a unit, as if their offences were indistinguishable. No one was really saying that. Wesley had gone much further, had been far more aggressive in his behaviour. When they confronted the boys with the allegations, Wesley denied everything. Tyrone owned up and apologized. Tyrone would always have treated the staff with respect.

'I didn't defy anyone,' Tyrone says now. 'I didn't directly go against anything they said. They didn't say to me not to do something, and then I carried on. I never had a chance.'

'I think that the school were trying to say to you, Tyrone, that they shouldn't have to tell you not to do things. You should know.'

The main thing he wanted to say, really, was that Tyrone's offences did not merit permanent exclusion, that a lively, physical teenage boy does not always understand the effect of his behaviour on other people. He could see that Tyrone had to change that behaviour, but he did not believe it was as serious as the school was saying it was. One of those pupils who made a statement about him had even been round to see him, at home, to ask if they could still be friends.

The hearing started at three o'clock, and they were still there at half past six. By the end, they were asking questions about how they might ensure nothing like this happened again, if they were to let Tyrone stay. Tyrone's dad hopes he gave them something to think about, at least made them consider the other sanctions that might be applied.

But on the other side, Mr Steer put up just as vigorous an argument. He said there had been a very serious breach of discipline, and that he had a duty to uphold discipline in the school. If they let Tyrone back in, how would the other pupils feel? This wasn't just a problem about Tyrone, but about the whole school.

But surely, Tyrone's dad felt, the discipline of the school had already been upheld. Wesley's exclusion had already been confirmed. There should not have been a need to exclude Tyrone as well. Was it right that Tyrone was asked to sign a statement confessing to a series of incidents of intimidation, without himself or Tyrone's mum being present?

He felt there was more than enough evidence for the governors to come to a different conclusion, and yet he left with the feeling that this had been a rubber-stamping exercise. He did not feel, at the end of the day, that anyone was there to change their mind. It was done and dusted. Let's err on the side of caution. What if something goes bad later on? What if there's another incident? The school's governors don't want to put themselves in a position where someone can accuse them later of not facing up to a problem.

Now they must wait to see if Tyrone will be offered a place at another school. There are some schools he just cannot go to. The one that failed its inspection, for example, is the one with spare places. To accept one of those would be like saying you wanted to work in McDonald's.

Tyrone has been looking down while his dad has been talking, staring at the hem of his T-shirt. Hearing the notion of his future life at some other school beginning to solidify in his father's words, he looks up. 'But I still want to go back to Seven Kings, Dad.'

'You can't become a different person, Tyrone. Be honest with yourself. If you went back and everyone else around you was the same, doing the same things, you would do them too. You'd find it very difficult.'

'If I go back I'll see how it goes, man. You have to try it and see how it is. I don't want to go to a different school with different friends.'

'I'm not under any illusions, Tyrone. If by some miracle you did go back, you wouldn't have many friends among the teachers. I would expect Mr Steer to ask them to tell him if you did anything at all that they thought was inappropriate. Would you really want to have that hanging over you?'

'I just want a little tiny piece of hope, man. I really want to go back to Seven Kings, Dad.'

'I think you have to understand that Mr Steer doesn't want you in the school. It's time to call it a day. Put what's happened behind you.'

He cannot do it. He has put so much of his life into Seven Kings. He has a class photo, just a small one. He has three Seven Kings blazers, one for each year he spent there.

'I don't want to call it a day, Dad.' He looks at him, imploring now, a child. 'I want you to help me, Dad.'

DOUG HARRISON

At school they are helter-skeltering towards the end of term. Doug Harrison is sitting in the regular senior-leadership team meeting, listening to lists of plans, instructions and policy decisions. Redesignation of the school's specialist status. Plans for the next school year. Cards for staff who are leaving.

Clive Rosewell reports that the new PE teacher has been in. 'He looked the part – he was wearing a suit. And he wanted to spend a day with us before term ended.' They all nod approvingly.

As the meeting breaks up, Alan has another piece of news. He has agreed to take an excluded boy from another local school. 'It's a political thing, almost. If we're arguing that Tyrone needs a school place by September, then we have to expect someone coming back.' He has been on the phone this week, trying to ensure that Tyrone is offered a place at a good mainstream school for September. Strictly speaking, it's down to the local authority to place him, but a personal recommendation helps.

'When this new boy comes in, I'd like to see him. Feel his collar a bit,' Alan says.

The boy will be given the full works, of course, whatever his past record. Just as Anthony was, when he arrived at the beginning of last year. There is a point at which the school has great leverage over a child who has strayed, and this is it. The right impression needs to be made from the start, if they are to continue in a positive, trouble-free manner.

The meeting over, Doug's first job is to phone Suzanne Levy at Redbridge College. With a heavy heart he has agreed that both Lindsay and Amina, the two girls whose attendance has been so poor this year, should go there next year instead of continuing at school. He lifts the phone. Lindsay was supposed to go to the college to enrol, but so far there has been no sign of her.

'Suzanne?... Yes... Lindsay's family are moving house this week. She hasn't been at school yesterday or today. She's not too well, apparently. Something wrong with her eye...'

Lindsay's attendance has continued to drop, and something had to be done. In the end they asked her if she still wanted to do a travel and tourism course at college. She said she did. Doug and Angela have been down there with her for a look around. She just needs to do this one small thing and she will have a place. But she has been hard to pin down.

At least he can see where Lindsay's coming from. There are things he can work on with her, albeit not desperately successfully. They have kept her at school this year, for most of the time. She has not yet dropped out completely.

With Amina, though, there is nothing he can grasp on to. In so many ways she is the sort of girl you would want your daughter to be. Intelligent, good at sport, good relationships with both boys and girls. Mixes well. Polite. Well behaved. Yet her attendance has dropped to 31 per cent. So, it has been decided that she will have a couple of hours' home tuition, two or three days a week, plus some courses at the college.

She was shocked when they told her what they had decided. She didn't want to leave school. She promised faithfully that she was up to date with most of her work and that she would be able to catch up, really, really soon. They had had that conversation so many times.

Sometimes he thinks the school doesn't help itself because they give the kids so many second chances. They set a deadline, and the deadline isn't met. The following week they give them another chance, and another. Sometimes the kids perceive that whatever they do it won't be the end of the line. They're not self-sufficient, they're spoon fed. But if you don't spoon feed them, the exam results will go down and the kids will suffer.

It's the same with discipline, really. So much of what they do is about flexibility. Yet he wouldn't have it any other way. Sometimes, as with Tyrone and Wesley, they are left with no choices. But that's really the point at which they admit failure. Normally there is a plethora of strategies they go through before they get to that point. Discipline, to him, isn't something you can separate out from the rest of what a school does.

The other day he had a visit from a senior member of staff from one of the new city academies. He had been interested to hear that Seven Kings had taken on three former police officers to cover for absent staff and do some mentoring. But it soon became clear that the academy was thinking of something more than that. They wanted someone to take on the role that the year heads play at Seven Kings, to hand over behaviour management to non-teaching staff. He can't see how that would work.

He is head of year ten at the moment, and has taken the same group through years eight and nine. He will be their year head next year, too. He has taught about half of them. Lots of the others have drifted in to see him about one thing or another. It's important. Otherwise you only see them when they're naughty. If you have to tell a child off, you need first to know how they are in lessons. You need to know a bit about their background, what life is like for them at home.

He goes to social events sometimes at the school where his wife works, and people say to him, 'Seven Kings? You don't get difficult kids there, do you?' It isn't like that. They don't have many discipline problems because they build up good relationships with the pupils. They put in time.

Yesterday, for example, someone reported that a year-ten boy had been seen smoking outside the tube station. He denied it. There wasn't much they could do. If they catch him smoking at school, they will have to tell his parents. Technically, if he reoffends, they should give him a temporary exclusion. But what happens when he reoffends a third time?

Do they have some rigid scale of discipline that ends with a boy being permanently excluded for keeping on smoking? It would not make sense.

Maybe, when they catch this boy smoking again, he'll come in and say he's really concerned about his parents' reaction. Maybe Doug will do a deal with him. No letter home this time, but if he gets caught again there will be trouble. That way, the boy will owe him. With a lot of kids you play them like fish. You have to keep them thinking it might happen. If you write the rules up on the wall with a list of punishments for breaching each one, you leave yourself with no choice. Anyone can be a year head if they take that approach.

You keep lines of communication open. Last week they'd had two boys who had fallen out over something or other. Sides were taken, there were rumours of appointments made for fisticuffs outside school. His job was to keep talking to both sides. He spent hours taking statements, listening to wildly contradictory versions of who said what to whom. He hopes that once it's all over he will still have a good relationship with all of them, and that they will all feel the school gave them a fair hearing. He won't add up the hours he spent, but it was worth it.

Most of these little disputes never come to him, but he keeps an eye on them. He will be walking past a group of kids and he will see someone looking a bit upset. He won't do anything dramatic but he will say, 'Everyone all right?' And then, maybe later, he will stop one and ask if there was any real problem. There are 101 ways of dealing with every little incident.

Sometimes the problems come straight to him. The other day a boy appeared in his room to complain that a teacher had wrongly accused him of stealing. He had put a tube of paint into his bag in the art room, the teacher had seen him and jumped to the wrong conclusion. So why, Doug had wanted to know, had the boy put the paint in his bag? 'Well, sir,' he said, 'because otherwise I thought the teacher would see I had it and then she would think I was stealing it.' Doug was not born yesterday. The boy got the same level of ticking-off that he would have had if the teacher had sent him for stealing.

Yet sometimes, as with Tyrone and Wesley, things go too far and they are left with no way out. The governors' hearing was amicable enough, he thought. It was what you expect. Tyrone's parents defended their son, though they did not defend what he had done. He is sure the school did the right thing. Of course, the families still have a right to appeal to an independent panel if they wish. But that could take months, and the boys would miss a lot of school in the meantime. In his thirty years' teaching, he has only been to one independent appeal. It was upheld. He does not think it would be in this case, for either boy. He still wonders what might have happened if they had not discovered the problem and stopped it when they did.

This, he thinks, is what his job is about. In a sense he is a sort of conscience for the school. A small voice, in all the endless meetings about initiatives, networks and conferences, that says, 'What about the kids? Are we actually talking about what happens to children, in classrooms? Are we still doing those basic things? The things we do well?'

DEBBIE ADAMS

She is in a good mood, this Thursday morning. There is a week and a half to go until the end of term, then she will have a week at her parents' in Kent, two weeks in Egypt with a university friend, a week in Italy with her family. Some time mooching around London.

She is on her way to Alan Steer's office for her 'transition meeting', which means they must talk about how she has fared in her first year of teaching. She is relaxed, though, because she has already been told she has passed. Her post will be made permanent. He will do most of the talking. He is expansive, full of bonhomie. 'Well, you're going to pass. That's the first thing. How *are* you?'

'I'm good.'

'Well, I *know* that!... You're a powerful lot of women in that English department.'

'Yes – luckily we all get on really well.'

'I'll avoid any stereotypes. You've got a lovely lot of people. I imagine you sparking off ideas and stuff. When I came in, science and technology was all male. It's got much better balanced. Mind you, languages will be all female from September.'

She says maybe some boys respond better to male teachers. She thinks about Haroon, the troublesome speech-maker, and about the little boy with the big mouth. But mostly, she thinks, it's been brilliant. Last night they had a year-seven celebration evening and some of her pupils taught their own lesson. Everyone laughed at their impression of her in strict mode. 'It's been a steep learning curve,' she says. 'Especially teaching A level. And grammar. Every week I've learned something new about it.'

'You've missed a generation.'

'Yes. We weren't taught grammar at school.'

'I used to sit in fear in my English lessons at school. I was at a boys' school in the 1960s. If you made a mistake the teacher would smack you round the back of the head until you found it and put it right. And you read in the papers about the good old days'.'

'Did it work?'

'Well, it did to a degree... No. Actually, I don't think it did. Because we all just sat there, terrified... I know it's a trite comment, but you never stop learning.'

'I know,' she says. 'I'm teaching Blake at the moment and I'd never read him before. I'm loving it. Nicole Ranson and I are going on a little trip to the Tate to look at his pictures. He lived on my doorstep so I'm going to trace where he was born in Soho and where his parents were born. I'll do a little Blake trail.'

'Well,' he says, 'you're a cracking young teacher and the school's absolutely delighted to have you.' He pauses. 'It's impossible for me to have these conversations without sounding pompous.'

Everyone is feeling the heat, and Debbie's classroom is particularly hot so this afternoon she will move into Nicole Ranson's room for a 'team taught' lesson. The two of them will teach a year-eight lesson on Blake's poem, 'The Tyger'.

As Debbie writes her learning objectives on the board, Nicole practises exaggerated Tyger movements. 'Stop, Nicole.

I'm not going to be able to keep a straight face.' She straightens it and lets the class in.

'OK. Today we're going to be presenting dramatic readings of "The Tyger" to the class. Just turn to the back of your book and find the page. Rifat, we'll talk in a moment. Could you open your book and write down the learning objectives, please? And could you please write down three things that make a dramatic reading?'

They all write for a minute. Then hands go up.

'Persuasive?'

'Suspense. Pauses?'

'Good. Now Miss Ranson and I are going to present to you – boys, please. Miss Ranson and I are going to present to you two very different readings of "The Tyger".'

They are transformed, now, into rather unenthusiastic year-eights. They stumble over words, they mumble, they read with their heads so low over the page that the class cannot see their faces.

Debbie reaches the beginning of the last verse with some relief. 'Ti-… erm. Tigger, tigger…' she begins, faltering. Then the laughter wells out of her and she doubles up, speechless.

The class bursts into spontaneous applause. 'Excellent, Miss!'

'Miss, you were brilliant. You were taking the Michael!'

'So, what was wrong with it?'

They are a-quiver. 'Miss! According to my knowledge of English I would give that two out of ten! You weren't paying attention! You were playing with your hair!'

'There was no eye contact!'

'And Miss Ranson was leaning on the filing cabinet. She looked as if she was asleep!'

Now Nicole strikes one of her poses, and Debbie begins to read the poem again in her most dramatic voice. Nicole is in her element. She is showing her claws; she's doing a sort of Tyger-dance round the room. She waves her Dread Hand. She stamps her Dread Feet. Everyone laughs.

'But, Miss,' Rifat says, 'you were hiding your face behind the book again!'

'That was because I was trying not to look at Miss Ranson.' She's still trying to suppress the laughter that is building insistently in her.

Now they split into groups. They have fifteen minutes to prepare their own dramatic readings. The room fills with clapping, foot-stamping, banging. There are freeze-frames, but mostly there is noise. So much noise, indeed, that it drifts out of the open door and away down the corridor.

After a while a face appears at the door. It's the head of English, Paul Lindsay-Addy. There is silence. Year eight look at him. Nicole and Debbie look at him.

He smiles. 'We're doing "The Tyger" too. And we'd like to challenge you to a competition.' Everyone cheers. The heat in the room has been sanctioned. For once, just once, the lid can come off. And they are suddenly united against their unseen opponents down the corridor.

They sit, waiting. There is a pause. Then some indefinable noise from Paul's room.

Debbie turns to the class. 'We can do *so* much better than that!'

Then it comes through, loud and clear: '"*Ty*-ger! *Ty*-ger! Burning bright..."'

As the rendition comes to a close she motions to the class to gather round. They creep quietly to the door. And on the count of five they begin to roar out the poem from the linings of their lungs: 'IN the FOR-est OF the NIGHT!'

Another pause. They creep back to their seats. Then Paul's face reappears. He claims victory, of course, but they know better.

The bell goes and the two classes meet head-on in the corridor.

'"What Imm*or*tal *Ha*nd or Eye..."'

'"Could FRAME thy FEARful SY-me-TRI!"'

As she tidies the classroom Debbie can still hear the sound of duelling year-eights receding in the distance.

ANTHONY

He stumbles down the stairs, yawning. It is late July, now. Since his GCSEs ended there has been a slightly lopsided quality to his daily life. The old structures are gone. He can sleep, as he has today, till eleven. He can receive visitors, as he did last night, at 2 a.m., leaning out through his upstairs window to see who's there, creeping down the stairs in the dark to open the door. If they fail to keep their voices down, though, there will be muffled protests from his parents' room.

In the morning he can let his mind remain blank while he listens to the sounds from below. His little brother, getting his books together and putting on his Seven Kings uniform. His mum and dad going out to work. Then he can let oblivion wash over him once more. That life is over.

Yet without any fanfare or warning, new routines have begun to creep into his day. It is as if they leave him no choice. They just gather quietly around him, one after another. It will be quiet, now, for an hour or two. He pads through the empty house to the kitchen and rifles through the fridge, looking for a soft drink. Flops down in one of the big chairs, facing the window.

The phone rings, and he answers it. 'Yeah, cool. Yeah. No one. Safe, man. Cool. Awright.' He replaces the receiver and sits down again.

At around lunchtime someone will be along. The doorbell will ring and it will be the Asian boys from school, or Rich, or Kofi. Sometimes a whole crowd will call, sometimes just one or two. He'll pull his hoodie over his T-shirt and they'll amble out together, down the street and away. Maybe they'll go to the park, to hang out, to have a laugh, to sit while the little kids play nearby on the skate park or the tennis court. There will be a crowd, people know where to find them. They'll have a smoke, maybe later on he'll swig from a bottle of K. Other boys get done over by the heavies who hang around. If they're pussy, if they look scared, they'll have their phones and money taken. But Anthony knows everyone, so he's left alone. Everything's cool.

The exams were OK, he thinks. He didn't revise, or at least not much. He did an hour for his biology exam, looking at an old exam paper, and actually it helped. The things he revised came up. And on the way into his maths exam this boy told him how to calculate VAT by taking 10 per cent, then 5 per cent, then 2.5 per cent, and adding them all together. That came up, too, so he was lucky. It helped, having the maths tutor his mum got him. English was hard. He doesn't think that the exam came on the right day for him. He felt a bit confused and sweaty. Nerves, maybe.

He hasn't heard anything definite about any jobs, even

though his mum has been writing down the addresses from electricians' vans and posting letters with his CV in them. If he can find an employer the JTL training scheme will sponsor him. A couple of weeks ago there was a missed call on his phone, and he thought it might have been an employer. But if it was, they didn't phone again. Anyway, he can go to college, but he needs C grades in maths and English for the best course. Or he can definitely get a job at Sainsbury's because they said after he'd done his work experience that they'd be happy to have him back.

He's not bored. Something always seems to be going on. Late at night when he's drifting the streets with his friends, wondering whether or not to go home, things happen. One night, down in Ilford, they shouted and waved as a stretched Humvee drove past. And the driver came back and gave them a ride, driving about Ilford looking out of the windows and waving.

Often it is something small that happens, running into this mate or that. He knows so many people Sometimes he'll be mooching along and he will see some of those crackhead boys who hang around. Usually he will stop for a little talk, maybe chill with them for a while.

'Awright, Anthony, mate?'

'Yeah, good, thanks.'

He doesn't do all that stuff. Too heavy. He sticks to weed. But they're OK. A bit hyper, sometimes, but they don't go right over the top and start shouting or anything like that. They steal stuff, to keep their habits going. Most of them are older, about twenty, but there is one boy his age. That's how he knows the rest of them, because he was introduced.

Once or twice a late night has drifted gently into an early

morning without a sigh. Scooting home around midnight the other evening they came across a house all taped up with police tape. He had his mobile in the air, filming, as they climbed in through a window, ran up the stairs and quickly down again.

His mobile went. A text, from his mum. 'Where are you? When are you coming home?'

He texted back: 'In a little while.' Then he deleted 'little', because he did not want to be dishonest.

They were skittery and jumpy. The house was full of empty plant pots where the police had sliced off cannabis plants and scooped them away. The shaky film on his mobile shows room after room, full of black pots. And a sparse, grimy kitchen with a camp-bed in it.

Someone said, 'What's that noise?'

Then someone else said, 'Someone in the cellar, man.'

And they made a quick exit, tumbling after one another out of the house. But they came back the next day, when it was light, for another look. There was no one there. His mum had been awake most of the night, worrying about him, because he didn't come home for hours and hours.

They did him a favour at school, he thinks, sending him home for smoking weed. He didn't think so at the time. Then he'd thought they'd made him look like a prick. They'd pissed him off. He didn't even care what the school thought of him. It was his mum: he felt like he'd let her down. They think he's dumb because he's high. They think if he's high he'll get off his head and start showing off, like a little kid, but when he's high he's no different: he knows everything just the same, he feels just the same. It doesn't touch him.

But he was more careful after that, and he didn't mess up

his GCSEs in the way he might have done. He's glad he's left Seven Kings. But he's also glad he went there. His mum wants him to change his life now, stop smoking and get a job. And he supposes he will, sooner or later.

Maybe his life will change in other ways too. Soon he won't be in the park at night, or rambling the streets. One night recently he went to a new bar in Ilford, called the EastSide Bar, with his friends. They went to see what it was like, and it was OK. Actually, it was good. They play music really loud, his kind of music – not even garage, or hip-hop or anything, just rap. His mum looked at him when he was going out, and she came over all funny. He was only in a shirt and jeans, but he did look quite smart. 'Look at you,' she said. 'My little boy, all grown up.' And he blushed.

ANGELA CASSIDY

At 8.45 a.m. she is on the phone to the mother of a boy who wants to change school. 'Yes... I know. He was a bit upset yesterday. There are some difficult characters in that class... Yes. I said to talk to you over the summer. See how he feels. Maybe by September he won't want to move.'

She glances at the fish tank. It is green with algae and she can hardly see the fish. Not that she cares much. Flaming fish. Alan keeps saying he's going to move them but it hasn't happened yet. She's had a bit of an end-of-term tidy up. The pile of objects by the window has shrunk. A multicolured duster, a rounders bat, a couple of window poles and a leg brace. By the door a new, end-of-term pile is growing. Coats and bags, mainly.

She must turn her mind elsewhere. A note from Himself. He would like the attendance done today, please. 'No change there, then,' she mumbles cheerfully. He always wants the attendance done, and the last day of term is not to be taken as an opportunity for slacking off. She asks some of the learning-support assistants to do a ring-round.

She looks up. A girl is hanging around outside her office, looking anxious. She recognizes her at once. A nice enough girl, if a bit needy, tends to pop in quite often with one small health problem or another. 'Come in, Zara,' she says, smiling her professional smile. 'What can I do for you?'

Zara comes in and sinks down on to one of the padded chairs with just a hint of drama tinting the edge of genuine distress. It is clear that something is more than ordinarily wrong.

She sits for a minute, trying to build herself up to saying something. Angela waits. Then she blurts it out: 'Miss, I think I might be pregnant.'

'I see,' she says. 'And how late are you?'

'A week, Miss.'

A small ripple of relief. It's probably a false alarm. When they come in saying they're three months gone there's real cause for concern. The routine is well worked out. Angela goes through it about three times a year, on average. The last day of term tends to bring these problems bubbling to the surface, and although it doesn't mean she must do anything differently it does mean she won't be here for Zara next week, or the week after.

'You're in year ten, aren't you, Zara?'

'Yes, Miss.'

'So, you're fifteen now?'

'Yes, Miss.'

'Well, the first thing to do is get a pregnancy test. Then you'll know for sure. It will very likely be negative. But if it's positive, you need to think what you will do next. Have you told anyone else, Zara?'

'Only my boyfriend. And my best friend...'

'How old is your boyfriend?'

'He's seventeen.'

'Well, really, Zara, I think it would be best if you could talk to someone in your family. Can you tell your mum?'

'No!' She looks really scared now. 'She'd go mad. I don't know what she'd do. She'd kill me...'

Angela looks at her. The phrase is a well-worn one, and usually not to be taken literally. Probably the girl is being over-dramatic. But it does happen. She cannot discount the possibility that the family might take drastic action. Neither can she refer her to a clinic for an abortion. If it was one of her kids, she would be horrified if another adult did that without telling her, but she can't make Zara tell her parents. Her view is always that these things should be dealt with in the family, where possible. 'Is there anyone else? An aunt, or a cousin, even?'

Zara is silent for a few minutes. 'Maybe I could talk to my cousin. She's twenty-five. She'd be OK about it.'

'I think that would be a good idea.' If it was her daughter, she thinks, she would be happy if she spoke to her aunt or one of her cousins. 'Would you like me to ring her and get her to come into school?'

'No, it's OK. She only lives round the corner. I often stop in there on my way home.'

'Good. But there is one other thing, Zara. You're only fifteen. You do realize your boyfriend is committing a crime?'

'Well, yes, but...' She peters out.

'I'm afraid I'll have to make a referral to Social Services. They probably won't do anything about it at this stage. But I have to do it because you're under age.'

'OK, Miss.' Despite everything, the fact of having had a conversation with an adult seems to have perked her up. She's still very tense, but she looks more certain. 'I'll get my cousin to lend me some money so I can do the test. Maybe it'll be OK. I've been late before.'

Angela guesses it will be OK. But she cannot make assumptions. One fact is clear: a crime has been committed. Although Zara says she has a boyfriend, Angela cannot take that for granted. She does not know whether that crime has been committed by a seventeen-year-old boy or by a member of her family.

Zara leaves, looking a little happier. Angela's shoulders sag with the realization that she has yet another child-protection form to fill in. She knows full well that Social Services will take no action. So much of this job is back-covering.

She looks down. One of the learning-support assistants has slipped a list of non-attenders on to her desk. 'Not well'... OK. 'Spoke to Dad. Late.' She looks at it for a minute, then crosses out 'Late' and writes 'Truanting'. Let's call a spade a spade, she says to herself.

One particular boy, Rafiq, is causing concern. His father says he left for school but he had been worried because he had a 'meeting' with one of his teachers this morning. That, she reflects, is code for a bollocking. So he probably sloped off instead of coming in. He wasn't at registration. And now they can't track down the class he's in because it's been moved from its normal room so that the builders can prepare for work over the summer. One of the support assistants goes out, again, to look for the class. Angela emails his teacher with little hope of a response.

She pulls the child-protection form from a pile of papers. Stares at it. 'I don't know the answers to half these questions. "Sisters or brothers?" Not sure. "Family stability?" What can I say?'

She doesn't spend enough time on attendance, she thinks, as she stares at the form. Really, the school needs someone to spend three days a week on it. A lot of it would be wasted time, of course. With the really hard cases, like Amina Simpson, for instance, it makes little difference. But if you don't do it you don't have the evidence to put before the magistrates, and Education Welfare want to know why. Then they'll send the file back for you to look at again. Show where you offered a part-time timetable. Show where you had the parents in. But it's right in a way. When you've been doing this for a long time, you can pick out the kids you might as well not bother with. But that wouldn't be the right way to do things. Because you can't know that it won't work.

That's why she has to leave. This job needs someone new, without the carapace of cynicism that has hardened around her over the years. She will be here in September, though. She's promised Alan she'll stay on for another couple of years. They need to split the job into several different ones. Someone to concentrate on first aid, someone for the physically disabled kids. Yesterday she spent a whole hour dealing with a fainting girl. Damn, she thinks. She needs to delegate more. She hasn't taught people to think for themselves.

The learning-support assistant comes back in. Rafiq's dad has been phoned again, and has reported that Rafiq is found.

He had a 'panic attack' on the way to school, so he's bringing him in now to see his teacher.

'Nice of him to let us know,' she says. 'Well, I don't want to see them. I'm not interested. I haven't got the time.'

It's break already, and the usual little group of kids has arrived, scattering bags and books as they delve for chocolate bars and drinks. Molly wanders in, accompanied by one of the support assistants. Angela has often worried about Molly, whether she should be here with her level of learning difficulties. Her parents have read all the research, and are determined that she should be in a mainstream school. Yet she doesn't seem happy. She doesn't fit. She hangs around with the physically disabled group, but she can't relate. The other day she was watching Samira, who has restricted height, bustling around the place. And she turned to her and said, 'You're just like a little dog. Did you know that?' Samira was upset. There were tears. She had to try to explain to Samira that Molly didn't understand, but she didn't want to know. She has enough problems of her own.

Poor Samira. She's another who has has been causing concern. She's a bright girl, outgoing, but she's tiny, physically frail and has a raft of health problems. She's also a teenager, and feels it's time she had a boyfriend. Her mum came in the other day to say she had discovered Samira visiting Internet dating sites. In itself, that might not have been too much of a problem but Samira had been giving out her phone number. 'I'm pretty, petite and funny. If you want to meet me ring 07939...' They'd had to explain that it wasn't a good idea. They tried to encourage her to join a youth club for physically disabled teenagers, where she might meet more people. But it's so hard to see what she'll do with her life. She's vulnerable even in the school corridor. How will she ever get on a tube train? And now one of the support assistants has reported that some year sevens have been teasing her in the corridor. That needs to be dealt with. Quickly. Their year head will track them down and talk seriously to them.

Mishti comes in silently. Angela hardly has to look up to know that it's her, with her distinctive, drifting walk. She has left already – she took her A levels last month. It will be strange not seeing her around next term. She has been a constant presence in the medical centre for the past seven years. They tried to persuade her to go out and eat in the canteen, or later in the sixth-form block, but they never succeeded. She just felt happier here. So she has become a friend to all of them, slipping from room to room, her quiet smile never changing. She has a slight limp, and a device to help her overcome a speech problem.

She sits down for a chat. Then she says, 'I've got a surprise for you.' She gets up and goes out, then comes back with a huge piece of paper, carefully bent double. She opens it out. It's a collage with photographs of everyone connected to the medical centre. Angela is there, and all the other staff. Shivanie and Jas. Dipti. Perin. Dozens of others. Everyone is gathering round now, pointing out different things. Angela gives Mishti a hug. Mishti starts to cry, wiping big tears from her cheek with a hand made clumsy by emotion. Angela blinks hard, and looks down at the child-protection form, which is still on her desk.

'What does the family want to change? I don't bloody know. Stupid form... Are you on that bus today, Mishti? If you are, you'd better get going.'

AUGUST

KESSIE

By mid-August it is as if she were waking from a long, sleepy time. Those first days after the exams finished seem long ago. It felt as though, having wound up her every fibre to its utmost, she had relaxed so far she could barely move. Staggering late from her bed in the mornings, snoozing through those grey, muggy early-July afternoons. Staring lazily at the big television, letting the American sitcoms wash over her in waves. Mooching in the shops with Grace, just about stirring herself to go to church.

Then the weeks in Brooklyn, with her uncle, her sister and her cousins. A whirl of sightseeing, shopping and family gatherings. But she missed her dad and her little brothers. In the end, she was glad to board the plane home, to cross London from Heathrow in the early morning, bleary-eyed, even though she had a knot in her stomach.

Jetlagged and light-limbed, she logged on to the computer

in the living room and waited for the green and white UCAS page to load on the screen. She tapped in her application number and password, then experienced a wave of relief as the confirmation flashed up before her. Aston University. Pharmacy. Accepted.

Grace had had bad news, though. The UCAS site had warned her she had not been accepted by Aston. They boarded the bus to Seven Kings for the last time in that strange state of limbo, knowing they would not be starting the next phase of their lives together but not understanding why.

Somehow she managed to slip past the room where Miss Jones and Mr Hayes were dealing with queues of people, all clutching their A4 sheets of results. It wasn't difficult. Outside the front of the school little knots of people were forming and re-forming; some former pupil who left at sixteen was roaring back and forth in a big convertible car. Kessie barely spoke to anyone before she was back outside the school gates, the full picture sinking into her head. Three Bs. There had been no miracle.

And yet she has her place at Aston, despite being a grade away from her offer. One day she will be a pharmacist. It has taken her till now, nearly a week later, to begin to feel she has done something of which she can be proud. She has worked so hard, and she has denied herself so many things. She did her best, with the help of God. She worked hard, she prayed, then went ahead and did what she could do. What more could she have asked of herself than that?

It will be strange going away, especially without Grace, yet in some ways she's ready. She has only realized it in these last weeks, but it has been happening to her, seeping into her, like a dye, for a long time. Once she was part of her family. Then, gradually, she grew apart and became this new, individual person. Kessie on her own, focusing on her work. Kessie getting the bus to school. Kessie going to church in the evenings with Grace. Her dad, her sister, her brothers were still gathered around her and she was part of them still, yet she was changing.

In her head she has completed that act of separation now; soon she will become physically separate too. But when she goes she will carry with her the gifts her family have given her, most of all the gift of themselves. They will always be with her; she will not be apart from them in her head. She will take her religion, and once she has located the Elim Pentecostal Church, she will be among friends. She will take the unshakeable belief, garnered in so many conversations with her teachers, that she has something special to contribute to the world. She will take her astonishing, dogged, constant, unflagging, indefatigable, self-possessed capacity for perseverance. And with all those weapons in her armoury, she will begin to build something new, something fresh. She will build a world that is uniquely hers.

GCSE DAY

Jemma makes slow, stately progress through the hall towards the tables where the results envelopes are stacked in alphabetical groups. Now she must hug Jacob, and now she must hug Naomi. Their embraces are solemn, in tribute to the weight of the occasion.

At last she reaches her destination and is handed the envelope containing her GCSE results. As she pulls out the white

A4 sheet and unfolds it, she seems unsure of how to arrange her face. She remains for several moments standing, staring at the list of capital letters with an expressionless gaze. She cannot react. It is a time neither for celebratory screaming nor for tears of wrath or disappointment. On the list are nine Bs, three As and an A star. Yet the As are not in the right subjects.

Slowly she takes control of the situation. 'What do I have to do now? They said I needed As in my sciences to do them in the sixth form.' She is saying this as she walks slowly back through the crowds, accepting the comfort of friendly arms slung around her shoulders as she goes.

By the time she reaches the door she's herself again. 'I need to talk to Miss Jones.' Her energy is coming back. She flits to and fro, waiting for her opportunity, casting glances through the door of the nearby classroom where the head of the sixth form is sorting out problems such as hers.

Seated now, she is soon confident again. 'I did get an A in my science coursework, and I had an A in the mocks and a predicted A in my GCSE. *And* my science teacher recommended I took two sciences...' She is selling herself hard.

'Why did you only get Bs?'

'I found the exams really difficult... I don't know, actually. I'm not sure.'

Miss Jones is reassuring. 'Well, I know how clever you are and I know how good you are at maths. I'll have to check, but I'm sure we'll be agreeable. I think we'll go with it, Jemma.'

She relaxes, and the big smile spreads across her face. Miss Jones laughs and points a finger at her. 'You'd better not let me down. You'll have to jump in running.' The expression makes Jemma laugh. 'You know what I mean. You'll have to work really, really hard. And if you're finding things difficult, you'll have to get help. We'll give you a couple of weeks to change your mind.'

As she leaves, Jemma regains her Tiggerish bounce. Nobody really doubts she can cope with science A levels, so long as she puts in the work.

Jemma's results have been one of the more ordinary bits of an extraordinary day. It is weeks since the BBC phoned to ask if they could spend today at the school, delivering reports for the main lunchtime and evening television news. Students were lined up for interview. There had been confident predictions, after all, that the results would be the best the school had ever had.

It was not until yesterday, though, that the full extent of the triumph became clear. Last year, 85 per cent of the school's candidates attained five good GCSEs. Several months ago, there had been whispered predictions of a possible 90 per cent this year. But the final tally, 93.5 per cent, surpassed all expectations.

As he prepares for yet another spot in front of the cameras, Alan Steer grants himself a moment of self-congratulation. Fifteen years ago 29 per cent of the pupils at Seven Kings had reached this benchmark, so the school has gone from just below the national average, which was then around 30 per cent, to almost forty percentage points above it.

What have they done? If Seven Kings is indisputably a good school – and it is – what has it done to get from there to here? Has he fed some magic potion to the staff and pupils to bring them to this point? He has not. Today's triumph is like a stalagmite, grown imperceptibly over the years through the accretion of countless tiny acts. As he says so often, the key is not knowing what you should do, it is doing what you know. Always.

In pursuit of this goal the Seven Kings pupils have been pushed, chased, prodded, cheered on and, if necessary, physically heaved over the finishing line. They have been interviewed regularly about their progress. They have been told not just what mark their work is worth, but why. They have been told, if their mark is a C, what they must do to make the next mark a B, and then an A. They have never been allowed to drift. They have been harried.

There have been small structural shifts. There is the boys' information technology GNVQ – the vocational exam equivalent to no fewer than four GCSEs. This year, through this one strategy, twenty or so boys who were at risk of not crossing the magic 'five A–C' line added four such grades to their tally. Lindsay and Amina were moved on to Redbridge College at fifteen rather than being allowed to spend their last year of compulsory education languishing, to the despair of their teachers.

And yet while the magic 'five A–C' barrier is important it is not their only goal. Certain things remain unacceptable. They will not push vocational courses to the detriment of their academic base. In a discussion paper Alan wrote last Christmas he said this: 'I have little commitment to specific vocational courses, other than their potential to motivate and provide success where both were lacking before. We will introduce construction. Beauty is too naff to contemplate, but fashion textiles would be good.' Nail Art will remain confined to the local college. He can think of schools, whose GCSE tally comes in even higher than Seven Kings', where huge numbers of pupils get construction, or beauty, but not English or maths.

Seven Kings knows its clientele. The parents in this area, so many of them second-generation immigrants from India or

Pakistan with high academic aspirations for their children, would not welcome the prospect of a wholesale move to fashion or manufacturing. But the school does not just play to its market. In any case, it has no real need to do so. Its pupils are allocated on a catchment-area basis, and there are so many applications it could fill their places several times over. It has a character of its own, which fits the market well but is also the product of Alan Steer's own strong opinions – the naffness of beauty courses is a key illustration.

There are certain basic touchstones on which everything rests. He insists on respect and discipline. The bases are always covered. There is never an opportunity for drift. Every day, non-attenders must be chased. Every day, orders must be given for shirts to be tucked in, beards shaved, unsuitable earrings pocketed. On the last day of term, right up until the moment the last bell goes, pupils must continue to be taught. These small acts so often pre-empt the necessity for higher-level remedial action.

When children walk from the litter-strewn, petrol-clogged street past the school's blue-and-yellow painted sign, they must see immediately what sort of world they are entering. That is why the school grounds are always immaculate, and why the flower-beds are carefully laid out.

These things may not sound vital to the well-being of a school. Indeed, there is barely one that could be considered, alone, an essential ingredient in the mix. But together, constantly reinforced, they are unshakeable. The business of running a good school, like that of running any successful organization, is not simple. It takes drive, leadership, hard work, commitment. They filter down.

He is unsure, though, whether he could walk into a failing

inner-city school and make these methods work. This was never a struggling school. It was, it now seems, a school that was not achieving its full potential in terms of exam performance. But it was always a nice, caring school. There is confidence here now, born of years of incremental progress towards the point at which the school stands today. It is not clear to Alan Steer whether it would be possible to reach this point by the same means from a different, less comfortable starting-line. In some schools, it might be possible to do all the same things and yet, instead of creating this impression of a great liner steaming majestically forward, merely to find oneself paddling furiously to stay afloat. This is one of several inbuilt advantages the school now has.

Another such advantage, without a doubt, is the school's pupils and their parents.

For many years the number of pupils who are entitled to free school meals has been taken as a fair measure of poverty, and therefore as a predictor of educational failure. Not so many years ago, eminent academics devised a method of calculating a school's 'value added' by comparing its free school meals claims with its exam results. Yet in this area, and others like it, wealth or the lack of it is a poor indicator of success or failure. Ruhy, a twelve-year-old refugee from Iran who lives in a rented flat with a mother who does not work. Yet one of her cousins has recently completed a PhD. Her mother expected to graduate until she was driven out of her university by religious bigotry. Shivanie and her older sister Sheena, who is dancing round the school hall now with a huge smile and a list of twelve As and A stars, are the daughters of a post-office worker, yet they have an uncle who is a professor. It was circumstance, not lack of inclination, that prevented their parents fulfilling their potential. As a result, their determination that their children should fulfil theirs is daily renewed.

There are, of course, pupils whose parents have already succeeded in education and business. A school with a good reputation, like this one, attracts them. Perin would almost certainly have gone to the local grammar school if it had had a lift. His younger sister goes to an independent school. Yet his parents, both pharmacists, have no regrets about their decision to send Perin here.

Indeed, the expression of quiet joy and gratitude on Perin's mother's face last week, along with those of other parents watching their offspring collecting A level results, spoke volumes. Nobody at Seven Kings had ever doubted that Perin could do it. Like so many others, he had arrived that morning seeming nervous, rather than with his usual air of calm confidence. He received the slip bearing the news that he had four A grades at A level with equanimity. It was, after all, only what he deserved. Afterwards he stayed around for a while chatting on the grass in front of the school with his friends Vijay and Ranjit, who also got straight A's. Had the news been less good, they would have received it with mild but accepting disappointment. Perin is a young man who knows his worth, and that there are few obstacles in his path which hard work and determination will not shift.

It is not only successful families, like Perin's, or aspiring families, like Shivanie's, who value education in this area. In so many other households, even those with no history of higher education, there is a strongly held belief that study is the way to a better life. Why else do the heads of the Seven Kings sixth form spend so much time trying to persuade pupils that there are other careers as worthwhile as medicine, the law or banking? If there is a new middle class emerging in Britain today, a class of people not born into affluence or privilege but who will be among the eminent doctors, lawyers and politicians of the future, it is to be found here, in areas like Seven Kings, and further into the city, in Newham and the like.

This school has more tangible, workaday advantages too. It has, by dint of its success, a great deal of money to spend. No one cares to say this in anything above a whisper, but sometimes they scratch their heads, wondering how best to spend it all. Secondary schools are a world away now from those down-at-heel days in the early 1990s when walls were scuffed and there was never enough money for textbooks. This one, in particular, gives the visitor the impression of walking into the premises of a successful business. The slate-and-stone water feature, the African sculptures, the legacy of a school art project, the neat reception area with its wobbly glass bricks and its video screens displaying recent school triumphs, all spell quiet confidence. There are electronic whiteboards in the classrooms, laptops for all the staff.

And the staff. What to say about the staff? While schools across London struggle to put faces in front of classes, casting around for supply teachers who often prove unsuitable, this school has a staff to kill for. There is some turnover, of course, but as usual this year it will be fully staffed at the start of September. There is still a small group – Doug Harrison, Colin Gratrix, Duncan Paterson and one or two others – who have been here since the school came into being thirty years ago. There are far more who, having arrived here since then, have stayed and built careers. To say that everyone is eternally happy in every moment of their working days would be an exaggeration, of course. But by and large they are committed to their work and, above all, positive in their attitude.

This, above everything else, is the essential strength of Seven Kings High School. Jemma, asking herself what is the point, seeing they are all here together between the hours of eight thirty and three thirty, of *not* getting on? The truth is that the staff like the pupils. And the pupils – whisper it – giving or taking a little, making the odd adjustment here for a clash of personality or a realignment there for an inevitable dressing down, quite like their teachers, too.

THE NEXT GENERATION

The next Seven Kings generation will be different from its fore-bears. While its parents and grandparents travelled the globe to find success and prosperity, its expeditions will perhaps keep it closer to home, here in London. Yet this generation has something it holds in common with its parents and grand-parents that will shape its future path more than anything else. It is big, and hard to grasp, but it must play a key part in deter-mining which of them will succeed and which will fail. It is this sense of the inevitability of progress, the belief in each generation of a family that the next generation will be more successful, more prosperous than the last. This next generation will go on an expedition, but it will be social rather than geographical. It will become middle class, and in doing so it will bring a new diversity to society. The success of these young people will change the world in which all of us will live.

This sense that they seem to have, of constant movement, onwards and upwards, is something that the British working class – if such a thing still exists – is widely believed to have found and lost again. Growing prosperity in the years after the Second World War, coupled with the advent of a free education system for all children up to the age of fifteen, brought major social change. A recent analysis of the experiences of three generations of Britons by London University's Institute of Education found that three-quarters of children born in 1946 had fathers in manual occupations, compared with less than half of those born in 1958 or in 1970. Between the 1950s and the 1990s, the proportion of young people who were expected to go to university at some stage in their lives rose from six per cent to more than 50 per cent. That change was not universal, of course, and some families were left behind. Success tended to be coupled with strong family support, high parental aspirations and a belief in education as a key to progress.

Yet the optimism that pervaded British society in the three decades after the Second World War did not last. Spells of high unemployment during the 1970s and 1980s, accompanied by the collapse of traditional apprenticeships, left generations of working-class youngsters with inadequate skills and a profound lack of self-confidence. Across the country, dispatches from the heartlands of the white working class have told a similar, depressing story. Some of those heartlands are not very far from Seven Kings and grew out of the 1950s and 1960s slum-clearance programmes, developments into which people moved with hope but without any great sense of achievement. Others were communities like the white working-class areas that still exist in London's Docklands and elsewhere, which have sunk into a sense of hopelessness with the decline of their traditional industries.

We do not hear much, these days, about upward social

mobility. Indeed, the evidence suggests there is not a lot of it about. The researchers from London's Institute of Education who studied three generations of children pointed to an increasingly polarized society. The benefits of an expanding higher-education system have gone largely to those who already come from privileged backgrounds, they say. Rising levels of prosperity have brought benefits mainly to those already at least part-way up the social ladder. Certain groups of young people have tended to be left behind – youngsters from Bangladeshi families, boys from Afro-Caribbean backgrounds, white boys too.

Here, on the outskirts of the capital, that old feeling of progress and optimism is thriving, not so much among the area's dwindling white population as among its burgeoning population of second- and third-generation immigrants. If the old British working class has lost its *raison d'etre*, its sense of direction, these families have found it. Here all is pushing, thrusting, full of energy. Seven Kings does not stand and stare, it does not have moments left in the day for vagueness or uncertainty. In the main, our seven young people know where they are going and what they will have to do to get there. There is a genuine belief, in this small but important stratum of society, that the next generation will have advantages the last one did not.

Yet there is little sense of grievance or of thwarted ambition at Seven Kings. And national statistics point to much greater levels of success than might popularly be assumed. Young people from ethnic-minority backgrounds account for 16 per cent of undergraduates in English universities while they make up just 8 per cent of the population as a whole. They account for 35 per cent of places in medicine and dentistry, 38 per cent in computer science and 31 per cent in law. That success story starts in homes like Perin's and Shivanie's.

So how will it look, this kingdom of the future, where Jemma and Perin, Shivanie and Kessie will reign, and where today's adults will grow old? How will they shape it in their image? Will they set it aloud with the sound of rap music, limousines and bling? Much of what the press has to say about today's teenagers points to a gloomy prognosis for the world they will lead and manage in the future. They are, according to the most reliable evidence available, more prone to anti-social behaviour, more likely to drink excessively and take drugs, to get into debt in pursuit of their consumerist dreams, and less likely to stay married than their forebears. On the basis of less reliable but equally oft-repeated evidence we might also surmise that they are also more likely to be violent, illiterate, uncultured and generally ill-educated.

To be brutally fair, some of this depressing stuff might apply, some of the time, to some of our seven youngsters. But none applies to any of them all the time. And some applies to none of them. If there are places in Britain where this popular but downbeat assessment of the world holds true, they lack some of the qualities to which Seven Kings can lay claim.

Ilford was always an optimistic, energetic place. It was a place, one among many on the outskirts of our major cities, for which people worked, to which they aspired. Its housing was generously proportioned and usually owner-occupied. There was nothing smart or leafy about it. Its red-brick terraces and semis, built in the early years of the twentieth century, sprouted pebbledash fronts and concrete forecourts. Yet it had a sense of purpose, an energy, which said that its people were on the move.

The houses left vacant by families who have moved on have been filled mainly be families with their ethnic origins in India or Pakistan. Four out of five pupils at Seven Kings High School have their roots in one of those two countries; many of the rest come from a huge range of different places around the globe. White children with parents and grandparents who were born in Britain are a small minority.

The new families have brought with them the aspiration that exists here and in similar places around the country. People who grow up here are not, for the most part, financially wealthy but they grow up with a sense that their families have travelled far and will go further. There is a kind of momentum, an optimism in their lives. They often have achievement in their histories.

Seven Kings, then, can tell us something about the future of Britain, of how our urban professional class will change and grow. After all, it will not be the left-behind who shape the world. Nor will change be driven by the already-arrived, whose values are well represented among the existing influential, well-educated classes. If the middle class is to change, it will be young people from places like Seven Kings who will make and shape that change.

The faces of Britain in the future, or at least those of the professionals in surgeries, solicitors' offices and schools, will be different. This will be the first way in which our 'kings' will change the world – simply by being in it, in its educational élite, among its driving forces and guiding lights. They will make it, by their presence, more diverse.

Does it matter? Yes. It matters because if the Seven Kings experience tells us one thing about diversity it is that with proximity comes understanding or, at the very least, acceptance. These young people have grown up in a diverse world and live comfortably with the different beliefs and lifestyles of their peers. For most of them race, gender and even disability are not big political issues. They are just part of who they are.

It matters too, because theirs will be a world far removed from the image of today's young that exists in the popular imagination. Theirs will be a world in which alcohol will play only a minor part; crime, anti-social behaviour and under-achievement none at all.

Theirs will be a world in which hard work will reap rewards. These people do not take their success for granted. They expect it, but they also know they must apply themselves to achieve it. Their acceptance of hard work will shape many other aspects of their lives. They know they will have no time to waste.

There will be little time, for instance, for political passions. If these youngsters are to change the world, they will do so being themselves more than by embarking on crusades. Of the seven, none has any strong interest in party politics and only one or two speak of wanting to right wrongs or make a difference. Sometimes they speak of helping others, of charity, but mostly they are too busy working, focusing on their future, for all that stuff. Theirs will be a post-Thatcherite world in which purpose and drive are focused not on ridding society of evils but on preserving and developing what is good.

For some, the desire to achieve will be entrepreneurial. Perin, for instance, knows his dad was trading shares in his twenties while his contemporaries were in the pub. Kessie, too, says she can see herself running her own small business. Many of these young people are perfectly poised to inherit a world in which individual effort, drive and flair are prized.

Theirs will not be a rebellious world, then, or a world full of conflict. Yes, some will test the boundaries set by their parents' generation. But Alan Steer says the pupils in his school are, by and large, a conservative bunch. They have no great desire to build anew what their forebears have built already. Even Jemma, with her questing, questioning personality, talks about re-creating the life she has here when she goes somewhere else.

But perhaps even more surprising is the conservatism these young people display not in their public, career-driven lives but in their personal lives. Statistics tell us that more than a third will be divorced at some time in their lives, that their children may grow up in homes where the old parents-and-kids family model has given way to something more complex. And yet for these young people, family – the family they have now and the family they hope to have in the future – is central to their lives. If they work hard, they do so to please their parents. Something about the chemistry in their homes makes them want the approval of their families just a little bit more than their less successful contemporaries, whose desire for parental approval is weighed with a competing desire for the approval of their peers. All expect to have careers, but their motivation for wanting to have them will be focused, at least in part, on families. They dream, for the most part, not of glamorous urban loft living but of solid homes with spouses and children.

Religion brings a sense of warmth and belonging that has much to do with this family orientation. Jemma talks of her church community as an extended family. It helps her to know who she is and where she belongs, and it connects her deeply and strongly to others with whom she can share it. When she talks about her faith she also talks about the people she connects with it. When Kessie talks about what church means to her, she talks about relaxing with her closest friends, the people with whom she shares a real sense of trust and understanding. Shivanie and Perin talk about religion perhaps as something more personal, more contemplative. Perin makes time to pray during his day. Shivanie gets bored sometimes during devotional singing, but feels her religion is something she carries with her. It roots her and gives her strength.

There is compassion, too, in the lives of these pupils, which seems to encompass them all, religious or non-religious. Tyrone's dad talked about wanting to have a warmer, less authoritarian relationship with his son than he had had with his own parents. Anthony acquired the sensitivity to know when his mother needed him to pour her a drink. These boys have grown up expecting warmth, fun and humour to be a part of their lives. Theirs will not be a strict, unbending world, but it will be one in which certain boundaries are not crossed, where traditional family and religious values – old-fashioned values, if you like – will play a major part. And yet they will shape their surroundings and bend them to an image that is all their own.

The picture that emerges, then, is of a very different urban class from the one that exists now in our big cities. It will bear little resemblance to that earlier, Ken Barlow generation of working-class youngsters who benefited from a university education and used it to escape the lives their parents led. Swept on by the social change and prosperity of the 1960s, many became more liberal, more political, less religious. They rejected their parents' values. But at the moment, these young people show little sign of that. Who knows? Maybe they will change their outlook when they go to university. But the signs are that when they go they will not go far. Lacking the grants that fuelled students' independence in the past, they will cling to their parental homes for longer, and thus to their parents' values. This new generation will be the one that begins to shift the British middle class from the liberal, left-leaning terrain it has occupied for so long. It will be the generation of the new traditionalists.

ANTHONY

Today is Anthony's sixteenth birthday. He does not want to hear bad news, but on the other hand it hardly matters any more what his results are. In the past week his whole life has changed.

It started with a phone call, a few days before he was due to go to Cornwall on holiday with his mum and dad and his little brother John. His mum had been writing down details from electricians' vans for months. Finally, it seemed, her efforts had paid off.

The lady on the phone wanted to know if Anthony would be able to come for an interview for an electrical apprenticeship. He wasn't sure. 'I'm going on holiday on Saturday.'

'Well, it's Wednesday now. Could you come on Thursday or Friday?'

'I dunno. The thing is, I've got to do my packing.'

This was true. He also had to get his hair cut, meet some mates, see a girl. In his schedule, there wasn't time for an interview. But the lady was insistent. In the end he promised to phone her back. The rest of the day took over and he forgot.

That night his mum came home from work to find a message on the answerphone. 'Anthony, you did promise to phone back about the job interview. Do you want this job or not?'

Before he was out of bed the next morning his mum had made the appointment for Friday, the day before they were to go away. It seemed to go OK, and they gave him a form to fill in and send back, which he did.

Then, when he came back from holiday, his mum checked again. This time they said there was a job for him, and they were sending a letter about the start date. Suddenly there it was, and they wanted him to start straight away. In August. He was still on his holidays, he felt. He had people to catch up with. He had been away, after all.

The firm were getting impatient. He phoned the lady back again, and they had quite a good conversation about it. In the end they were happy for him to start work at the end of August. So that is what he'll do.

From next week he will be an electrical apprentice, working towards something called a Joint Industry Board qualification in electrics, which will take four years. He will work forty-eight hours a week, including two hours' travel each day, and a day each week at college. He will earn £150 a week. If he qualifies he will be able to work anywhere in the world, and earn good money. Probably, he thinks, he will get through it. It will be all right.

So, as he slopes into the school hall with his friends around him, he's feeling mellow. The envelope being pressed into his hand cannot bite or sting him. He pulls out the page, and a warm glow spreads through him as he reads down the list. Four Bs, three Cs and an E - in drama. And he has his four GNVQ grades to add to that, too. Eleven good GCSEs. He tucks the envelope into his pocket and walks back down the school drive for the last time. Mum will be pleased, he thinks.

SEPTEMBER

TYRONE

As the new Autumn term begins Tyrone is still in limbo, uncertain of his future. Then everything seems to happen at once. He is invited to Beal High School, a few miles from his home, and arrives at 8 a.m. with his mum and dad and his best, most co-operative demeanour. There is an interview. A warning that he will be there on approval: he can be summarily dismissed if he goes astray. Then a two-hour dash to the shops for a uniform, and back for lessons at eleven. Suddenly he is transformed into a fully fledged Beal pupil, with a brand new brown blazer to prove it. Seven Kings is in his past.

A couple of weeks later he is standing outside the classroom in the early autumn sunshine with a little group of boys around him. He should be inside but he's loitering, spinning out the last moments of his lunch hour. Under his new blazer his shirt hangs loose. The conversation is casual, exploratory. It has been a time of uncertainty. He is still in the process of rooting himself in this strange new environment. 'Tyrone! Inside! Now!' The teacher's tone is sharp and he must respond.

'Miss,' he says, 'I didn't know. There's so many bells here...' She gives him a look, and he goes indoors.

This afternoon is a catering lesson. He will make quiche. There are many different experiences in this new place and this will just be one. Some pupils here learn textiles, or child development. It's a different world from the one he has left.

In the corridor he is slowly regaining his old self, if a bounceless, subdued version of it. Every minute or so a newly familiar face will appear in the crowd as he travels through, and there will be a grin, a raised hand, a cheerful word. But without Jerome or Calvin bobbing along next to him he is somehow marooned, rudderless. He's slowly finding a new direction but he must begin to rebuild, now, everything that he has lost.

In the catering room he pulls on a yellow apron, then seeks out a carrier-bag of ingredients he left here earlier. Peppers, bacon, cheese. He has never eaten anything like the thing he'll make today, and neither does he want to. Yet he wants to get it right. His teacher, Miss Young, has shown them how. But he cannot remember the detail.

'Miss,' he begins, 'what am I meant to do now?'

'Pastry first, please,' she says. 'Five minutes to make the pastry, two minutes to line the tin.'

The lesson is like a race: fifty minutes to make the quiche and bake it. Soon the girls' table on the other side of the room is forging ahead. Miss Young is giving them a commentary: 'The boys are catching up... well done! First one in the oven!' Soon she is next to Tyrone, grating cheese while he chops peppers.

'Good boy,' she's saying. 'Well done. Good, good, good!'

His quiche is one of the last to go into the oven but when it emerges, glossily brown, he beams with a sort of muddled pride. 'It looks like a pizza,' he says. 'I could almost eat it.'

By now the bell has gone and the school has emptied. He casts his eye around for his one real friend here, a boy in the year below him he knew before, but he's gone already. Soon, he thinks, he will have other friends. They won't be like his old friends, though. He still misses them. He still sees Jerome every day.

But he thinks he'll be all right here, he'll find a way to be. He'll find a little crew, like he had before. Maybe it won't be a hard-working crew, or even a well-behaved crew, but it will be his little crew. He will be able to do his thing. He will be popular, and stay on the tracks. Inside, he still feels like a good boy.

POSTSCRIPT

If this book is about anything it is about journeys. It is about the road on which seven young people have travelled together. It is about Ilford as a stopping point on the way out of London, and the various migratory journeys its people have undertaken before coming together here. And writing about them has been a journey for me, too.

When I first talked to Alan Steer about the book, he expressed concern that comprehensive schools tended to be portrayed in clichés. The urban secondary became either a hell-hole where no child could thrive, or a victim of terrible social ills, a place where heroic staff struggled against insuperable odds. Seven Kings is neither.

My year at Seven Kings changed my view of education, and of the young. The daily life of the education journalist – or of any kind of journalist, for that matter – involves getting your nose right up to the sharp end of a subject. We tend to talk to the people who shout loudest. Sometimes – and this has been the case recently with Seven Kings – they are shouting about their successes. To be honest, though, it is more interesting when they are shouting about things they want changed. Frequently, the teacher's voice is heard through the medium of the teachers' unions, who often have something to complain about.

What surprised me about Seven Kings, then, was its optimism, its common purpose and its sense of shared endeavour. There were disaffected pupils, as there would have been anywhere else, and probably miserable staff, but they were in a minority. For the most part people were happy to be there. The incumbents of Seven Kings were not fighting a daily battle for survival. They were just getting on with the job. Of course, not every school is like that, but I do think its experience points to new hope in the education system, which wasn't present a decade ago.

I used to visit schools a lot in the mid-1990s when I was an education correspondent on the *Independent*, and they were often depressing places with mud-scuffed doors and peeling paint. Teachers, and head teachers, felt weighed down by an avalanche of government initiatives. They felt hardly anyone ever said anything nice about them.

Education differs from other walks of life in that it is peopled by educationists – that is, by people whose business is learning and who, as a consequence, tend to be open to learning. It is a world in which people reflect constantly on their own practice, on what they should and should not do. It is a world in which – when it works properly – people apply their minds to what they do, forever renewing and refining. If my experience at Seven Kings is in any way representative, it is a world in which the role of ideology in that ongoing debate is dwindling. As the old sense of beleagueredness has begun to dissipate, a more pragmatic, efficiency-driven approach has begun to take hold.

Alan Steer described how in his early days at Seven Kings, during the mid-1980s, there were constant ideological battles, over whether he – or anyone else – had the right to tell teachers what to teach, over the introduction of the National Curriculum and precisely *what* they should be teaching. Should the English curriculum focus on the 'canon' of great British literature or encompass all the cultures of the world?

Now the focus seems to be not so much on what should be taught but on how. And I cannot recall a single instance during the year in which I heard two or more people having a purely ideological dispute. Like their pupils, the staff were too busy getting on with their jobs to bother themselves with such things.

This apparent lack of ideology, the feeling of being on an old battleground left vacant by combatants who had moved on, caused me to question myself.

Like many now in middle age I grew up in a liberal, argumentative, fractious world in which the young were often at ideological odds with their elders and each other, where to be young – perhaps even to be truly alive – was to be political, to debate, to challenge. At Seven Kings the pupils followed the example of their teachers and quietly accepted their lot. At first I found this hard to comprehend – Perin, for example, not wanting to waste his time complaining when he was misled about lift access to the tube. What did he do? Did he write to Ken Livingstone? Why not? Well, he said, he was sure someone else would have raised the issue. I think he had better things to do with his life than get upset about a lift.

Sometimes I didn't have the mental or linguistic tools

to see where my subjects were coming from. It took many months, after I'd heard Kessie's dad explain his educational philosophy largely by reference to the Old Testament, for me to assimilate what was being said. Eventually, though, it sank in – I think. There are so many valid discourses that do not even nod to the conversation the liberal intelligentsia of Britain has been having with itself for a century or more about the best ways to bring up the young to aspire and achieve.

That battle has been waged back and forth over a vast tract of ground. In the late nineteeth century, it alighted for some years on the question of girls. Should they be allowed to go to university and enter the professions? Later, the provision of a free secondary education was a key issue, and then selection, single-sex schooling, religious schooling, the sponsorship of state schools by private individuals and corporations, selection again. The story continues. Yet for most of the seven in this book, those issues did not seem particularly relevant. They tended to focus on something much simpler: that if they went to school and worked hard they would succeed, and their future would be brighter as a result. That is not to say that intellectual debate about education is not important or relevant: it is. It just doesn't speak much to these schoolchildren, even to their parents, about what matters to them.

The key to understanding these young people, I now think, was in being able to see clearly – as they so often could already – what worked for them. Kessie's evangelical Christianity and Perin's quiet focus on the things that mattered to him were right because they worked as strategies *for them*. If they substituted their own modus operandi, their own focuses for the old verbal, vocalized, discursive, chafing means by which so much of the older generation had done its growing up, that was their right.

Writing this book did not make me less ideological, or less argumentative. Yet I can see now that maybe not everyone has to be that way. We are entering a world in which ideology will be less central to our debates and disputes. Perhaps we will focus a bit more on what works, and a bit less on the wider political frameworks around which we build our thinking.

Sometimes, of course, the strategies these young people employed conflicted with the expectations of adults. Jemma, whose approach was much more similar to the tradition in which I grew up, liked to debate, dispute and argue. In the context of Seven Kings, where a calm obedience was expected, this caused her some problems. Tyrone and Anthony, too, failed at times – or refused – to fit in with the demands of school rules and discipline. From my more confrontational, anti-establishment, middle-aged perspective, I felt a sneaking sympathy for some of their transgressions. Jemma refusing to shut up about how her technology lessons were a mess because the teacher was away. Anthony repeatedly regrowing his little beard after he had been told to shave it. They were asserting their individuality in their own ways – and in ways I could recognize. I have come to understand better, though, how an avoidance of such conflict can also be a useful strategy.

I found myself heartened by the many ways in which some of these young people were able to get by with a minimum of conflict. The kindness, the tolerance, the warmth of the relationships they had with their parents and each other was heartening. Alan Steer once remarked that he wondered what the world would make of the pupils of Seven Kings High School – after all, they were just ordinary kids. Would people

really want to read about their lives? It was a moment of revelation for me. I found myself responding that, actually, I found
each one absolutely *extra*ordinary. Yes, of course they were
normal kids. But put together they had drive and purpose,
which could not fail to gladden the heart. All of them, even
those who had problems, had genuinely redeeming qualities.

There were bumpy patches along the route for all of us. I
wondered how Anthony's parents would react to seeing his
reprimand for drug-taking described in print, and whether
Tyrone's parents, reeling after his permanent exclusion, would
want to carry on. But they reacted with an openness and
generosity that moved me. It was necessary, though, to
disguise the identities of pupils with whose personal traumas
and misdemeanours Doug and Angela dealt during the year,
and in some cases to change details of incidents to protect
those involved. But in the end all these issues proved relatively
uncontroversial and we were able to agree a version of events
that seemed fair to everyone.

At the beginning of the year I had asked the parents of the
seven main characters in this book to sign letters agreeing to
let them take part. Those letters said pseudonyms would be
used for pupils – though not for staff – but three students,
Jemma, Perin and Shivanie, said they would like to appear
under their real names. Shivanie's sisters, Dipti and Sheena,
asked for their real names to be used too, as did her friends,
Jas and Geeta. Tyrone and Anthony chose alternative names
for themselves, and I gave names to all other children who
appeared.

The seven main characters read the parts of the book that
described their lives, and five were broadly happy with what
they saw. Sadly, the other two were not. Ruhy – I borrowed

this name from a family friend who is also from Iran – wanted me to take out all the parts that explained how and why she came here, and anything that she felt might be construed as negative about Iran. To describe her as a refugee, she felt, was tantamount to describing her as a criminal. Refugees, she said, were people who jumped on trains at Calais and came here illegally. My response, that I certainly didn't see it this way and didn't expect the book's readers to either, was of no comfort to her. In the end we compromised. I took out some of the most contentious details, and tried to make it clear that the parts she disliked were not her own recollections – she does not remember anything about them – but her mother's. I told her I believed that she, like so many refugees, past and present, would make a huge contribution to the life of Britain. I also told her I hoped this book would help to change attitudes so others would not feel in the future as she does now. And I told her I was sorry. I should have spelled out more clearly from the outset how keen I was to tell that part of her story along with all the others.

Kessie, too, was unhappy with the way I described her, and here we hit stalemate. At the end of the school year, I had told her that I saw her as a mature, hard-working, focused young woman, and that I felt both her religion and her close relationship with her father were strong features in her life. She agreed with that, and that was what I tried to put across. But Kessie wrote to me after reading the first part of what I had written to say that she found it insulting, that it made her family circumstances sound desperate and that I had described her as being under pressure when she was not. I have tried to ensure that there is no such implication – certainly none was ever intended.

I asked for a cross-section of Seven Kings life, and by and large I think I got one. With hindsight, I think the biggest omission was that none of the central characters was a practising, religious Muslim although about a third of the school's pupils would fit that description. I was at Seven Kings on 7 July 2005 and in the ensuing weeks, and I have to say that if any tensions arose as a result of the London bombings that day, I was not aware of them. The reaction in the school was personal, and human – are our families, our friends' families, hurt? – rather than political or sectarian. But I think it would have been enlightening to see at close range how a young Muslim might have dealt with the aftermath, and with the linking of Islam and terrorism in the public mind.

It has been strange, starting a new school year without visiting Seven Kings. I can't say I miss the early starts. But I do miss the company of all those who appeared in this book. An exercise like this one is bound to be fraught at times, yet I think that for the most part we got through it with a minimum of conflict – so maybe I did learn something from Seven Kings' non-confrontational approach!

Throughout the year during which I was a frequent visitor to the school, countless small acts of kindness and friendship were offered to me by so many people. This whole book, I hope, is a tribute to the tremendous warmth of the atmosphere at Seven Kings High School, which affects everyone within it. The stories of these seven young people point to the future of Britain. With them in it, shaping all our destinies, how can it fail to be a bright one?

ACKNOWLEDGEMENTS

The co-operation and friendship extended to me during the research for this book by the staff and student body at Seven Kings High School have made its execution a real joy. It is hard to pick out individual names, for they are too numerous.

However, with apologies to all those I am unable – or have forgotten – to mention personally, I should pick out a few names. I would like to thank Alan Steer in particular for agreeing to take the school into what must have seemed a potentially risky venture. He knew Seven Kings would emerge well from any honest portrayal of its daily life, and I hope he feels it has done. All the four staff members featured, Alan Steer, Doug Harrison, Debbie Adams and Angela Cassidy, gave their precious time unstintingly and without question. All of the pupils, particularly the seven whose lives were portrayed in detail, were a joy to know, as were their parents and siblings. Even when there were tricky moments, they offered me their trust and friendship in a way that was generous and open-hearted.

ACKNOWLEDGEMENTS

Among the many others who contributed, I would particularly like to thank Joan Morgan, Alan Steer's PA and the school's data manager, for all her help and support during the year. It was much appreciated. Thanks, too, to the staff in the school's front office, who were always happy to help out when I needed to find someone, forgot my pass or lost my dinner key – thank you, Dawn, in particular, for the latter.

The school's senior management team gave a great deal of time and energy to making the project work, and its governors, in particular Pat Green, gave their support and approval. Without John Dunford, general secretary of the Association of School and College Leaders, finding a suitable school and persuading its head to the project would have been difficult if not impossible.

I would also like to thank my agent, Tif Loehnis, for applying her brilliant mind to a rather underdeveloped idea and for turning it into a book that was much broader and more interesting – at least for me. Thanks, too, to everyone at Atlantic Books, particularly Toby Mundy, for believing in it and for making it happen.

Ruhy Parris lent her name – for which thanks should go, too, to her mother Shahla Haqjoo. My sister Judith Thompson, my mother Joan Abrams and my brother Julian Abrams all read the first draft and made helpful comments. My partner, Phil Solomon, as always, gave me unquestioning support and back-up, for which I remain eternally grateful.